T0326303

Dominique Lecourt

NLB

Marxism and Epistemology

BACHELARD, CANGUILHEM AND FOUCAULT

Translated from the French by Ben Brewster

'The Historical Epistemology of Gaston Bachelard'
first published by J Vrin, 1969
© J. Vrin, 1969

'For a Critique of Epistemology'
first published in one volume by François Maspero, 1972
© Librairie François Maspero, 1972

'Introduction to the English edition'
first published by NLB, 1975

This translation first published 1975
© NLB, 1975

Verso
UK: 6 Meard Street, London W1F 0EG
US: 388 Atlantic Avenue, Brooklyn, NY 11217
versobooks.com

Verso is the imprint of New Left Books

ISBN-13: 978-1-78663-240-1

Typeset in Monotype Ehrhardt by
Western Printing Services Ltd, Bristol
Designed by Gerald Cinamon

Printed in the United States

Translator's note: I should like to thank B. R. Cosin and *Theoretical Practice* for permission to use the former's translation of part of *Gaston Bachelard's Historical Epistemology* as a basis for my own translation.

Introduction to the English Edition

The essays in this collection, written over a period of three years, are explicitly placed beneath the sign of an encounter. A theoretical encounter: the one which has brought together, in France, dialectical materialism – Marxist philosophy – and a certain epistemological tradition inaugurated by Gaston Bachelard. The site of this unexpected encounter: the work of Louis Althusser, which is available to the British reader today thanks to the remarkable translations provided by Ben Brewster. Let me say straight away: for more than ten years now this encounter has whipped up an incredible series of political storms in the Marxist camp. On this side of the Channel the whirlwinds of these storms have not yet stopped forming and reforming.

This would all be very monotonous if history had not saved up for us the surprise of a sudden inversion: until 1968 the wind of criticism was set from the right, from 'Garaudyism', from that so-called 'Marxist humanism' which had been given free rein by the Twentieth Congress of the CPSU and which has since come to grief on the reefs of the most traditional clericalism. Althusser was then accused of 'scientism' and 'dogmatism'. These attacks took as their main theoretical target the notion of 'epistemological break' which he had borrowed from the works of Gaston Bachelard. Bachelard had coined it to remind the historians of science, too inclined to continuism, that a science is only installed by breaking with, by *cutting* itself off from its own past; that the object of a science is therefore not an immediate given and does not pre-exist the process of its production. Althusser adopted it to combat neo-Hegelian caricatures of Marx and to re-affirm a truth intolerable to all opportunisms – that *historical materialism*, as founded by Marx in *Capital*, really is, in the fullest sense of the word, a *science*. A revolutionary science whose object has been constituted in a rupture with the ideological and philosophical notions hitherto supposed to explain what a society is, what history is, etc.

But now, from the heart of that burning month of May which promoted and then cast down, at a stroke, so many illusions among petty-bourgeois intellectuals, there arose the ultra-left breeze which, its voice slowly growing stronger, took up the same arguments in a different tone. The very term science soon seemed suspect, on the pretext that in our society the sciences are enrolled in the service of capital: Althusser was found guilty of having wished to apply it to Marxism; this was seen as the mark of his theoreticism, the proof of his revisionism. Once again the main theoretical target of all these criticisms was the notion of 'epistemological break'.

It was in this conjuncture that, as a student in philosophy and a political militant, I set to work with the aim of disentangling what was at stake in this remarkable inversion. *Gaston Bachelard's Historical Epistemology*, written under the guidance of Georges Canguilhem and published thanks to him, dates from the autumn of 1968.

The articles collected together in *For a Critique of Epistemology* develop and correct certain remarks which the academic form of my first study had led me to leave in the shade and attempt to bring out more the political aims of what I should willingly call the incursion of a Marxist–Leninist in the domain of epistemology. It was a question, through an effort of internal criticism, of passing the system of Bachelardian categories through the sieve of dialectical materialism in order to determine within what limits, and hence with what reservations, the notion of 'epistemological break' could be relied on to sustain historical materialism's claim to scientificity.

But in this attempt to bring the question into focus, it was not long before I started a hare in the field of epistemology itself, for I still had to explain how it had been possible for the original epistemological tradition I was discussing to have been constituted marginally to what was practised under the name of epistemology or philosophy of science, particularly in the Anglo–Saxon countries. The introduction to *For a Critique of Epistemology* bears the traces of this: I point out there the opposition of the Bachelardian categories to all positivism in epistemology and to all evolutionism in the history of the sciences. But I also leave a redoubtable riddle unsolved: that of the (historical and theoretical) non-encounter of two tendencies of a single discipline, despite their strict contemporaneity, the riddle of a protracted mutual ignorance. *The New Scientific Mind*, Gaston Bachelard's first great epistemological work, was published in 1934, the same year in which Karl Popper's famous book *The Logic of Scientific Discovery* appeared in Vienna. During the subsequent thirty years the works of the one and the other have been developed, enriched, corrected and broadcast without it ever being possible to register either the beginnings of a confrontation or a sign of any emulation between them. Indeed, the French public, with the exception of a few specialists in logic rather than epistemology or the history of the sciences, are ignorant of Popper's name, and his work has not yet been translated into our language. As for Bachelard, I do not think I am wrong in stating that the majority of English readers will learn how to spell his name when they open my book. We lack a history of epistemology – a history which would necessarily take the form of a *comparative epistemology* – to explain this strange situation, for it is clear that arguments based on the intellectual chauvinism of either side are not sufficient. There is no question of my being able to fill this gap in a preface: it would demand long analyses which I reserve for a later study. However, two recent events oblige me at least to set the reader straight about a serious misunderstanding which may be encouraged by this lacuna and whose theoretical consequences threaten to be serious. These two events are, in chronological order, the translation of Althusser's works into English and, on the other hand, the appearance a short while ago of Thomas Kuhn's *The Structure of Scientific Revolutions* in French. A number of British commentators have seen a 'convergence' if not an identity pure and simple of the epistemological positions defended by Althusser and by Kuhn. Many French critics – including Marxist ones – have thought that they could detect an accord between Kuhn's theses and the Bachelardian epistemological current.

Hence we are now called upon to wonder if the day of the long postponed encounter has not come and reserved for us the ultimate surprise of an intersection of these two parallel epistemological traditions: have they not both, from either side, reached results which coincide, at least in part, in their latest representatives?

To put it plainly: I think this is completely wrong. And this for a reason of principle: for a reason of *position* in philosophy, and hence of philosophical *tendency*. Indeed, it seems to me, as I attempt to prove throughout these essays, that the dominant tendency of the Bachelardian tradition is materialist whereas the tendency of 'Popperism' and its variants is, despite certain appearances, frankly idealist.

I shall not evade the difficulty; I shall examine two texts in which the proximity of the two traditions might seem flagrant: on the one hand, Bachelard's *The Rationalist Activity of Contemporary Physics*; on the other, *The Structure of Scientific Revolutions*. These two books do indeed seem to be in accord in essential matters: both present a *discontinuist* conception of the history of the sciences. Elsewhere both present, unevenly developed, a reflection on the scientific division of labour and its material instances: books, manuals, scientific instruments, the constitution of groups of investigators, etc. Finally, even at the level of vocabulary they seem to echo one another, since Bachelard and Kuhn both speak of the 'normality' of science. Such are the appearances. They go against my thesis.

Let us therefore return to Bachelard's text. I think I can argue that its central notion is that of 'epistemological value': made explicit in the first pages of the work, it provides the guiding thread for a demonstration intended to establish the conditions which should be fulfilled by the 'philosophy of scientific culture' which the author wishes to initiate. This philosophy, explains Bachelard, should reveal the history of the sciences as the progressive emergence and permanent reorganization of 'epistemological values'. How are we to interpret this ambiguous expression? To my mind it cannot be understood unless one perceives in it the intention of a double polemic. Against the French philosophical tradition dominated by the spiritualist current of the 'philosophy of values' (ethical, aesthetic and religious values), Bachelard demands for epistemology the right to deal with values too; he even suggests, with a certain insistence, that the practice of the science might well be the site at which the most assured rational values are constructed. Witness this other text, contemporaneous with the one we are discussing:

If one were to draw up a general table of contemporary philosophy, one could not but be struck by the tiny space occupied in it by the *philosophy of the sciences*. In a more general way, *philosophies of knowledge* seem in disfavour in our day. The effort to know appears to be sullied with utilitarianism; however unanimously accepted, scientific concepts are held to be mere utility values. The man of science, whose thought is so opinionated and ardent, whose thought is so living, is presented as an abstract man. By degrees all the values of the studious man, of the skilful man fall into discredit. Science is no more than a minor adventure, an adventure in the chimerical countries of theory, in the obscure labyrinths of artificial experiments. By an incredible paradox, to hear the critics of scientific activity, the study of nature leads scientists away from natural values, the rational organization of ideas is prejudicial to the acquisition of new ideas.[1]

The expression epistemological *value* is thus caught in the tight network of a polemic which inscribes it in a determinate conjuncture in the history of philosophy in France: its function is to remind the professional philosophers that it would be greatly to their advantage not to neglect the acquisitions of the contemporary sciences.

But with this expression Bachelard is also aiming at a tendency within the philosophy of the sciences itself: the positivist tendency. Against the dissertations about the 'value of science' which have been traditional since Poincaré, against the sceptical and relativist professions of faith to which they have given rise, Bachelard invites the epistemologists to *take cognizance* of the constant emergence of new epistemological values in contemporary scientific practice. This is what is clearly indicated in the book on which we are commenting:

In the destiny of the sciences rational values *impose themselves*. They impose themselves historically. The history of the sciences is guided by a

1. 'Le problème philosophique des méthodes scientifiques. Discours au Congrès international de Philosophie des Sciences, Paris, October 1949,' in Gaston Bachelard, *L'engagement rationaliste*, PUF, Paris, 1972, p. 35.

kind of autonomous necessity. The philosophy of the sciences should systematically take as its task the determination and hierarchical classification of epistemological values. Wholly vain are general discussions about the *value of science* unless the details of the value of scientific thoughts are gone into . . . but the influence of sceptical theses with respect to scientific thought remains visible even today . . .[2]

The notion of epistemological value thus also has the function of combating what a few lines further on he calls a 'vague relativism' and an 'outmoded scepticism'.

At the same stroke the positive meaning of the notion is revealed: it will lead us to the quick of the debate we wish to institute with Kuhn's theses. This positive meaning is, in its turn, double:

(a) Bachelard is stating, in the ambiguity of his metaphor, the philosophical thesis that underpins all his epistemological work: that the truth of a scientific truth *'imposes itself' by itself*. In Spinozist terms: 'veritas norma *sui*' (the truth is its own measure). In Leninist terminology: Bachelard is posing the thesis of the objectivity of scientific knowledges. He is posing it, not discussing it. He does not seek to found, to *guarantee* this objectivity. He is not concerned to pose to scientific knowledge the traditional question of its claims to validity. This point is crucial, for we maintain that this position is a *materialist* position. A position which enables Bachelard to take a step outside the theoretical space of what idealist philosophy in its classical period called the 'problem of knowledge'. This position even enables him, as I have tried to show in my first essay, to provide the outline of a descriptive theory of this space.

(b) A second decisive thesis implied in the Bachelardian metaphor: an epistemological 'value' *devalues* what it is not: what is anterior and exterior to it. On the one hand it judges what precedes it, on the other it disqualifies the survivals of its past in the present. It has a 'critical' effect of demarcation on these survivals. 'Sic veritas norma sui *et falsi.*'[3] This is expressed in passages such as the following:

The history of the sciences will then appear as the most irreversible of all histories. In discovering the true, the man of science bars the way to an

2. Gaston Bachelard, *L'activité rationaliste de la physique contemporaine*, PUF, Paris, 1951.   3. Cf. Spinoza *Ethics*, Book II, Proposition 43.

irrationality. Irrationalism can no doubt spring up elsewhere. But from now on there are forbidden routes. The history of the sciences is the history of the defeats of irrationalism. But the fight is without end . . .[4]

Bachelard expresses this thesis a hundred times in his last works: in it he sees what he rightly calls the very *dialectic* of scientific thought.

Hence one can argue without paradox that Bachelard is defending a position which is both *materialist* and *dialectical* in philosophy. From this position in philosophy he is able to revolutionize the status of epistemology: to institute what I have called a historical epistemology and to demarcate himself radically from every form of positivism.

What in fact will be the task of the epistemologist once the two philosophical theses above have been posed? His work, insofar as it is properly epistemological, will consist of studying the concrete modalities of the realization of the process of production of scientific truths in the actual history of the sciences. This is indeed what Bachelard undertook: his entire œuvre, in its permanent recommencement, does indeed bear the mark of two conjoint and constant preoccupations: to assure–reassure his position in philosophy (which amounts to affirming–reaffirming, in a polemic constantly returned to against all the variants of philosophical idealism, the two theses I have just disengaged) and to reflect, in their revolutionary currentness, all the events which induce reorganizations and mutations of scientific work in the physico–chemical sciences. But he finds these events *at the conjunction of two distinct processes*: a process *inside* scientific practice which corresponds to what in his vocabulary he calls an increasing 'specialization' and 'socialization' of scientific work, a more and more rational 'division' of tasks and a closer and closer 'cooperation' of the workers inside the 'scientific city'. The forms of this internal process are, according to him, determined by the *norm* constituted by the truth of scientific knowledges: insofar as it is a process of the production of *knowledges*, this process, which, like every process of production, is carried out in (or rather *beneath*) historically determined relations (of production), is indeed subject

4. *L'activité rationaliste*, op. cit., p. 27.

to the norm of the true: its norm *is* the true. But on the other hand, this internal process, intrinsically normative, is inserted in the overall process of social practice. But this insertion has its effects even *inside* the internal process. Hence Bachelard's constant concern for the intervention of non-scientific determinations *in* scientific practice; hence also the analyses outlined on a number of occasions of the material instances which govern these interventions: an analysis of the pedagogy of the sciences, of the constitution of scientific libraries and of the status of scientific books. Hence also the famous theory of scientific instruments. What is important in these pages, which are often disappointingly brief, is that they strikingly reveal a principle of analysis which is in solidarity with Bachelard's materialist philosophical position. This principle can be stated as follows: the effects of the external determinations ('social', 'economic', 'ideological' and 'political' determinations) are subject to the internal conditions (the norm of the true) of scientific practice. Here is a principle which rules out from the start all epistemological economism, sociologism and psychologism: it is indeed impossible to achieve a *genesis* of scientific concepts on the basis of what are known as the social, economic or psychological (or even biological) 'conditions' of scientific practice. It is this which is very clear in the difficult question of the intervention of the *subjects* (of the scientists, of their individual psychological reality) in scientific practice. Once he has repudiated the idealist philosophical question of the guarantee of the objectivity of scientific knowledges and thereby given up looking for the 'cause' of scientific production in a subject, individual or collective, Bachelard establishes without ambiguity the terms in which the real problem of the psychology of the man of science must be posed. It is necessary, he proves, to start from the internal process, for which the scientists are only the *agents*: as such they have to submit to the norms of the process; if they refuse, they immediately set themselves outside science. But to get there, being also 'subjects' of ideology (having a consciousness, wishes, ambitions, political, religious and ethical ideas, etc.), they have to make an effort – Bachelard says: a rationalist effort – and this effort is the whole process of the *formation* of the scientific mind. An effort which *splits* the scientific subject, which demands of him, often to the point of his being existentially torn, that he make a *break* with the 'spontaneous' interests of life. . . . This break is never definitely guaranteed insofar as the subject – be he *le savant Cosinus* – never succeeds in being a 'pure' agent of scientific practice. . . . That is why, on this path, the asceticism of which Bachelard often stressed, he constantly comes upon *obstacles*. Obstacles which are crystallized and systematized in their philosophy and which, by this bias, produce braking effects in scientific practice itself. Thus it is clear in what precise sense Bachelard can speak of the 'normality' of science: in order to designate the specific character of that special production the production of scientific *truths*, and in order to suggest the impact of this character on the agents of that production.

If we now turn to Kuhn's work, we find a very different definition of what he calls normal science. It is the set of convictions shared by the scientific group considered at a given moment; a conviction that the group defends against every threat and every blow by rejecting what is heterogeneous to it. Hence the famous formulation:

'Normal science' means research firmly based upon one or more past scientific achievements, achievements that some particular scientific community acknowledges for a time as supplying the foundation for its further practice.[5]

These groups which live in so-called normal science live, as is well known, within what Kuhn calls a single '*paradigm*'. Margaret Masterton has clearly shown the rather loose extension given to this notion by Kuhn.[6] For the moment all we need do is refer to the passage in which the author justifies the use of the term in his essay:

By choosing it, I meant to suggest that some accepted examples of actual scientific practice . . . provide models from which spring particular coherent traditions of scientific research.[7]

5. Thomas S. Kuhn, *The Structure of Scientific Revolutions*, second enlarged edition, International Encyclopedia of Unified Science, Volume II number 2, University of Chicago Press, Chicago and London, 1970, p. 10.
6. Margaret Masterman, 'The Nature of a Paradigm', in Imre Lakatos and Alan Musgrove (eds.), *Criticism and the Growth of Knowledge*, CUP, Cambridge, 1970, pp. 61–6.   7. Kuhn, op. cit., p. 10.

Examples follow: Aristotle's physics, Newton's principles, Lavoisier's chemistry. . . . And he concludes provisionally:

Men whose research is based on shared paradigms are committed to the same rules and standards for scientific practice.[8]

The notions of normal science and paradigm are thus in solidarity and constitute the theoretical armature of Kuhn's epistemology. But the mere comparison of the two passages cited brings up a crucial question: what is it that constitutes the normality of so-called normal science? To what *normativity* does normal science conform? The most immediate answer will be: the paradigm is the norm for normal science. Kuhn's text says so plainly. But we will be permitted to repeat the question vis-à-vis the paradigm: what is the basis for the normativity of the paradigm?

To this new question Kuhn provides a first answer: it is the *decision* of the group which *chooses* to hold such and such a scientific theory or discovery to be paradigmatic. In order to deal with it he uses an analogy:

This essay aims to demonstrate that the historical study of paradigm change reveals very similar characteristics [to those of a change in political institutions] in the evolution of the sciences. Like the choice between competing political institutions, that between competing paradigms proves to be a choice between incompatible modes of community life.[9]

Much might be said about the idealist conception of political revolution governing this analogy.[10] But no matter: for our purposes we shall only retain the philosophical thesis it is trying to illustrate: it is the assent of the group which assures the normativity of normal science in proceeding to the *choice* of the paradigm. Feyerabend has seen the difficulty of such an answer, and that ultimately it repeats in its own way the old aporias of conventionalism: on this basis, he says, there is no way of distinguishing scientific research from a gang

8. ibid., p. 11.   9. ibid., p. 94.
10. Stephen Toulmin is right to have pointed this out ('Does the Distinction between Normal and Revolutionary Science Hold Water?' in *Criticism and the Growth of Science*, op. cit., p. 41), but the epistemological transposition of evolutionist notions he then proposes in order to resolve the difficulty seem to me to be open to the same criticisms as those I make of Kuhn's 'solution'.

of criminals.[11] Less cavalier, John Watkins makes the same objection: it is impossible, he says, to distinguish between science and theology if one holds to Kuhn's concepts.[12] These two criticisms are correct insofar as they are aimed at *the question* Kuhn is unable to resolve: that of the objectivity of scientific knowledges. Feyerabend and Watkins are right to stress that the answers given by Kuhn to this question are not satisfactory.[13] In the meantime the author himself is aware of this, for he proposes a second type of answer. When in fact he comes to explain the mechanisms of the choice he began by discussing, Kuhn resorts to a new analogy, which, on reflection, is in contradiction with the notion it is supposed to illustrate. This analogy is taken from the experimental psychology of the processes of perception; on one occasion he invokes the experiment of Bruner and Postman on the perception of anomalies in a series of playing-cards presented at slower and slower speeds: on another he appeals to Stratton's famous experiments with goggles involving the transformation of the visual field.[14] In both cases, his purpose is to show that the inauguration of a paradigm induces a new structuration of the scientists' 'world view'; and hence that a change in paradigm such as is produced at every 'scientific revolution' implies a mutation in that structure. In this he sees an argument in support of his non-continuism. But the whole difficulty is the problem of the status of this analogy: if it is a strict analogy (i.e. the equality of two relations), then it must be admitted that it quite simply contradicts the idea of a choice and decision supposedly presiding over the adoption by the group of a paradigm, for, as a good 'Gestalt', the form precisely imposes itself by itself and the whole 'mystery' the theory is supposed to clear up resides in this apparent defeat of

11. P. K. Feyerabend, 'Consolations for the Specialist', in *Criticism and the Growth of Knowledge*, op. cit., pp. 199–201.

12. John Watkins, 'Against "Normal Science"', in ibid., p. 33.

13. Let me add, however, that the criticisms of Feyerabend and Watkins cannot be decisive because they are situated *on the same terrain* as Kuhn's demonstration: they do not, as I propose to do, attack the very *question* posed by Kuhn but the answers he gives it. That is why the discussion recorded in *Criticism and the Growth of Knowledge* has the curious feeling of a dispute in which everyone can at any moment say to his opponent or opponents 'I agree with you completely', while at the same time maintaining the specific difference of his own position as energetically as possible.

14. Kuhn, op. cit., pp. 62–4 and 112.

voluntary motivations. If it is not a strict analogy, then there is only one alternative. Either it is just an *image*, as a number of passages from Kuhn suggest, and it tells us nothing about the theoretical mechanism it claims to explain. As proof, these few lines in a central passage from the book: 'In their most usual form, of course, gestalt experiments illustrate only the nature of perceptual transformations. The tell us nothing about the role of paradigms.'[15] Or else it is more than an analogy: it is a relation of identity. Kuhn also sustains this thesis in the following text:

Either as a metaphor or because it reflects the *nature of the mind*, that psychological experiment [Postman's experiment] provides a wonderfully simple and cogent schema for the process of scientific discovery.[16]

Here we fall back from conventionalism on to a weak form of the most traditional *apriorism*. This is not surprising if it is true that conventionalism is merely a 'sophisticated' (and hence enfeebled) form of this apriorism. Scratch a conventionalist and you will find an apriorist.

I propose to take Kuhn's oscillations on this point as symptomatic: honest enough to recognize that they are all as fragile as one another, he picks up one answer after another to an insoluble question. The very question that Bachelardian epistemology refuses to ask; the question on the repudiation of which it has established its own terrain: the old idealist question of the objectivity of scientific knowledges (how is it to be guaranteed? how is it to be founded?). No doubt Kuhn poses this question in terms that seem 'concrete', current and scientific: there is no question in his work either of a *cogito* or of a transcendental subject, it is a question of 'scientific groups', of laboratories, and it is in this that the book 'speaks' to the scientists of today – better no doubt than Bachelard's works – but it is essential not to be taken in by words: the theoretical core of this work is an old philosophical notion, an old idealist question accompanied by the cortège of answers it imposes, in the circle of which Kuhn – and not he alone – has allowed himself to be trapped.

That is why, despite the 'discontinuism' and a few other appear-

15. ibid., p. 112.   16. ibid., p. 64.

ances, it seems to me, decidedly, that the two tendencies of contemporary epistemology cannot meet. I repeat: this is because of a reason of position *in philosophy*. The one is, timidly and confusedly but indisputably, ranged in the materialist camp, the other is inscribed in the orb of idealist philosophies.

Dominique Lecourt
Paris, 1973

Part One

Gaston Bachelard's
Historical Epistemology

Foreword

The present study by M. Dominique Lecourt reproduces a *mémoire de maîtrise* which seemed worthy of publication as much for the intelligent sobriety with which it interrogates Gaston Bachelard's epistemological work as for the discernment with which it singles out the points at which to bring this interrogation to bear.

If in his study he does mobilize certain epistemological concepts imported from a source he does not conceal, M. Lecourt can justify himself, first by the discretion he demonstrates and second and above all by the fact that these concepts were invented and essayed in order to conform, in a domain to which Gaston Bachelard never applied himself, to certain norms and exigencies of Bachelardian epistemology.

The index of principal concepts which terminates this study will be useful to all those for whom the reading of Gaston Bachelard's epistemological work is, in conformity with what he himself wished, an effort.

Georges Canguilhem

Introduction

Commentary on a commentary, reflection on a reflection, is this work a matter of historical erudition – as its title would suggest – or one of philosophical ratiocination, since it presents itself as a 'philosophical memoir'? Such is the question justifiably posed before such an undertaking. Another form of this crucial question: is it a matter of exhibiting a curious variety, the historical species, of the genus which tradition has delimited by the name of epistemology? In that case, one would speak of 'historical epistemology' in the sense in which one speaks of 'historical geography' to designate a special branch of the discipline 'geography'. Or is it a matter of isolating in the history of epistemology the instant bearing the name Gaston Bachelard so as to recall it to memory? In this sense, 'historical epistemology' would have to be taken to mean 'historical monument': a witness of the past which, although it has gone by, still deserves to be remembered.

Here it is a question of something quite different: Gaston Bachelard's work, by an inner necessity peculiar to itself, escapes the clutches of these tedious alternatives. What it reveals to us is the fact that epistemology *is* historical; its essence is to be historical. If we take as a first definition of epistemology what etymology tells us about it, we can say: the discipline which takes scientific knowledge as its object must take into account the historicity of that object. And the immediate counterpart to this revolutionary proposition: if epistemology his historical, the History of the Sciences is necessarily epistemological. Once the tedious alternatives have been rejected, we are caught in an engaging reciprocity.

It *engages* us indeed, beyond the play on words, in thinking that of the concepts which are at work in it: epistemology and history. That is, in answering the question: what theoretical mechanism is concealed by the mystery of this double inauguration? or rather: by virtue of what necessity does the problematic installed by Bachelard in epistemology carry its effects beyond its own field into that of the history of the sciences? Still more precisely: what regulated system of concepts functions in Bachelardian epistemology to *give rise* to the construction of a new concept of the history of the sciences?

But we are *caught* in it: it is indeed clear that to say 'historical epistemology' is already to imply in the definition of the discipline the concept whose construction becomes possible as one of its effects. The aporia would be complete if we were to ignore the special status of epistemology: its object refers itself to another object. It is a discourse which is articulated on to another discourse. Literally, it is a second discourse whose status thus depends in the last analysis on the structure of the first.

Now, I shall attempt to prove that Gaston Bachelard's discovery is precisely to have recognized and then to have theoretically reflected the fact that science has no object outside its own activity; that it is in itself, in its practice, productive of its own norms and of the criterion of its existence. This bold thesis produced by a philosopher who took it upon himself to be and to remain the modest pupil of contemporary scientists revolutionizes the field of epistemology. I shall be concerned to show by what theoretical effort Bachelard was able to produce it, within what network of concepts he was able to express it. Without anticipating the details of the analysis, a mere over-view of his work justifies the claim that it is all organized around a reflection on Mathematical-Physics; precisely on the riddle of the hyphen between them which contemporary science showed had necessarily to be resolved in theory.

Let me leap straight to my conclusions: by adopting as its object scientific knowledge in its movement, epistemology is dealing with a *historical process*. A whole field of real problems opens to its inquiry; outside the tranquil universe of the ideal problems posed by the philosopher about 'Science', about its foundations, its method, its reality, its status with respect to other forms of knowledge. . . .

It is thus clear from now on that this thesis runs counter to the convictions by which philosophy has lived hitherto. I propose to show that it runs counter to them in a very special way, in a *non-philosophical* way, although the collision takes place *in* philosophy. We shall find that on certain questions which the theoretical conjuncture has turned into 'sensitive points' – e.g., the question of intuition or that of quality – Bachelard rejoins the philosophers from a different starting-point. I take the risk of claiming that this meeting is not a matter of chance; it pertains to the fact that the problems philosophy poses also have a relation to scientific knowledge, but in a different modality, which it will be incumbent on me to determine.

A non-philosophical meeting in philosophy; indeed, I hope to prove that the theoretical discipline inaugurated by Gaston Bachelard poses vis-à-vis the sciences different questions on a different terrain; it invalidates the notions of previous epistemology, and – what is more serious – it disqualifies the problems of traditional philosophy; it puts them out of court. In other words: it *stands in for* – it occupies the place of – previous philosophy, but *elsewhere*. Here doubtless we have the ultimate and profound reason for the *dépaysement*, the lack of bearings one feels in reading Gaston Bachelard's texts: it is another country that one finds; a new world by the grace of a new style constructed with new concepts.

In fact, one could not but notice that Bachelard's work is shot through and through with a constantly recurring polemic against the philosophers. Philosophy is present in it as a hydra before it is thought as a spectrum. I shall argue that the necessity of this polemic is inscribed deep in Bachelard's thought: in *opening* the field of historical epistemology, he *uncovers* – lays bare and to the quick – what philosophy is eager to *cover up*: the real – historical – conditions of the production of scientific knowledges. This philosophical recovering is revealed by a systematic *displacement* of problems: Bachelard's undertaking is to restore them to their rightful places, i.e., to their senses, obviously at the cost of returning philosophers to theirs. Hence there was a destiny in his theoretical thought which had to turn this peaceful man into the philosopher fighting on every front.

But Gaston Bachelard is not content to describe the mechanisms and effects of philosophical intervention in scientific knowledge; he also tries to find out *why*. It is clear, in his eyes, that what I have called the 'displacement – re-covering' cannot arise without an interest to order it. In other words, not only does Bachelard exhibit the unthought of philosophical discourse (the re-covering), he also sets us on the road to the unconscious whose effect in the philosophical text that un-thought is. In that unprecedented book *The Formation of the Scientific Mind*, and then continually in the rest of his work, he makes visible the *values* which order – in all senses of the word – philosophical discourse, ideological values whose intervention in scientific practice constitutes what Bachelard designates by a new name: the 'epistemological obstacles'. This new word is a new concept which, for reasons pertaining, as we have just seen, to its nature, philosophy could neither produce nor even recognize.

It is in this way that I shall take seriously the notion of 'psychoanalysis' which appears in the sub-title to the book. I shall see in it an unprecedented project, often more admired than understood, whose necessity Bachelard was first able to conceive. In it, better perhaps than elsewhere, we find out why according to Gaston Bachelard the specific determination of philosophy is its relation to the sciences, how philosophy is defined in and by this intervention, how it is extra-scientific values that it imports into the scientist's activity, that it superimposes on the operations of scientific knowledge. But also revealed is the main victim of this intervention: the scientist himself who, whether consciously or no, borrows from philosophy the concepts it has formed to reflect his own practice. It ultimately reveals why it is that 'science does not have the philosophy it deserves'; what it is that it loses thereby; but also how it can acquire it. This book, which Bachelard wanted to be easily accessible, will undoubtedly bring us to the most difficult, most secret parts of Bachelardian epistemology.

Indeed, new tasks can now be assigned to the epistemologist. An open and mobile philosophy is required that respects the always new and unexpected openings of scientific thought. That is to say, philosophy must renounce systematic form, the comfort of its closed space, the immobility of 'closed reason' and *take risks*, along-side the scientists, behind them, in as yet uncleared 'fields of thought'. As we shall see, it is to this that the set of concepts elaborated and reworked by Bachelard responds and is engaged; constitutive of his epistemology, they find their most noteworthy, because operational, expression in his last works: *Applied Rationalism, The Rationalist Activity of Contemporary Physics* and *Rational Materialism*.

It is surely not without interest to state it: it is at the beginning of *The Rationalist Activity of Contemporary Physics*, in 1951 – i.e., almost a quarter of a century after his first works – that Gaston Bachelard devotes a long introductory chapter to the definition of the 'tasks of a philosophy of the sciences'. A remarkable manifestation of that openness which he demanded other philosophers make their main concern, this fact has a further import. If it is agreed that its location is of some importance, it can be inferred:

– That it is a reflection on the techniques and concepts of the new Physics which summoned Bachelard to conceive of new tasks for the philosophy of the sciences, or, what comes to the same thing, to establish the basic concepts of a new epistemology. His whole work confirms this for us;

– But above all that it is tardily, at the end of a long theoretical effort to disengage the specificity of the concepts of the new science that this epistemology can conform to its own concept – already at work but unthematized in the writings of the preceding period – and *formally* engage philosophical thought in a new problematic.

To my mind, it is very significant that it is the same book which, a few pages later, takes as its theme the problems of the History of the Sciences and reflects them for themselves; no longer incidentally, as was the case in the other books. The Lecture at the Palais de la Découverte on the *Actuality of the History of the Sciences* merely returns to and extends the considerations of the book of 1951.

I see in this a justification for the thesis I have already advanced: the institution of a new problematic in the History of the Sciences is the effect, outside its own field, of the Bachelardian epistemological revolution.

It is also from this double statement that I obtain my authorization for the order of exposition adopted here. It consists of first showing how Gaston Bachelard, thanks to an upheaval in Mathematical–Physics, simultaneously *recognizes* the object of science and that of philosophy; or rather, but in different senses, recognizes that neither the one nor the other has an object; and goes on to show that this double recognition, once its theoretical implications have been thought, produces a double and reciprocal foundation: that of historical epistemology and that of epistemological history.

It goes without saying that these theoretical positions which I am defending do not emerge without my setting to work a certain number of principles of reading. In particular, if what I have said is correct, it is clear that the architecture of Bachelard's *text* is complex. Several levels can be distinguished in it, levels which may overlie one another from one chapter to another, from one paragraph to another and even from one sentence to the next. This intricacy, which is not a confusion, pertains to the complexity of the situation of Bachelardian epistemology. It might be schematized provisionally as follows:

– the text tells us something about scientific knowledge; in the practical state, this is epistemology functioning;

– the text tells us something about philosophy; this is epistemology functioning on the polemical divide;

– at the same time as it can be seen functioning, a precise epistemological doctrine, formed out of a 'body of concepts' that are well-adjusted, is being elaborated, specified and expounded;

– on my own behalf, let me add that the fact of this elaboration, in the field of philosophy itself, may manage to inform us as to the interplay which constitutes the latter.

In defending these theses and principles, I believe I am being faithful to Gaston Bachelard's thought: fidelity, in this case, does not seem to me to consist of making myself the mirror of his work, or even, to use one of his expressions, of producing its 'pleonasm'; but rather of showing by what difficult routes it managed to be an open philosophy, a thought which suggests other thoughts, an epistemology which has not yet taught us its last lesson. The highest of these being doubtless the one I shall attempt to disengage at the end by showing how Bachelard, faithful to his principles, was able to make his thought conform to the rapidity of scientific advance and to proceed to the heroic re-working of his own concepts.

Gaston Bachelard's work is such that, having completed our study of it, here we are, summoned to set to work in the school of the latest advances of scientific thought. I hold this summons to be the ultimate answer to the questions I posed at the beginning and which might be summed up in this one: 'Why then read Gaston Bachelard in 1968?'

Recognitions

The year 1927, in which Gaston Bachelard submitted his two doctoral theses, saw Max Born state the probabilistic theory of the electron, Heisenberg formulate the uncertainty principle and Lemaître the hypothesis of the expanding universe. Run through the preceding decade and it is clear that it is no less rich in scientific achievements of the first importance. In 1925, Millikan had discovered cosmic rays, in 1924, Heisenberg had established Quantum Mechanics, and 1923 was the date of publication of the first works of Louis de Broglie on Wave Mechanics; slightly exceeding the limit I have set myself, I can add that Einstein's work on the Special and General Theory of Relativity appeared in 1913. It is easier to understand what Bachelard meant, much later, in 1951, when he wrote in *Rational Materialism*: 'one decade in our epoch is equal to centuries in earlier epochs.'

Without it being possible in 1927 for him to know of all these achievements, Bachelard was from the beginning acutely aware of this acceleration of scientific time. But what drew his attention was above all the *novelty* of these theories and of the concepts they brought into play. He was witnessing something he was already calling a 'mutation' and was later to think in the concept of 'rupture'.

Gaston Bachelard was, so to speak, quite particularly destined to feel these upheavals, since they concerned the discipline he regarded – and his opinion on this point was never to vary – as the 'queen of the sciences': Mathematical–Physics. It was in this science that he had found his master in the person of Gabriel Lamé,[1] for whom he expressed a never-ending admiration. Now, it was the

---

1. Gabriel Lamé, mathematician and engineer, born 1795, died 1870. Bachelard organized all his *A Study of the Propagation of Heat in Solids* around Lamé's *Leçons sur la théorie analytique de la chaleur* (Lectures on the Analytic Theory of Heat), Paris, 1861.

basic concepts of Mathematical–Physics that the Theory of Relativity brought back into question: space, time, localization . . ., all these notions had to be re-examined; at the same moment, alongside traditional Physics a new science was growing up: Micro-physics. The question Bachelard posed here was what meaning to give to this 'alongside' (*à côté*): should the new discipline be seen as a region of Physics, one of its appendages – however strange – and thus one of its extensions? or on the contrary, should it not be thought that Physics as a whole must come under the jurisdiction of its principles?

A double problem is thus posed straightaway: that of the *epistemological status* of the new science, and through it, the more general problem of the relations between 'regions' of knowledge (*savoir*); that of the *historical status* of the new with respect to the old, or again: is it necessary, in the domain of knowledge (*savoir*), to rely on a chronological succession in order to think a history? These two questions are conjoined to such an extent that they pass for a single one in Bachelard's earlier works.

Let me add that in this conjunction, it is the historical aspect which seems dominant, because of its paradoxical form; the effect of Bachelard's long theoretical labours is to prove that only an answer to the epistemological question can give the elements with which to think the historical question rigorously. We are thus privileged to be the spectators of a real disentanglement.

No doubt it would be an insult to Philosophy to contrast the list of its productions between 1913 and 1927 to that of the scientific achievements in the same period.

Nothing would be found; nothing new; nothing, at any rate, whose novelty poses or resolves the same question as the new theories of physics. This disparity Gaston Bachelard felt to be all the more scandalous in that the scientists brought into play in their activity notions which *also* appear in Philosophy; we might say: on which philosophy has *lived* as long as it has existed. Such for example are the notions of reality, of matter, of space, of time. . . . It seemed to Bachelard that these notions are the object of a double treatment; they function in two heterogeneous systems of concepts.

It is this double treatment that is already attentively examined in the main Thesis of 1927, entitled *An Essay on Approximate Knowledge*. Let us note for the moment that in it Bachelard is concerned to show how, when they function in scientific discourse, these concepts are susceptible to precise definitions, fine variations and fruitful rectifications. . . .

He also shows:

– that Philosophy uses these concepts as if science said nothing about them, or as if what it did say about them was not its concern;

– that Philosophy, when it takes science as its object, discusses an ideal science very different from science as it actually exists. In an expression he was to use in *The Formation of the Scientific Mind*, it is revealed that 'all philosophy has a science of its own'.[2]

Reflecting on a Mathematics and a Physics which did not have the revolutionary character of those then just emerging, he respected even at this time the motto which was to remain his to the end: *'Se mettre à l'école des sciences'* – 'Go to school with the sciences'. He was convinced that philosophical notions such as reality and truth could be rectified to advantage by so doing.

One can understand that this philosophy had to be an exception. Convinced of the 'philosophical interests' of scientific thought, by the position he adopted, which is probably to be explained largely by his past as an auto–didact in philosophy, free with respect to all the schools, he was already in a position to grasp the revolutionary character of the new theories from the only point of view which could reveal it as such: that of the man of science.

'One of the most obvious external characteristics of relativist doctrines is their novelty', wrote Gaston Bachelard at the beginning of his work of 1929: *The Inductive Value of Relativity*; and, five years later in *The New Scientific Mind*: 'There is no transition between Newton's system and Einstein's system. One cannot get from the former to the latter by collecting knowledges, taking double pains with measurements, slightly modifying principles. On the contrary,

---

2. *La formation de l'esprit scientifique*, p. 55 (for full bibliographical details of Bachelard's works, see the first Appendix to Part One).

an effort of total novelty is required.'[3] This text alone could be the object of a long commentary, but for the moment let us bear in mind its claim that relativist theories demand of scientists an *effort* of novelty; it is just such an effort that Bachelard demands correspondingly of the philosopher.

How is the novelty to be characterized initially, or, what comes to the same thing, what are the most apparent motifs of the effort to be made? The first element of an answer is given to us a few pages later in *The New Scientific Mind*: with relativist science there occurs an *explosion of the concepts* of Newtonian science. In fact, Bachelard is examining a notion to which he will return on several occasions later in his work, the notion of *mass*.

He writes:

Relativity has split the notion of mass as fixed by its purely Newtonian definition. It has led in fact to distinguishing between mass calculated along the trajectory (longitudinal mass) and mass calculated along a perpendicular to the trajectory, as a sort of coefficient of resistance to distortion of the trajectory (transverse mass).[4]

This split in the concept of mass demands an effort of conception, because, writes Gaston Bachelard – immediately presenting the philosopher's objection in the form of 'it is said that . . .' – it seems artificial. It forces one to review a commonplace notion that one believed, for evident reasons, to be *natural*. What is revealed in the first two chapters of *The Philosophy of No* is that Newtonian mechanics did not demand such a revision. In fact, we lived in the Newtonian world as if in 'a spacious and bright dwelling'.

This now obligatory dissociation between commonplace, natural notions and scientific, artificial notions is at the centre of Bachelard's reflections from then on.

Its implications seemed to him to have a primordial philosophical

---

3. *Le nouvel esprit scientifique*, p. 42. This passage can be compared with the conclusion to the chapter: 'To sum up, a general view of the epistemological relations between contemporary physical science and Newtonian science reveals that there is not a *development* from the old doctrines towards the new ones, but far rather an *envelopment* of the old thoughts by the new ones' (ibid., p. 58).

4. ibid., p. 47.

interest; they are undoubtedly the first of the lessons the philosopher can learn with the scientist, and also not the least.

Less apparent, but just as instructive, he believes, is the revision of the principles of traditional Physics made by the doctrines of Relativity. This revision takes the form of a *relinquishment*. In *The New Scientific Mind*, Bachelard writes: 'It is after the event, when once one is installed in relativist thought, that the numerical results produced by Newtonian astronomy are rediscovered – by mutilations and relinquishments – in the astronomical calculations of Relativity.'[5] This text, to which we shall return later, shows that the scientific advance here has been made by a mutation in principles; it is clear in what sense Bachelard was able to write at the beginning of *The Inductive Value of Relativity* that this science was 'without antecedents';[6] there you have the last word of its novelty.

Now, something strange and monstrous, Philosophy continued to use the same words, the same concepts, in the same senses as in the time of Newtonian science. Much worse, when it claimed to reflect the new doctrines, as we shall see, it followed the opposite procedure to that of the scientist and insisted on 'explaining'[7] the new by the old. What Bachelard is conscious of is thus a *discrepancy* (*décalage*) between the discourse conducted by Philosophy and that of the new science. Philosophy, when it speaks of space, of time, of motion (and it does not refrain from doing so), seems to him to be *delayed*, to lag behind a scientific revolution. We shall see that on this point Gaston Bachelard constantly deepened his thought: it becomes clear, in particular, insofar as he acquires new epistemological concepts, that Philosophy did not even think Newtonian mechanics adequately, by a necessity affecting its essence.

But let me leave this point to return to that critical moment in which the installation of a new science makes the discordancy of the two discourses blinding. I have characterized this discordancy as a *delay* of Philosophy. For Bachelard the fundamental characteristic

5. ibid., p. 42.
6. *La valeur inductive de la rélativité*, p. 6.
7. The central thesis of the philosophy of Émile Meyerson (1859–1933). In 1921 he wrote a work entitled *De l'explication dans les sciences* (On Explanation in the Sciences). I shall return to it at length in Section 3 of this Chapter.

of scientific thought lies in its *movement*: it *is* movement. Philosophical thought, on the contrary, for profound reasons which will emerge later, finds itself attributed a 'tendency to immobilism'; let us say, for the moment, that it gives proof of immobility.

In this respect the two Theses of 1927 are very significant: they constantly valorize the progressive, mobile character of scientific thought. Bachelard neglects no metaphor to make us aware of this: sometimes borrowing from the vocabulary of biology, sometimes – less often – from that of strategy. In the *Essay on Approximate Knowledge*, conceptualization is successively defined as an 'energy',[8] a 'force',[9] an 'activity' or a 'movement'.[10] Further on, it is defined in terms of struggle and combat. We even find the two registers crossing at the end of the book, where Bachelard writes: 'a truly dynamic knowledge, grasped in its act, in its effort of *conquest* and *assimilation*' (my emphasis).[11]

In the face of this burgeoning activity, Philosophy remains pale and 'petrified'. There is a riddle here that haunts Gaston Bachelard's thought and writing. He laboured all his life to understand the *wherefore* of this inertia and to free the philosophers from it. But even in 1927 he had the first inklings of an answer: it seemed to him that the discordancy only occurred because of a profound resemblance between the two discourses. As I have noted, the sciences bring into play the *same words* as philosophy; but these words, writes Bachelard in his Thesis, are naturally charged with ontology. They are crammed with being.[12]

Everything seems to be at stake here: when a philosopher reads a word he tends to see in it a *being*; the scientist sees in it a *concept* all of whose being is resolved in the system of *relations* in which it is inscribed. The whole *Essay* would have to be invoked here in support of this thesis. I shall have to be content to invoke a few of its major themes, whose persistence in the later works is the mark of their importance.

Of this type seem to me to be all the reflections, all the demonstrations whose aim it is to prove that the *extension* of a concept has

8. *Essai sur la connaissance approchée*, p. 21.   9. ibid., p. 24.
10. ibid., p. 28.   11. ibid., p. 243.   12. ibid., p. 53.

precedence over its *comprehension*. In *The Coherent Pluralism of Modern Chemistry*, published in 1932, we read: 'It is extension that illuminates comprehension.'[13] Which is converted into a norm: 'A study of extension (must be) substituted for a study of comprehension.'[14] To leave the problematic of chemistry, which will perhaps be judged too favourable to my demonstration, *Applied Rationalism* tells us about mathematical notions: 'It is by extending an idea to extremes that one grasps its maximum comprehension'[15] and further on, in another connexion: 'There is a proportionality between the extension and the comprehension of a concept.'[16] Despite the terminology they borrow, these remarks are not the fruit of a study of Formal Logic; they derive from a direct reflection on the structure of scientific discourse.

It seems to me that the valorization, constant in the two theses, of the notion of *order of magnitude* should be attributed to the same concern to ensure the primacy of relation over being. Thus, in the *Essay* we read:

At the school (of science), one learns to think in accord with the order of magnitude of the phenomena studied. . . . The order of magnitude may be considered as a first verification. Often it is even a sufficient proof in itself alone. Not only does it justify a method, but also, however aberrant the atmosphere surrounding it, it appears as the sign of an existence, as a decisive mark of the ontological faith of the physicist which is all the more striking the greater the imprecision of the entity suggested.[17]

A remarkable passage in that it imputes to the Physicist a displacement of ontology, from being onto relation.

A displacement corroborated by the later developments of Physics, since in an article in *Recherches Philosophiques* (1933) entitled *Noumenon and Micro-physics*, we can read the following proposition as the conclusion to a demonstration: 'The substance of the infinitely small is contemporaneous with its relations.' In this way Gaston Bachelard was led to propose the word *exstance* to replace the word

13. *Le pluralisme cohérent de la chimie moderne*, p. 61.   14. ibid., p. 99.
15. *Le rationalisme appliqué*, p. 94.   16. ibid., p. 125.
17. *Essai sur la connaissance approchée*, p. 78.

substance, which he held to be useless and dangerous;[18] I shall return to this.

Correlatively, other notions once considered to be 'primary' such as the notion of simplicity, turn out to be downgraded by this promotion of relation and order. Thus, in *The New Scientific Mind* he writes: 'In reality there are no simple phenomena, the phenomenon is a tissue of relations,' whereas in the *Essay* he had already suggested that simplicity is a function of the order of approximation envisaged.[19] All this is summed up in a lapidary sentence from *Noumenon and Micro-physics*: 'In the beginning was the Relation.'

Now, as we have seen, where there is really only a system of relations, words induce the idea that there are entities. By which Philosophy allows itself to be seduced, taking them for hard currency. The Philosophers do not know how to read the scientists. They do not see that the sciences secrete a philosophy which is not necessarily that of their statements but rather that of their stammerings, their hesitations, and ultimately of their advances. For Gaston Bachelard it is incumbent on the epistemologist to get to the secret of the sciences, to discover what the spontaneous ontology of language obliterates, starting from a principle which was to remain one of the corner-stones of his philosophy: a *word* is not a *concept*; which implies the definition of the concept by its function in a system of inter-conceptual relations.

Thus, from one wherefore we have now been thrown back on to another: why does philosophy make this mistake? By what aberration, by what inner vice is it condemned to understand nothing of scientific discourse? Another form of this question: should we despair of philosophy? the answer Bachelard will enable us to give

18. For example, in *The Philosophy of No* (English translation, p. 66) and, later, in *Applied Rationalism*, where he writes: 'Comparing the thought of the contemporary physicist with that of the eighteenth-century physicist, it is clear that the old qualification *"electric"* hardly suits the electron. The electron is no longer electric in the sense in which fluids were called electric in the eighteenth century. The *centrality* of the notion marked by the qualification *electric* has shifted. The electron is no longer truly an electric substance, it is very precisely an exstance' (*Le Rationalisme appliqué*, p. 39).

19. *Essai sur la connaissance approchée*, pp. 101ff. Notably he writes: 'This simplicity can in no respect be the proof of the reality of a law. It is only a point of view of knowing and, even within knowledge, it is completely relative.'

to it involves simultaneously the status of Philosophy, the nature of scientific knowledge and the function of the new epistemology.

I have tried to show that the principle of this question – and hence of its answer – lies in what Bachelard is *conscious* of and considers as a *symptom*: the inability of philosophy to grasp the new as a problem is for him the index of a flaw in its constitution. In other words: the most visible effect of the epistemological deficiency of philosophy is its impotence to think the History of the Sciences as it was lived at the beginning of the twentieth century: in upheaval, revolutionary, in full mutation.

From the first – in a very special modality – epistemology and History of the Sciences are linked in Bachelard's thought. They are so linked by necessity, even though the system of concepts which explains this necessity has not yet been elaborated.

2. THE PHILOSOPHICAL DISPLACEMENT

If the man of science wished to pose the philosophical question he tries each day to resolve in his own practice, he would probably formulate it as follows: 'On what conditions will the knowledge I produce be scientific?' If the philosopher wished to echo this, he would transcribe it: 'What are the foundations of scientific knowledge?' There is a very good chance that the scientist would subscribe to this second statement. However, the question is not the same; the philosopher has resorted to a real *substitution*. Let me go further: having posed *his* question will prevent the philosopher ever answering the scientist's one.

To my mind, it is this subtle play made behind a verbal screen that Gaston Bachelard was able to reveal. It is this subterfuge of philosophy that he constantly denounced. For it really is philosophy that is guilty, in the last analysis leading the man of science into error just where it might have redressed it. Such is the secret of the destiny linking the philosophy of the philosophers to the spontaneously not very clear-sighted philosophy of the scientists. It cannot be grasped unless it is seen that this *spontaneity* is, so to speak, a product of *importation*.

I have to concede, as Lenin did in other connexions (which could be shown to be less foreign to ours here than might appear): 'There is spontaneity and spontaneity.' There is indeed, besides the one I have just described, the one that made it possible to state the initial question. It involved the posing of the problem of the *constitution* of scientific knowledge (*savoir*), of its organization, of its *principles*.

These problems are, broadly speaking, those confronting Bachelardian epistemology, faithful to scientific thought. Bachelardian epistemology refuses to pose the question of the foundations of knowledge oɪ of the *guarantees* of knowledge (*savoir*) that traditional philosophy thinks within that of the duality of the Universe and the Mind. For the last two have no meaning with respect to the activity of the scientist as such.

It remains, according to Gaston Bachelard, to ask what strange perversion drives philosophy to divert the questions of the man of science from their meaning. For the moment I am content to observe, with him, that the philosophical problem of knowledge is formulated in favour of a *displacement* of the philosophical problem of scientific knowledge.

This displacement is made on condition of a preliminary distinction between Universe and Mind, or again, between the Real and Thought. This distinction is the work of philosophy. Now it is its well-foundedness that Bachelard is attacking; in his eyes, it amounts to the establishment of an imaginary hiatus in the place of the hyphen linking Physics to Mathematics. The mystery of this operation is the object of a lengthy elucidation in Bachelard's work. Made explicit at the beginning of *The New Scientific Mind*, it is expressed in a remarkable way on the first page of *Applied Rationalism*: to the 'dialogue of the experimenter equipped with precise instruments and the mathematician aspiring to inform experiment closely', corresponds in Philosophy the dispute between the Realist and the Rationalist. The former exchange information, the latter arguments. A pitiful situation for Philosophy, in which the dispute is never closed through the absence of any possible agreement between the interlocutors. Each is on his own side, one standing for Thought; the other for the Real.

This point seems fundamental to me, not only because it is the object of a continuous philosophical meditation by Bachelard between 1927 and 1953, but because it also gives us access to what, for him, constitutes the essence of scientific thought, and enables us to glimpse the essence of philosophy. Indeed, I think that the persistence for a quarter of a century of his polemic against what he calls 'Realism' – a term whose definition can be seen to vary between a sensualist empiricism and a realism of the essence of a Platonic type – that the obstinacy of his efforts to refute Meyerson – whose name still appears in his texts of 1953, more than thirty years after *Identité et Réalité* – can only be understood if it is clear that in them Bachelard was denouncing the *essence of philosophy*.

The initial conceptual couple installed by Philosophy may be read: Real/Thought or Being/Knowledge or again: Reason/Experience; but also as Being/Thought or Real/Knowledge, or any combination you like. They are nearly all condemned in Gaston Bachelard's work. In each of the couples the two terms are face to face: the 'philosophical' problem consists of linking them together. The foundation of each is thus looked for in the other.

Now, there are two possibilities, and only two: either the foundation of Knowledge is sought in Being, of Thought in the Real, and one is in some way or other a 'realist'; or else the foundation of Being is sought in Thought and one is in some way or another an 'idealist'. Bachelard's thought fights on both these fronts; what it makes visible is the fact that the ones are no better than the others: it is the couple itself which has to be rejected.

Once the initial distinction has been established, the field of philosophy is open; there is no stopping its production of other couples of concepts; let me list those which constitute most especially objects of reflection for Bachelard:[20] subject/object, concrete/abstract, given/construct, natural/artificial, intuition/deduction, wealth/poverty.... Before following the Bachelardian analysis in detail, let me take it upon myself to push the list to its end, which will then release its meaning; it seems to me that the last of the couples can be formulated thus: *philosophy/science*, where 'philosophy'

20. See the *Index* in the Appendices to Part One for the main texts on this point.

appears on the side on which are also found the given, the concrete, wealth; on the contrary, science is called abstract, artificial, poor.

In his Speech of 1949 on 'The Philosophical Problem of Scientific Methods',[21] Bachelard said: 'If a philosopher speaks of knowledge, he wants it direct, immediate, intuitive,' and he added: 'The man of the sciences, whose thought is so opinionated and ardent, whose thought is so living, is presented as someone abstract.' Many other texts could be cited in support of this one; but let me rather pose it a question: '*Who* places philosophy in this comfortable situation of having a direct grip on the real?' Answer: a philosopher.

This reveals the sense of the initial distinction; and at the same time a singular and constitutive operation of philosophy is unveiled, one by which it thinks the distinction Being/Thought under the domination of the hierarchized couple: Philosophy/Science. I shall show, from the texts, that Gaston Bachelard *discovered* that philosophy only established the former couple to provide a basis for the latter.

At the beginning of *The Formation of the Scientific Mind* we read: 'In this book, I propose to show (the) mighty destiny of abstract scientific thought. To do so I shall have to prove that *abstract thought* is not synonymous with *scientific bad conscience*, as the banal accusation would seem to suggest.'[22] Philosophy is both judge and party to the dispute: it is Philosophy that accuses and states the law about which the scientist, having contravened it, has a bad conscience. This passage would suffice to prove that the final couple is indeed the truth of the third (abstract/concrete).

In *The Rationalist Activity of Contemporary Physics*, a long reflection on the notional constitution of Bohr's magneton comes to a conclusion in the following ardent text:

What a knot of primary notions! what a unique enrichment of the particle principle! Meditating on this notional structure, the philosopher would have a fine opportunity to take back the judgement in which he denounces the *abstract* character of scientific thought.[23]

21. A speech at the *Congrès international de Philosophie des Sciences* (1949).
22. *La formation de l'esprit scientifique*, p. 6.
23. *L'activité rationaliste de la physique contemporaine*, p. 167.

It is clear here that the disappearance, at the level of modern scientific practice, of the couple Real/Thought would have the effect of inverting the relationship: Philosophy/Science. In other words, we have here a demonstration of my thesis in the opposite sense to the first text cited. The examples could be multiplied: the couple abstract/concrete is present everywhere; everywhere brought back into question as the favourite resort of the philosopher to affirm his superiority over the scientist.

We shall see that one of the tasks of Bachelardian epistemology is to invert these couples, to distort them in order to show their inanity; without anticipating too much on later developments, we shall find Bachelard affirming sometimes the concretization of the abstract, at others the de-realization of the real, or again the construction of the given, and, inversely, the intuitive value of the construct. . . .

In the *Essay on Approximate Knowledge*, we read:

The datum or given is relative to the culture, it is necessarily implied in a construction. . . . A given has to be received. It will never be possible to dissociate completely the order of the given and the method of its description. . . . Between these two terms – which represent for me the minimum opposition of the mind and the real – there are constant reactions which arouse reciprocal echoes,[24]

which Bachelard returns to in lapidary fashion in *The Inductive Value of Relativity*: 'Once a given has been received, it is already understood.'[25] Once again, it is a matter of disqualifying a typical couple of philosophy. The proof is constantly present, in two passages from *The Rationalist Activity of Contemporary Physics*: modern science, says page 87, destroys the notion of a datum or given 'so traditionally received in Philosophy', and, further on: 'The traditional philosophical notion of a datum or *given* is highly improper to characterize the *result* of laborious determinations of experimental values.'[26] Lastly, to round off the demonstration, let me cite the following passage from *The Coherent Pluralism of Modern Chemistry*, a book which appeared in 1932: 'There is a tendency to attribute

24. *Essai sur la connaissance approchée*, pp. 14–15.
25. *La valeur inductive de la rélativité*, p. 241.
26. *L'activité rationaliste de la physique contemporaine*, p. 124.

to the datum or *given* an inexhaustible diversity . . . a prodigious and gratuitous *diversity*, multiple both in forms and in substances',[27] in which it is quite clear that with the given, it is wealth that Philosophy is in fact attributing to itself.

But allow me to take the opportunity offered by these examples to advance a few remarks which justify, to my mind at least, the method of reading I am using. One thing is indeed clear: in Bachelard's text, philosophy is never present in person, never expounded for its own sake. It is never seen to emerge save *in actu* in the objections or reproaches it makes against scientific knowledge. This confirms what I have said about the architecture of Bachelard's discourse. Let me add that, in principle, the philosophical notions are isolated by Bachelard and then transported outside the system that has given them birth into domains to which they are foreign; domains in which they are literally and visibly *'dépaysées'*. Think, for example, of the so strange – and probably, for a Kantian, so scandalous – use he makes of the notion of 'noumenon'. I draw the following lesson: in Gaston Bachelard's text, the fate of a whole philosophy often hangs *on a single word*.

Between the conceptual couples instituted by philosophy, which does have to *recognize* the existence and validity – however minimal – of scientific knowledge, it is a matter of establishing a harmony. This is the office of the notion of *truth*. A philosophical concept *par excellence* which, in the field of philosophical thought, stands in for the scientific notion of objectivity, by displacing it. This is a point to which I shall return; I must be content here to pose the question: *who* will state the truth? once again: the philosopher; since he is on the side of the real, since the real is given to him without mediations, since he is from the outset the depository of the unity of the couple. *He*, the man of the least effort, will be able to judge the 'heroic work of the man of science'.

In psychological terms, Bachelard invites us to read in this notion of truth the whole 'self-sufficiency' or 'conceit' of the philosopher. In other words: philosophy installs a system of concepts in which it is sufficient unto itself; it is itself the legislator there, ordering the

27. *Le pluralisme cohérent de la chimie moderne*, p. 11.

degrees of knowledge by auto-placing itself at the top of a hierarchy which it has itself established.

I should like to show, in conclusion, that one particular problem crystallizes all the oppositions. The theoretical conjuncture had made it into a 'point of philosophical sensitivity'. This is the problem of qualities, placed on the agenda by the appearance of micro-physics, which, as we have already seen, brought the sensorily given back into question.

In *Rational Materialism*, Bachelard writes:

The scientist is challenged to know matter 'to the core' (*dans son fond*). To the *quantitativism* of matter is thus opposed a *qualitativism*. And the philosopher claims that only highly nuanced intuitions can make quality tangible to us. He grasps quality in its essence, as one tastes a fine wine. He lives the nuances. He lives quality 'immediately', as if sensuous life further super-individualized the individuality of the matter offered to sensation.[28]

It does not matter much to us whether one can give a name to this 'philosopher'; what is most significant about this discreetly ironic text seems to me to be the illustration it gives of the status of this kind of philosophy. In the challenge it throws down before the scientist we can see the polemical obverse of the proposition that sustains it, according to which 'science cannot know everything'.[29] Or, in a less discreet form: let science keep its place; philosophy has its word to say.

In the same work there is a text to which I shall have occasion to return in detail: 'The colour of a cherry, if one takes that colour as the object of an immediate experience, is hardly more than a sign of its ripeness. This is the experience of the housewife at the market-place . . .,' or again, adds Bachelard, that of the painter at his easel.[30] He concludes: 'These utilitarian or aesthetic . . . experiences should be studied in the domains in which they arise, if need be in the

28. *Le matérialisme rationnel*, p. 62.
29. I have borrowed this expression from Pierre Macherey who, in a series of lectures at the École Normale Supérieure in 1967–8, used it for the same purpose: to characterize philosophies which exploit the difficulties of the sciences for their own ends.
30. *Le matérialisme rationnel*, p. 195.

echoes of subjectivity which give them the facile glory of the philosophies of intuition. But they cannot be central themes for the philosophical problem of the objectivity of the qualities of matter.' Thus, in this text we see Bachelard operating a *correction*: for the imaginary – and displaced (out of their 'domain') – problems of traditional philosophy he substitutes the problems that are actually posed in the practice of contemporary science; one word is enough to characterize them: objectivity.

I shall stop quoting here; but analogous texts could be found in many of his works, in particular in *The Coherent Pluralism of Modern Chemistry*[31] and *Applied Rationalism*.

I am therefore justified in claiming that what Bachelard discovers is the fact that the system of concepts installed by philosophy has the effect of *repeating* the real problems of scientific knowledge while subjecting them to a displacement. The result – which we can finally see to be the *aim* – of the operation is to place philosophy in the commanding position in the hierarchy of knowledge established by it.

It is already clear what Bachelard meant when in *Applied Rationalism* he wrote: '(Many) philosophies present themselves . . . and claim to impose a *super-ego* on scientific culture.'[32] It will be even clearer when we have studied the particular cases of the philosophy of Émile Meyerson and of Realism.

3. THE PHILOSOPHY OF THE IMMOBILE

From 1927 – and for ever afterwards – Émile Meyerson embodied the pretentious philosophy that glories in the perennial nature of its questions and aims to subordinate scientific knowledge to its degrees. In the Preface to his work on Relativity, which is entitled *Relativist Deduction* (*La déduction rélativiste*), Meyerson writes: 'It is a matter of drawing from the relativist theories information about the principles of scientific reasoning in general,'[33] in other words: of making

31. Notably *Le pluralisme cohérent de la chimie moderne*, pp. 34–5 and 72–3.
32. *Le rationalisme appliqué*, p. 79.
33. Émile Meyerson: *La déduction rélativiste*, Paris, 1925, p. xv.

those theories leave the domain of precise questions in which they have come to light and which gives them meaning, for the 'generalizations' in which philosophy reigns. Later in the same book we can read the following disguised confession:

Let us be content to conclude that, in this matter, the scientist will be obliged to guard himself carefully from the temptation, which constantly obsesses him, to encroach on the domain of philosophy; for every man, including the scientist . . ., produces philosophy as he lives.[34]

Let us, in our turn, be content to note that the modesty of the terms cannot mask the ambition of the proposal: to establish the legislation of philosophy. Allow me to leave until later my examination of the final proposition which, in Bachelard, finds a quite different echo.

Relativist Deduction finds a response five years later in *The Inductive Value of Relativity*. The refutation could not be clearer; sometimes it is a chapter heading that responds to Meyerson: thus, the last chapter of the *Essay*, entitled 'Rectification and Reality', confronts the work of 1907: *Identity and Reality*. Often the opposition is focused in a phrase, an expression which is adopted and turned inside out by Bachelard, in passing.

Émile Meyerson writes, citing a Belgian professor:

One gets rid of what is *relative* to the various observers in order to obtain the *absolute*, represented here by a distance. All the observers study the same geometrical space, and it is in this setting, placed once and for all, that physical phenomena unfold.

'This', Émile Meyerson goes on,

is a remark eminently suited to make tangible to us the extent to which the thought process obeyed by the relativists conforms to the eternal canon of the human intellect, which has constituted not only science, but, before it, the world of common sense. Indeed, this world of absolute invariants, placed in the eternal setting of space, is not only the world of the mechanics of Galileo and Descartes, it is also that of our immediate perception.[35]

This text is characteristic and instructive: it is necessary to take

34. ibid., p. 76.   35. ibid., p. 69.

the opposite view on every point to grasp Bachelard's thought . . . and also the essence of the theory of Relativity, for it is a fine illustration of that philosopher's science unceasingly denounced by Gaston Bachelard. For our purposes, let us note that it is quite clear in what sense and on what conditions Meyerson can speak of relativist 'deduction': one must previously have posed the existence of 'an eternal canon of the human intellect' in order to affirm, correspondingly, that there is a *continuity* between science and the world of common sense, with the reservation of a *reduction* of space to a 'setting' (*décor*). The visible effect of these intra-philosophical processes in the historical conjuncture is to misrecognize the 'novelty' of these relativist theories. In the same book, Meyerson affirms that he 'is unable to doubt the strict continuity between the most recent avatar of scientific theories and the phases that have preceded it'.[36]

But now we come to the heart of the matter: 'The real of relativist theory is, quite certainly, an ontological absolute, a veritable being-in-itself, and even more ontological than the things of common sense and pre-Einsteinian physics.'[37] The ontological inebrity of this text cannot mask the difficulty Meyerson experiences in safeguarding the absolutes; he needs, as Gaston Bachelard says somewhere, 'hoards of erudition and patience'. A whole section of the book, and, it must be said, a very strange one for a reader of Bachelard, is devoted to conjectures – ornamented with the promising title 'Glimpses of the Future' – about a possible return to 'classical' conceptions of space and time. Émile Meyerson confesses: 'Reason has to do violence to itself to adapt itself to the forms imposed on it by Relativism.'[38] Allow me to set beside this passage the one from *The New Scientific Mind* where Bachelard writes: 'The mind has a variable structure from the moment knowledge has a history.'[39] We might say that the principles of Meyerson's philosophy are the absolutes of Reason, whereas Gaston Bachelard, following Georges Bouligand, proclaimed the arrival of the time of the 'decline of absolutes'.

36. ibid., p. 71.   37. ibid., p. 79.   38. ibid., p. 366.
39. *Le nouvel esprit scientifique*, p. 173.

The implicit postulate that explains the predominance of measurement in physical science is the profound conviction that the real is intelligible,

writes Meyerson, 'but', he objects,

that is an untenable opinion. Nothing is more manifest than the fact that our intellect is on no occasion content with a mere description of the phenomenon, that it always goes further, and that the knowledge it aims for is not purely external and destined solely to facilitate action, but rather inner knowledge, enabling it to penetrate the veritable being of things.[40]

The world of common sense, even, is only a stage on this road. Ignoring the purely descriptive conception of science revealed in this text, let us note that it constitutes the last word – according to Gaston Bachelard – of philosophies of this type: the systematic depreciation of scientific knowledge in favour of another kind of knowledge, which it claims is more profound because it is more immediate. Something I have summarized as: 'Science cannot know everything.'

Note, finally, that of necessity a philosophy which affirms the unity and eternity of Reason, which seeks in the categories of Thought the guarantee for scientific knowledge, must one way or another establish a continuity between the world of common sense and that of science.[41]

Beyond Émile Meyerson, a whole philosophical current is denoted by the name 'Realism'. The following provisional definition can be found in *The Inductive Value of Relativity*: 'I call realism every doctrine that maintains the organization of impressions at the level of the impressions themselves, that places the general after the particular, as a simplification of the particular, that believes, consequently, in the prolix richness of individual sensation and the systematic impoverishment of the thought which abstracts.'[42] All characteristics that can quite strictly be applied to the Meyersonian doctrine. At the opposite extreme to this strict definition, Bachelard's last great epistemological work contains the following thesis:

---

40. *La déduction relativiste*, p. 13.
41. That is the fate of all Classical Philosophy, with the exception of the philosophy of Spinoza.   42. *La valeur inductive de la relativité*, p. 206.

'All philosophy, explicitly or tacitly, honestly, or surreptitiously, makes use of the *realist function*. All philosophy deposits, projects or presupposes a reality.'[43]

I think it is extremely important to measure the *dispersion* (*écart*) to which these two texts bear witness. To my mind it amounts to a transition from the definition of realism as a philosophical doctrine to its recognition as an epistemological function. This very fact invites us to register and reflect on the variations produced on the term 'realism' in Bachelard's text. Not for the satisfaction – already legitimate in itself – of establishing in it the sense or senses of a word, but with the idea that what we shall find is actually valid for all philosophy.

I think I can show that this will be a question of the last of the recognitions: the one that will free scientific thought from the distorted representations which philosophy has given of it, and in which it thought it was reflecting itself. The essence of scientific thought will thus appear; but also the essence of philosophy will be precipitated – to coin a phrase – and the tasks of a new discipline pushed to the fore.

It has seemed to me, on reading these texts, that the (philosophical) problem of Realism was posed by Bachelard vis-à-vis three precise (scientific) notions: the notion of *object*, that of *experience* or *experiment*, and that of *data* or the *given*. These notions are the site, in his work, of a constant play and work. For they constitute part of the language apparently common to the scientist and the philosopher. It is clear that the notions of the Real, of Reason, of Nature and of Mind . . ., do not intervene as such in the scientist's activity; they are external to the practice of the scientist and he only gives them credit at the moment when, leaving the laboratory, he poses himself questions about his own work which he knows to be philosophical.[44]

But the notions of experience or experiment, object and datum or given are both intra-scientific and philosophical. I intend to prove

43. *Le matérialisme rationnel*, p. 141.

44. Louis Althusser recently proposed (lectures at the École Normale Supérieure, 1967–8) to distinguish between the 'spontaneous philosophy of the scientist' and his 'world outlook'. I feel that this distinction correctly handles the one Gaston Bachelard is setting to work but not thematizing here.

how Bachelard grasped that they were the site of constant slides, the bias by which philosophy intervened surreptitiously in the practice of scientific knowledge. The result is a *struggle* between antagonistic, contradictory forces. In which these notions are literally 'crucial'.

At the beginning of *The Rationalist Activity of Contemporary Physics*, we read: 'The notion of object seems to me to be revolutionized by the displacement demanded by micro-physics.'[45] To find what is the precise nature of this displacement, we can read for example in *The Dialectic of Duration*, a work which appeared in 1936, two years after *Thought and the Moving* (*La Pensée et le Mouvant*) which it refutes: 'We have reached a level of knowledge at which the scientific objects are what we make them, no more and no less. . . . We are *realising* by degrees our theoretical thought,'[46] or again in *The Formation of the Scientific Mind*: 'The object may not be designated as an *immediate* "*objective*"; in other words, a march towards the objective is not initially objective. It is therefore necessary to accept a true rupture between sensory knowledge and scientific knowledge.'[47]

By the play on words that he suggests (object-objective), Bachelard is, as always, inviting us to beware of the spontaneous ontology of language. He puts us in a position to detach ourselves from it. It is at this point that Gaston Bachelard, aware of the fact that 'the old words are not sufficient to say everything',[48] attempts to invent some new ones. Thus, in *The Philosophy of No*, he proposes the notion of a *super-object* (*sur-objet*). He defines it as follows: 'The super-object is the *result* of a critical objectification, of an objectivity which only retains that part of the object which it has criticized.'[49]

In *The New Scientific Mind* he had already tried to lead us out of the spontaneity of language by another play on words: 'Above the *subject*, beyond the immediate *object*, modern science is founded on the *project*.'[50] But, succumbing to the fate of those who try to say

45. *L'activité rationaliste de la physique contemporaine*, p. 16.
46. *La dialectique de la durée*, pp. 63–4.
47. *La formation de l'esprit scientifique*, p. 239.
48. *Le rationalisme appliqué*, p. 134.
49. *The Philosophy of No*, p. 119.
50. *Le nouvel esprit scientifique*, p. 11.

something new and have to use ordinary language to make themselves understood, in *Rational Materialism* he abandons the neologisms of earlier years and uses another procedure – one frequent in his work – which I should like to call: 'disqualifying qualification': instead of saying object, Bachelard writes: 'secondary object'. The qualification 'secondary' having the effect of ruling out all the empiricist implications that might have been slipped into the word 'object'. Taking up the discussion about the tetrahedral representation of carbon, he writes: 'As we shall see, the debate definitely turns on an object without a direct realistic value in ordinary experience, on an object which has to be designated as a *secondary object*, on an object preceded by theories.'[51] And he adds, justifying my insistence: 'I repeat these philosophical observations again and again because I venture to uphold the thesis of a rupture between scientific knowledge and ordinary knowledge.'

What Bachelard is revealing here is the fact that when a scientist and a philosopher pronounce the word object, when they introduce it into their discourse, they are not discussing the same thing, or, rather: philosophy is discussing a *thing* and the scientist is discussing a *result*. We understand why Bachelard wrote in *Rational Materialism*: 'The object is only instituted at the end of a long process of rational objectivity.'[52] A proposition strictly impossible for a Philosopher. On this point the 'work' of philosophy can be characterized as follows: it takes as its theme the object-result, a scientific concept, and inserts it in the philosophical couple subject/object. What it says about it is still valid only for the object-thing of philosophical discourse.

The same demonstration could be repeated vis-à-vis the notion of experience or experiment, or vis-à-vis that of data or the given; or again vis-à-vis the derived notions of observation, facts, etc. The same conclusions would be drawn: philosophy plays on these words in order to erase or fill in the discontinuity between ordinary immediate experience – the *lived* – and the production of scientific thought. It disengages concepts which, as such, have meanings

51. *Le matérialisme rationnel*, p. 142.   52. *Le matérialisme rationnel*, p. 187.

through the places they occupy in the system of scientific thought, it reduces them to nothing more than words which it inserts as such into its vocabulary and uses in a diversionary way. Recognition of the essential progress of scientific knowledge in order to annul it, such is the constant procedure of the Philosopher.

But we have gone one step further: it is now clear that the criterion of scientific thought cannot be sought in an object outside knowledge, a philosophical function of a hallucinatory type. The firm ground, the only firm ground once, like Gaston Bachelard, one is convinced of the eminently progressive character of scientific thought, is the process of objectification which Philosophy failed to think.

But to think scientific knowledge as a process is to displace the traditional questions; it is to refuse to think 'Knowledge' without specification; it is to refuse to admit that a knowledge might reach being itself, without mediation; in the last analysis it is to affirm that the essential discursivity of scientific knowledge is the pledge of its objectivity.

To close, I shall now rapidly show how the change in terrain we have just witnessed rebounds on the philosophical notion of truth. This repercussion might be defined as follows: its effect is to reveal the notion of truth as philosophical. No sooner is this effect produced than it leads to another: the notion of *error* – thought in its relation to that of truth – has to be corrected.

In fact, Gaston Bachelard often returned to this point to show that he gave a quite new sense to error. So much so that it has been possible to write that the positivity of error belongs to the 'axioms' of his epistemology.[53] Here we see in what way the question of error is indeed essential to his epistemology; it is a point of demarcation for him vis-à-vis the Philosophers

Even in the Thesis of 1927, Bachelard writes:

The problem of *error* seems to me to come before the problem of truth, or rather, I have found no possible solution to the problem of truth other than dispelling finer and finer errors.[54]

53. Georges Canguilhem: 'Sur une épistémologie concordataire', *Hommage à Gaston Bachelard*, 1957, p. 5.
54. *Essai sur la connaissance approchée*, p. 244.

In *Applied Rationalism*, he writes:
If one poses the problem of error on the plane of scientific errors, it emerges very clearly, or rather, concretely, that *error* and truth are not symmetrical, as a purely logical and formal philosophy might lead one to think.[55]

If scientific thought is a process for which neither its point of departure nor its point of arrival are that 'presupposed, deposited or projected' real which philosophy cannot do without, but an always-already-thought, organized real, it is clear that error is no longer an accident on the road, but an essential, necessary and driving moment of knowledge. But also: there is no eternal instance that can decide in sovereign fashion on the true and the false, since philosophy no longer has this privilege. If so, error will only emerge as such after its rectification in a historical process. Thus we find, at the end of this polemic against Realism as an ideological philosophy of science or as a fundamental scientific ideology, that with Gaston Bachelard, history is introduced into epistemology.

I have borrowed the terms philosophical ideology or ideological philosophy from a vocabulary which is not that of Bachelard; but it seems to me that it does enable us to explain the extension acquired in the course of his works by the term Realism. Overstepping the bounds of its original terrain, the notion serves progressively to designate all sorts of philosophies: Empiricism, but also Phenomenology in *The Rationalist Activity of Contemporary Physics*, Existentialism, but also, as we have seen, a purely logical and formal philosophy. The only *raison d'être* for this extension is the *function* (the 'realist function') performed by philosophy alongside science; this function, as I have demonstrated at length, is to displace the scientific concepts to ends which are external to scientific knowledge. It seems to me that strictly speaking one could say that it is a matter of a general ideology of science, in the sense defined by Louis Althusser. I dare even to think that Gaston Bachelard would have been so generous as to have accepted this vocabulary, seeing in it the new words capable of expressing adequately what was most new in his thought.

55. *Le rationalisme appliqué*, p. 58.

4. MATHEMATICS AND LANGUAGE

I shall attempt to prove that in Gaston Bachelard's eyes every 'ideological' conception of scientific knowledge depends in the last analysis on a misrecognition of the role and nature of *mathematics*. It is indeed a constant theme from the *Essay* to the works of the 1950s that mathematics cannot be conceived as a *language*, even a well-made one. This insistence I shall treat as an *index*: if Philosophy, when it wishes to explain the function of mathematics, repeatedly states that it is a language, it is certainly no accident. That Bachelard constantly and radically opposed this thesis by showing that it missed the essentials of scientific thought, cannot be seen as a coincidence.

In *The New Scientific Mind*, Bachelard writes:

> What might give rise to the idea that the scientific mind remains basically of the same kind through the most profound rectifications, is an incorrect estimation of the role of mathematics in scientific thought. It has been endlessly repeated that mathematics is a language, a mere means of expression. It has become customary to think of it as a tool at the disposal of a Reason conscious of itself, the master of pure ideas endowed with a pre-mathematical clarity. Such a segmentation might have had some meaning at the origins of scientific thinking, when the first images of intuition had a suggestive force and helped theory to constitute itself.[56]

I close this long passage here, but it is the whole of the beginning of Chapter III that should be discussed in this commentary. The quotation I have just given would be enough to prove that we have not left the heart of our problem, if it is true that it reveals that the eternity of an immobile Reason depends in the last instance on a certain conception of Mathematics.

In *The Formation of the Scientific Mind*, Bachelard shows how the whole philosophy of *observation* dominant in the eighteenth century had as a 'leitmotif' the separation of Mathematics from Physics. He quotes De Marivetz, who had offered the following opinion: 'The phrase, *to calculate a phenomenon*, is very improper; it was introduced into Physics by those who know better how to *calculate* than how to

---

56. *Le nouvel esprit scientifique*, p. 53.

explain.' Bachelard comments as follows: 'It would be enough to force slightly the words of this opinion on the role of mathematics in Physics to discover the epistemological theory constantly repeated nowadays that mathematics *expresses* but does not explain. Against this theory I believe myself that mathematical thought forms the basis of physical explanation and that the conditions of abstract thought are from now on inseparable from the conditions of scientific experiment.'[57] Here too we can see Bachelard amending the philosophical couple abstract/concrete vis-à-vis the recognition of the real relations between Mathematics and Physics.

It is interesting to see that, in the *Essay on Approximate Knowledge*, Gaston Bachelard, still at this point the prisoner of philosophical phraseology, already feels all its inadequacy. Thus one can read this strange sentence: 'Physical science has found in mathematics a language which detaches itself without difficulty from its experimental basis and, so to speak, thinks all by itself.'[58] The 'so to speak' (*pour ainsi dire*) cannot hide from us the fact that a language which thinks all by itself is precisely no longer a language in the eyes of classical philosophy.

The essence of Mathematics, for Gaston Bachelard, lies in its power of *invention*; it is the driving element of the dynamism of scientific thought. In *The Philosophy of No* he writes:

When one follows the efforts of contemporary thought to understand the atom, one comes close to believing that the fundamental role of the atom is to oblige men to do mathematics. *De la mathématique avant toute chose. . . .*[59]

Behind this *bon mot* we are invited to read a very profound conviction. In the already cited article in *Recherches Philosophiques*, 'Noumenon and Micro-physics', he develops his thought as follows:

The real of Mathematical-Physics enriches itself by a double dynamism: in studying it, one has as much chance of discovering phenomena as theorems. Anyway, it is always necessary to reach the point of *realising* the

57. *La formation de l'esprit scientifique*, p. 231.
58. *Essai sur la connaissance approchée*, p. 10.
59. *The Philosophy of No*, p. 32.

theorems thus discovered. For this task, it is no longer a question, as was constantly repeated in the nineteenth century, of translating into mathematical language the facts released by experiment . . .

Indeed, 'the power of discovery has almost entirely passed to mathematical theory'.

Twenty years later, things are even clearer: in *The Rationalist Activity of Contemporary Physics*, we read: 'It is essential to break with that stereotype dear to sceptical philosophers who will see nothing in mathematics but a *language*. On the contrary, mathematics is a *thought*, a thought certain of its language. The physicist thinks the experiment with this mathematical thought.'[60] To give this text its true significance, it should be realized that when Bachelard writes 'sceptical philosophers' he is not aiming at any particular school of philosophy but at philosophers in general who are sceptical about the power of invention of mathematics: on the other hand, other texts have to be adduced to grasp what Bachelard means by 'thought' when he writes that mathematics is a *thought* (*pensée*). Now in *Noumenon and Micro-physics*, we read: 'A good physical hypothesis is necessarily mathematical in kind', and in the *The Rationalist Activity*: 'Scientific hypotheses are from now on inseparable from their mathematical form: they are truly mathematical thoughts.'[61] Hence Mathematics must be understood to provide Physics with its body of hypotheses – in short to provide its theories.

And we find Bachelard expressing clearly what he could only suggest in the *Essay*: 'It has been too quickly said that mathematics is a mere language which expresses observational facts in its own way. This language is, more than any other, inseparable from thought. Mathematics cannot be *spoken* without being mathematically *understood*.' This is what Bachelard was trying to say twenty years earlier when he wrote that mathematics was a language that thinks all by itself.

But let me push the demonstration a little further: it emerges at the same moment that these 'sceptical philosophers' ally in a single thought, without any contradiction, the *formalism* of mathematics

60. *L'activité rationaliste de la physique contemporaine*, p. 29.   61. ibid.

and the *empiricism* of the object. Mathematics is attributed the role of a 'universal instrument of representation'[62] pre-prepared for any discourse. In other words, the mathematician is an *interpreter*: he substitutes the clear form of his language for another already present but *latent* language. However little we can understand it, the real is loquacious. This implies a whole conception of knowledge as a mere translation, as a reading of another text inscribed in 'the real'.[63]

Bachelard's theoretical genius is to have seen, by means of the treatment that this conception reserves for mathematical thought, that it is the conception of all previous philosophy.

This mistake provides us with the key to so many others, but we still have to discover the reason for it. We shall find that this investigation leads us, in Bachelard's wake, outside philosophical thought and outside scientific thought itself. But I shall not anticipate: I would rather illustrate the conclusions I have been able to formulate vis-à-vis mathematics in general by a reflection on one particular notion.

This notion, which has an important role in Bachelard's thought, is the mathematical notion of an *operator*. All of Chapter IV of *The Experience of Space in Contemporary Physics*, a work which appeared in 1940, is devoted to it, as well as Chapter VIII of *The Rationalist Activity*. To use an expression of Bachelard's from the former work,[64] this notion enables us to fight on two opposite fronts: against mathematical formalism and against philosophical realism. We can make 'the same answer to both: mathematics surpasses in inventive thought both conventions and experiments'.

What formalism takes for a 'form' must be considered as an 'operator'; the operator thus appears as a plan for the realization of mathematical laws. We find Bachelard, in the matter of piezo-electricity, defining the laboratory crystal as follows:

'The crystal created in the laboratory is no longer truly an *object*, it is an instrument. More accurately, in the same style as that in which mathematics speaks of operators, the crystal, technically

---

62. Another loan from Pierre Macherey.
63. Cf. on this Louis Althusser in *Reading Capital*, NLB, London, 1970, Part One.
64. *L'expérience de l'espace dans la physique contemporaine*, p. 94.

formed, is an *operator* of phenomena.'[65] Allow me to turn the metaphor around: it will then seem that mathematics, the crystal of thought, is that without which Physics could not advance.

It is thus its misrecognition of the role of mathematics in scientific thought that prevents philosophy from thinking the sciences as a historical process of production of knowledges. It is to this that Gaston Bachelard always brings us back, and he is prepared to characterize all philosophy by reference to it.

5. PHILOSOPHICAL TOPOLOGY

Once, like Gaston Bachelard, we have recognized that the criterion of scientific knowledge is not to be sought, on the pretext of a foundation, outside its own field; that the process which it constitutes is a process of progressive objectification by successive rectifications which reveal, by way of recurrence, the raw material on which thought works – and which one can call the 'given' if one really wants to – as a tissue of errors; once we have proceeded to these recognitions, as I have shown, we are in a position to assign to philosophy its true nature, since it becomes obvious that it is philosophy which has prevented this operation of recognition from being immediate; it is philosophy which, by the constitution of inadequate couples and the institution of an overbearing jurisdiction, has prevented what is perfectly obvious from being seen as such; not only by the philosophers, but also, what is more serious, by the scientists themselves when they come to pose themselves philosophical problems.

This set of results, the polemical acquisition of which we have been able to witness, makes it possible to characterize all philosophy with respect to Scientific Activity as I have described it. In this sense it can indeed be said that 'science orders philosophy'; that is how Gaston Bachelard is able, in a text from *The Applied Rationalism*,[66] to propose the operational metaphor of a *philosophical spectrum* which I shall reproduce and comment on here:

65. *Le rationalisme appliqué*, p. 202.   66. *Le rationalisme appliqué*, p. 5.

A first observation: by reproducing it in this way, I am unfaithful to Bachelard's text in omitting the central line with its inscribed blanks. This is from a necessity of exposition, since the terms that appear in them in Bachelard designate the new epistemology, all of whose concepts we have not yet put into place.

But the blanks I have left are not totally indeterminate: indeed, we can say of them that they will provide a place for a doctrine which respects scientific procedure in its reality, i.e., in its structure (in the arrangement of its forms) and in its progress. We can even go further and state that this doctrine will have to respect *both* the rational aspect of the production of concepts and the experimental aspect of what I shall provisionally call the application of science. That is why I have to inscribe, not one but two blanks in my schema. It should also be added that these blanks must be – highly – co-ordinated, otherwise some metaphysics would install itself in the gap between them, overjoyed to have rediscovered a couple it could make its own.

One step further: the new epistemology, constructed as close as possible to the activity of scientific knowledge, is what enables us by its central place to see the truth of all philosophy. It is that from which all philosophy receives its truth, it is the principle of organiza-tion of the *'philosophical topology'*[67] which is presented to us here.

I say: 'all philosophy', and not just all philosophy of the sciences,

---

67. ibid., p. 7.

for it is clear that all philosophy is in some respect or other, whether it wills it or not, a philosophy of the sciences. Precisely to the extent that all philosophy contains as one of its principal parts a 'Theory of Knowledge'. All this, as we have seen, is what Bachelard obliges us to think. In fact, the spectrum presented here offers us a kind of 'range': from philosophies which present themselves as strictly linked to scientific thought such as positivism and formalism, we pass on to much looser 'philosophical functions' under whose headings all philosophies can find a place.[68]

We must now follow closely the explanation Bachelard gives of this topology; which amounts to giving a commentary on what I have hitherto left in the shade: the vertical arrows linking the doctrines together. A first remark, quite formal but not without importance: these arrows are symmetrical and inverted with respect to the central line. In other words, by folding the schema about its centre, they can be made to coincide.

What would this fold signify? that each of the doctrines can be inverted into the apparently contradictory doctrine without its nature being changed thereby. This should not surprise us after the analysis I have made of 'Realism' (i.e., of one of the terms of the topology), but it does enable us to fix the theoretical reason for the reversal we have already seen functioning.

This reason is that the *nature* of each of the doctrines resides not in itself but in the *fold*, the fixed point in philosophical space. In this case the vectors which appear between the doctrines are not physically oriented; the symmetry is purely geometrical; if one *is* at the point marked 'conventionalism' one is at the same place as the point 'empiricism' since ultimately only the absolute value of the dispersion counts.

The same thing has been expressed in other terms vis-à-vis something else: 'Two systems of thoughts which rediscover the same

---

68. The reader who wishes to see the 'spectral analysis' at work on a particular notion should look at Chapter VII of *The Rationalist Activity*, which begins: 'By itself the notion of spin could be the object of a congress of philosophers in search of precise discussions. This notion would be highly appropriate to the determination of a spectral analysis of philosophies of knowledge' (*L'activité rationaliste de la physique contemporaine*, p. 163). It is to the outline of that analysis that Bachelard proceeds in this chapter.

elements with the same relations but simply the opposite way round are basically reducible to a single form.'[69]

But there is more, says Gaston Bachelard, proceeding with his commentary on the philosophical spectrum: it is possible to consider that on each side of the fold the doctrines are complementary and themselves ordered with respect to the outer extreme; Idealism on the one hand; Realism on the other. It is these two extreme points that ensure the consistency of the 'inferior' doctrines, so much so that it would not be incorrect, it seems to me, to duplicate the inscribed arrows with inverse arrows. Note besides that these new arrows would represent what the *philosopher* is conscious of in his relation to the sciences: a Philosopher *lives* his relation to scientific knowledge 'in an idealist light' or 'in an idealist system', for example.

Such are the lessons we can draw from 'Bachelardian topology'; bearing in mind the results we have already obtained.

I think we can draw several supplementary conclusions of the highest importance. I shall state the first as follows: 'philosophy has no object'.[70] It does indeed seem that all philosophy is determined specifically by its *dispersion* from scientific practice. Philosophy has no other essence than this dispersion; it is precisely for the reduction of this dispersion to zero that Bachelard, as we have seen, worked throughout his life.

But one question remains unanswered: why, ultimately, this dispersion of philosophy? We have certainly seen what took up its abode *in* the dispersion: misrecognitions of the historical production of concepts through a mistake as to the role of mathematics in scientific knowledge. But we have not yet determined why philosophy, consciously or no, *undergoes* this dispersion.

It is to this, precisely, that Gaston Bachelard invites us. Let us say it in a word: the dispersion appears as a *function* organized according to certain ends. Now, even before recognizing them, we can safely say that these ends are both extra-scientific – which does not surprise us – and extra-philosophical, which might do so if we had not,

---

69. *Les intuitions atomistiques*, p. 3.

70. This thesis was expressed in this form by Louis Althusser in his lectures at the École Normale Supérieure in 1967–8. I believe that it coincides precisely with Gaston Bachelard's thought.

following Bachelard, constituted a topology whose most obvious characteristic is that it is a *closed* field.

What we are given to understand is the wherefore of the eternal mistake of philosophy. That is how I propose to read *The Formation of the Scientific Mind*; I well know that the richness of this work far surpasses the remarks I am about to present here, but on reading and re-reading it according to the principles I have set myself, it seems to me that in doing so I reach the essentials of this admirable text.

It seems to me that what emerges luminously from *The Formation of the Scientific Mind* is the fact that philosophy has the function of importing extra-scientific *values* into the sciences. Vis-à-vis these values, Bachelard answers *two* distinct but often confused, because imbricated, questions. The first, immediately visible, singled out by all the commentators, and part of the 'elementary Bachelardianism' of the philosophy student, concerns the *terrain of origin* of these values: everday life, prime experience, pre-scientific knowledge; such are the answers – for me provisional ones – that can be given to it.

The second, less obvious, concerns the *wherefore of the valorization* of this terrain of origin. This second question is not susceptible to an immediate answer.

In this theoretical reflection, which Bachelard describes at the beginning of Chapter VII as a 'Reflex Psychology',[71] it is at the level of their *effects* (reflections) in objective knowledge that Bachelard grasps these values. We must bear in mind this *indirect* determination if we want to understand correctly what Gaston Bachelard means by that still enigmatic metaphor, the notion of an 'epistemological obstacle'. Convinced that, for Bachelard, a metaphor cannot stand in for a notion.

If we take the central notion of an 'epistemological obstacle' at the level of its effects, the latter can be said to amount to *filling in* a rupture. Hence the epistemological obstacle, polymorphous in its nature, has only one effect. It is by working at the level of this single effect that we have a chance of specifying the concept; now, it

71. *La formation de l'esprit scientifique*, p. 132.

emerges that if this effect is always the same, its *place* in the knowledge process is variable. It can arise at the moment of the constitution of the knowledge, or at a later stage in its development, once it has already been constituted as a scientific knowledge. In the first case it can be said to be a 'counter-thought', in the second a 'suspension of thought' (*arrêt de pensée*). But this variation in identity is only of terminological interest. It designates the obstacle as a point of *resistance* of thought to thought. To be explicit: if it is agreed that scientific thought is eminently progressive and that its advance is constituted by its own re-organization, the epistemological obstacle will be said to emerge every time – but only then – a pre-existing organization of thought is threatened. Let me add that it appears *at the point* at which rupture threatens – points which other efforts than Bachelard's have been able to show to be the sites of an 'over-determination'. But, instantaneous in its emergence, it is clear that the obstacle is *solidary* with a determinate structure of thought which will seem, retrospectively, following the terminology of *The Philosophy of No*, to be a 'tissue of tenacious errors'.

Now, whenever it shows itself, the obstacle whose effect is to patch up – if only for an instant – the threatened fabric, invariably proceeds *by a displacement of interests*; these are Bachelard's own words.

In one case, the obstacle displaces the question even before it is posed, if I may so express myself; i.e., it prevents *the* question being posed, substituting an imaginary question for a real question.

In the other, it diverts the question from its meaning.

In other words, I shall say that in one case it prevents scientific thought from arriving, in the other, when it has already arrived, it demotes it to the rank of ordinary thought. For everything, ultimately, amounts to the re-establishment of the broken continuity between scientific thought and ordinary thought. It is clear that the first obstacle – meaning the most immediate, but also the most permanent and finally the most resistant – has at its terrain of origin the precise point at which ordinary thought begins; in sensory experience. In fact Bachelard constantly denounces it throughout his work as an eternal primitiveness of knowledge (*savoir*).

But there is much more in *The Formation of the Scientific Mind*. In it Bachelard undertakes to demonstrate the sources of the undue valorization of primary experience. Reading Chapter VII, entitled 'Psychoanalysis of the Realist', we see that the 'realist function' we now know to be an appendage of all Philosophy, organizes in a systematic way the tissue of errors which produces the most tenacious obstacles at the points of rupture.

Now, what is the principle that organizes the Realist's thought? Let us follow Bachelard in the details of the analyses he gives. Let us take the constantly invoked case of the science of the eighteenth century; what Bachelard tells us about it is very remarkable: the determinant element in his eyes seems to be the *social status* of this science: it is a drawing-room matter, it has the mark of *leisure*, of *ease*, of *idleness*,[72] even of frivolity:[73] Bachelard even ventures the expression 'simpering mathematics' (*mathématiques minaudées*). By this very fact, the interests for science are *false* in their principles.[74] They are analogous to the interests that this society had in literature or travellers' tales. In short: Nature is conceived as a Book whose pages have only to be turned to know it and appreciate it. It seems to me that there is something profound here, something to which I shall return later: it is the way one relates to scientific knowledge which determines – in a modality which will have to be specified – the representation one has of the internal structure of scientific learning (*savoir*). That is what Gaston Bachelard is suggesting to us when he shows (for he does show it, even if he does not prove it) that it is ultimately the fact that scientific books were related to as literary books which was determinant in the ideology of science which dominated in the eighteenth century.

This makes it more understandable that he is so insistent on citing the literary prefaces to pre-scientific books. It is certainly not for the pleasure of opening to us a department – however 'curious' – of his Museum: it is rather to arouse our attention – even by a horrified shudder – to this point, which to my mind is so fundamental. Meanwhile, Bachelard is very careful to show that this social representation of science has its effects in the most authentic scientific works

72. ibid., p. 30.   73. ibid., p. 34.   74. ibid., p. 40.

of the period – those of Réaumur, for example, which remain in the eyes of the History of the Sciences a scientific achievement 'for ever'.[75]

The importance conceded in this work to the problems of the teaching of the sciences will therefore come as no surprise; Gaston Bachelard sees in the education system the representation a given society adopts for itself of its learning (*savoir*). The fact that the work ends with what he calls 'an educational utopia' is enough to prove that he was far from considering that our society – his own, that of the 1930s – had eliminated from the representation of its learning (*savoir*) all the ideology, so visible in the eighteenth century, of leisure-science; Bachelard rediscovers it, displaced, camouflaged, but still just as active, in the conception of science as a part of a 'general' culture.

On several occasions this thesis turns into a celebration of the successive specializations of scientific disciplines. Thus: 'Specializations, in the domain of scientific thought, are special types of advance. To follow them in retrospect is to take the very viewpoint of precise advances.' A few lines earlier the polemical value of these affirmations stands out: 'It is perhaps astonishing that scientific specialization is so facilely, so constantly denounced as a mutilation of thought.'[76]

If my thesis is accepted, this 'facileness', this 'constancy' will be seen as the effect of a typically philosophical *resistance*. The most remarkable text in this respect is undoubtedly the one to be found in the *Bulletin de la Société Française de la Philosophie*, 'On the Nature of Rationalism', beginning as follows: 'It is specialization which gives the rationalist tonus! It is specialization which makes a vigorous mind! It is specialization which gives you the certainty that you are today in yesterday's line! Naturally, if you remain in the philosophical elements of rationalism, it is a rationalism which does no work, it is a rationalism which you do not endanger. . . .'[77] Here, the celebration becomes a hymn and an exhortation.

But let me admit that I have taken the most favourable part by

75. An expression used later in *The Rationalist Activity* and in the lecture on *The Actuality of the History of the Sciences* (1951). I shall come back to it.
76. *L'activité rationaliste de la physique contemporaine*, pp. 13 and 10.
77. April–June 1950; reprinted in *L'engagement rationaliste*, pp. 45–88.

choosing the example of the eighteenth century, about which it will at least be granted that it has an important role in the book, and return to Bachelard's text.

One cannot fail to be struck by the constant reference it makes to the Alchemists. What is the significance of this insistence?

He tells us himself: following Hélène Metzger, he shows that 'Alchemy, properly considered, is not so much an intellectual initiation as a moral initiation.'[78]

It would be very easy for me to show once again how it is a false relation to science which determines the representation of its structure; one might even see that in this case the relation imaginarily instituted between the science and its object is the inverse of the first one: in the ideology of observation, the object is available, always-already-given; in the alchemistic ideology, it is hidden, never-yet-attained.

But what should hold our attention is the fact that the Alchemist serves more than once as a reference to characterize some contemporary philosophical doctrines. Thus, two pages before the last quotation, we could read:

One might almost say that the alchemical experiment develops in a Bergsonian duration, in a biological and psychological duration. . . . Each being needs its correct time, its concrete duration, its individual duration, to grow and to produce. If so, when one can accuse the time that languishes, the vague ambiance which fails to mature, the soft inner pressure which idles, one has all one needs to explain from the inside the accidents of the experiment.[79]

This reference to Bergson is not the only one in the book on this point; besides, it is one of Bachelard's constant procedures to compare certain contemporary philosophical theses with pre-scientific texts. For in his eyes they share the same ideology, whose dominant values are external to the pure effort to know, and which are borrowed from certain practical ideologies such as morality or religion, the cement of a given society. In the style of Bachelard, on this occasion, it could be said that the fundamental ideology of science,

---

78. *La formation de l'esprit scientifique*, p. 51.   79. ibid., p. 49.

which is conveyed in a systematic form by philosophy, depends on social values such as morality, religion or politics.

Such is the ultimate explanation that we can give for the 'valorizing interests' which constitute the skeleton of the 'epistemological obstacles'.

If we want confirmation of this, it can be seen that where the 'substantialist' obstacle is concerned the main equation seems to be as follows:

$$\text{substance} = \text{inside} = \text{precious}[80]$$

and that Bachelard concludes his development thus: 'The realist accumulates in the substance, as a prudent man does in his barn, powers, virtues, forces, without realising that every force is a relation.' Thus it is indeed social attitudes that pass into knowledge through philosophy. The substantialist takes the word 'property' literally, and feels for it the 'solid pleasure of the proprietor',[81] the phrase is Bachelard's.

Similarly, if one wished to sum up Chapter VII in a compressed and caricatural way, one would pose the following three 'axioms':

'All Realists are misers'
'The Realist is a glutton'
'Nothing is more *methodical* than alimentation for the Bourgeois.'

But let me leave these considerations here. It is time to conclude.

What Bachelard demonstrates is that every epistemological obstacle intervenes in scientific knowledge by way of the intermediary of philosophy as the representative of ideological values hierarchized at the point where their system is in danger.

It follows that philosophy is nothing but this function of intervention. It seems to me that there are in this the elements for a Theory of philosophy and the construction of the concept of a History of philosophy. That would be the object of another study; it cannot be discussed here.

80. *La formation de l'esprit scientifique*, p. 98; 'Every container seems less *precious*, less *substantial* than the *matter* contained – the bark, so indispensable functionally, is appraised as a mere protection for the wood. These containers are seen as necessary, even in inanimate nature.' The whole chapter should really be cited.
81. E.g., ibid., p. 101.

What will be discussed is what Bachelard was able to think thanks to his recognition of scientific thought as a historical production of concepts and to his leading philosophy back to its truth, i.e., to its source. There are two new problematics installed at the end of this long labour: *historical epistemology*, as a regulated system of concepts, and the *history of the sciences* as the object of a theoretical thought.

The New Problematics

It is now, therefore, the time of the 'anabaptist philosophers' that Bachelard prayed for in *The Philosophy of No!*

For these new epistemologists will still, in a certain sense, be philosophers. This sense is even a very precise one; we shall see that it finds its definition in the blank space I have left in the 'philosophical spectrum' constructed by Bachelard.

They will be 'anabaptist' in that they will forswear all the beliefs, all the dogmas of traditional philosophy. We now know that we are in no danger if we take these terms completely literally.

They will establish themselves on this territory, still virgin land when Bachelard reached it, for which scientific knowledge itself, in its actual practice, is both the ground and horizon.

But it is clear that these philosophers will already be historians, and the historians of this country will necessarily be philosophers. Indeed, in Bachelard's work on the concepts of traditional philosophy in the light of scientific thought, we have already seen History appear in person, emerging from the shades in which classical philosophy and epistemology had buried it. There is a theoretical necessity in this appearance, as there was in the repression. But only a careful and exact scrutiny of the articulation of the new discipline's new concepts can bring it to light.

I. A NON-PHILOSOPHICAL PHILOSOPHY

It is in its very refutation that the necessity of philosophy has arisen. Indeed, insofar as we have recognized that philosophy was defined not by its object but by its *function*, and determined this function as an intervention in the area of (*auprès de*) the sciences, to that extent, in order to annihilate what I shall call the 'philosophical instance', it is essential that the conditions which give it consistency be themselves suppressed.

Which means, given the analyses I made in line with Bachelard in the last chapter, that all ideology – moral, political or religious – must be driven out. In other words, science must be installed in an ideological vacuum, that is, in a social vacuum.[1] This operation can be performed in thought: the result is to construct a *utopia*. But Gaston Bachelard leaves utopias to the poets; it is *this* world that the epistemologist discusses.

Another way of annihilating the philosophical instance: suppress all science; in that case philosophy would be, as it were, 'an ambassador without an embassy'; its existence stripped of all purpose, it would disappear. But the sciences do exist.

So there is a clear necessity for a discipline of philosophy because, *in the facts*, there are sciences coexisting with ideologies. But philosophy must be reversed: far from being the spokesman of ideologies vis-à-vis (*auprès de*) the sciences – its mission must rather be to neutralize their discourses and so to hinder as far as possible the emergence of obstacles. At the very least, it will adopt the mission of *distinguishing* within given discourses between what derives from scientific practice and what originates in ideological discourses.

It is just this function of *vigilance* that Bachelard assigns to the new epistemology. 'Escorting' the advances of the sciences, its constant concern will be to 'sort out the philosophical interests' which arise in the scientist's route.

In other words, it treats problems completely alien to traditional philosophy: it poses questions which Philosophers cannot – or will not – see as interesting. It goes without saying that these 'problems' may vary: insofar as a science advances, the 'values' which it secretes change and the footholds it gives to ideology shift. On the other hand, the emergence of a new science may change the theoretical conjuncture; finally, the dominant position of a determinate science

1. This argument, that I have taken over from Gaston Bachelard, could, I suggest, acquire precise theoretical status in the framework of the Marxist science of history or 'historical materialism'. Cf. Louis Althusser: 'Matérialisme historique et matérialisme dialectique', *Cahiers Marxistes-Léninistes* no. 11, April 1966.

in this theoretical conjuncture may come back into question – I am thinking in particular of the mathematical physics which was dominant in Bachelard's time, but had not always been and perhaps will not continue to be for ever.

For all these reasons, the new discipline will be an 'open' philosophy. Bachelard asserted that 'The philosophy of scientific knowledge must be *open*. . . . It will be the consciousness of a mind which founds itself by working on the unknown.'[2] Merely stating these principles shows that it is so open that, if the evolution of the scientific conjuncture demanded it, a non-Bachelardian epistemology in the Bachelardian sense of the term could be conceivable.

Being open, the new philosophy will be non-systematic: it will reject that *tendency to become a system* which Bachelard saw as a characteristic of traditional philosophy. Coming from Bachelard this is not a matter of the reproach which common sense directs against philosophy, for the wrong reasons, but an imperative which stems from the very nature of scientific knowledge. Science is not *one*, there are unevennesses of development between the different branches of scientific knowledge; Bachelard makes this clear at the beginning of *The Formation of the Scientific Mind*. Hence, to use his own expression, there can be no unitary epistemology. Or better: it is at the level of each concept that the precise tasks of the philosophy of the sciences are posed.[3] Thus a 'differential philosophy' will be constructed; the new discipline will be a philosophy of the *concept*.

Finally, attentive to the real conditions of the scientist's work, to the specificity of the different regions of science and to the evolution of their relations, and vigilant as to the insertion of scientific learning (*savoir*) into the world of culture, this new discipline will be a historical philosophy.

One last word on my method of exposition before leaving these generalizations for the details of the organization of concepts. Indeed, it goes without saying that the *order* I have adopted is in no sense historical; I do not claim to show first of all the formation of the concepts so as then to show them at work. This is clear enough from

2. *The Philosophy of No*, p. 9. 3. ibid., p. 12.

the fact that I have continually borrowed from *all* of Bachelard's works; a more genuinely historical treatment I am reserving for the last part of this book. The analysis I perform here is situated for the moment on a quite different plane. Let us say that it has been my ambition to display the *logical architecture* of Gaston Bachelard's epistemology. Or better still: I hope I have shown the *pre-requisites* of historical epistemology, which is itself – in a sense still to be specified – a prerequisite of epistemological history. What you are now about to read is an account of how these prerequisites form a consistent and co-ordinated doctrine. One should not be surprised to rediscover converted into norms some of the concepts which we have already seen in a polemical light; it is clear also that since Bachelard's epistemology is more mature in his later works, I shall appeal primarily to them and not need to recall the earlier texts in which the same concepts were already at work, but in a more imprecise and even more irresolute form. I shall make such a return only in those few cases in which the evolution of the concept has assigned it a clearly different meaning in the later works.

2. DIALECTIC

Exactly such a concept is that of *dialectic*, which undergoes a certain evolution between the first and the last works. Nonetheless, one must beware of seeing in this evolution a reversal of its meaning. It would be better to say that the function of the concept changes and that as a result its meaning swings from one end of the notion to the other.

Hence to clarify things we must throw light on the *function* of the concept: it is in the end to be found inscribed in the dialogue between the Mathematician and the Physicist, the purveyor of hypotheses and theories on the one hand, and the master of experiments on the other. A dialogue that cannot be grasped, as we have seen, without occupying that central position – so difficult to win – that Bachelard assigns to epistemology.

What is the exact meaning of this? An exchange of information whose final result is to *adjust* theory and experiment. But since we cannot have recourse to a fixed object, this adjustment must be thought not as a *formal adequation* but as a *historical process*. In a history which implies no security, no destiny promising theory that it will always find the means to realize itself. This history, then, is a risky one, and in it the two protagonists must unite their efforts.

Another word for this risk: *failure*. At any given moment the language of the physicist and that of the mathematician may be in contradiction. Philosophy will hasten to see in this a 'crisis' of science. For the mathematician and the physicist, it will just be the chance for some work: for the former to review his theories and formulate other hypotheses; for the latter to refine his experiments and check his instruments. In short, a re-organization of knowledge (*savoir*) will take place; it is this re-organization that Bachelard calls *dialectic*.

What he means to designate by this term is thus the specifically progressive approach of scientific thought. But we have seen that in order to think the particular style of this movement it was necessary to unlease a lively polemic against 'realist' philosophies: this is undoubtedly why in the earlier works the concept of dialectic is inflected more in the direction of the rupture which experiment imposes on knowledge (*savoir*) as it passes from one state to the next. Whereas in the last works, it is rather the progressive character of the later moment which is emphasized. It is undoubtedly legitimate to think that this variation, which does not cast doubt on the meaning of the concept, is related to the fact that at the close of his work Bachelard had available other concepts with which to think the 'rupture' aspect; I shall return to them.

It is enough to note that in this definition, the concept of dialectic does not coincide with any of the concepts designated by the word dialectic in traditional philosophy. I will not rehearse here the proof of this which Georges Canguilhem has given in his article on 'The dialectic and the philosphy of no':[4] but I would like to point out that when the situation of Bachelard's epistemology with respect to previous Philosophy is taken into account, this concept *could not* be

4. 'La dialectique et la philosophie du non', *Études d'histoire et de philosophie des sciences*, Vrin, Paris, 1970.

the equivalent of any philosophical concept whatsoever. I hope that I have demonstrated this in my first chapter.

3. TECHNICAL MATERIALISM

Scientific thought, therefore, progresses by oscillations, by re-organizations of its bases proceeding from its summit; but this movement takes place only in and by scientific experimentation. That is, by taking up the position of the other interlocutor. Here then is what scientific experiment in its technical detail forces one to think – a task unknown to philosophers, and one for which Gaston Bachelard lays down the principles.

The texts in which Bachelard inaugurates this theory of scientific *instruments* as 'materialized theories', and of their setting up, are famous. His theses form a completely new body of doctrine, which he calls 'instructed materialism' or 'technical materialism', i.e., the study of the material which science uses for the organization of its experiments.

This body of concepts was progressively elaborated in Bachelard's thought, its essential basis a reflection on the role which instruments play in Micro-physics. Its form, its field and its tasks are laid down in *Applied Rationalism*, but it is interesting that as early as 1927 in his *Essay on Approximate Knowledge*, Bachelard insisted on the role of instruments in physical knowledge, which he thought the philosophers neglected.

But if theories materialize themselves in this way, and if epistemology must therefore watch over the construction of an 'instructed materialism', this is in order to produce phenomena which will be strictly defined as *scientific phenomena*; in order that no ideological intervention can be made in the functioning of scientific knowledge under the cover of natural observations.

Bachelard gives a parodic appellation to this production of specifically scientific phenomena: *phenomeno-technics*, which is radically incompatible with a phenomenology that can only talk about phenomena, never produce any. In *The New Scientific Mind*, Bachelard asserts that 'the true scientific phenomenology is therefore essentially a phenomeno-technics. It instructs itself by what it constructs. . . . Science raises up a world no longer by a magical force immanent in reality, but rather by a rational force immanent to the mind.'[5]

And more sharply in *The Formation of the Scientific Mind*: 'Phenomeno-technics *extends phenomenology*. A concept has become scientific insofar as it has become technical, is accompanied by a realization technique.'[6]

Thus the essential element of the activity of scientific thought is to produce *couplings* of the abstract and the concrete via the installation of theoretically defined instruments and via setting up apparatuses according to programmes of rational realization. Or again, to use another of Bachelard's expressions, to *concretize* the abstract.

It is at the centre of this process, unthinkable for the philosopher, that the thought of the epistemologist must install itself.

Consequently, *experience* again becomes a central philosophical theme, but with a completely new meaning. Thus Bachelard writes: 'A well-conducted experiment always has a positive result. But this conclusion does not rehabilitate the absolute positivity of experience as such, for an experiment can be a well-done experiment only if it is complete, which can be the case only if it has been preceded by a studied project, starting from an achieved theory. In the end, experimental conditions are the same as preconditions of experimentation.'[7]

The 'objects' of these experiments must also be understood in a new sense. Amongst other examples, Bachelard gives this one in *The Rationalist Activity of Contemporary Physics*:

The meson, at the junction of the most abstract theory and of the most painstaking technical research, is now a particle endowed with that double ontological status required of all the entities of modern Physics.[8]

5. *Le nouvel esprit scientifique*, p. 13.
6. *La formation de l'esprit scientifique*, p. 61.
7. *Le nouvel esprit scientifique*, p. 9.
8. *L'activité rationaliste de la physique contemporaine*, Chapter 4, section IX. Here one must examine the whole of this long section. I see it as a very precise illustration of the theses which I am defending. The first lines read: 'The existence of the meson poses philosophical problems which would themselves take a whole book to examine, for one

It is therefore understandable that Bachelard should conclude: 'If one is to hold one's position at the centre of the working mind and of worked matter, one must abandon many philosophical traditions of the native translucence of the mind and of the reality of the sensory world.'

4. APPLICATION

What is now clear is that we have determined the epistemological disciplines which, at the level of scientific activity, will fill the blanks which I left in the spectrum. We can call them 'Applied Rationalism' on the one hand and 'Technical Materialism' on the other.

But to give them these names – as Bachelard does – is immediately to set up in each of them a *distinction* which produces a fruitful *reciprocity* between the two doctrines. Indeed, in other words, in the Rationalism, that is to say, in the production of concepts, even at this stage attention must be paid to the conditions of their application, or as Bachelard puts it, one must 'integrate into the concept its conditions of application'. Such a rationalism, then, is not unitary – or monolithic – but already divided; or to put it better, it is a dialectical rationalism.

In the 'Technical Materialism', the problems of setting up experiments must integrate into their solutions the theoretical conditions of their formulation.

The two disciplines are thus not only co-ordinated, but reciprocal. This reciprocity in its turn makes possible an important distinction between what I shall call problems of scientific research and those which one could more strictly call problems of experimentation.

The first effect of this distinction is the devalorization of the notion of 'method'. Or rather, the idea Bachelard often repeats with respect

---

would have to evoke cosmological problems which are posed in terms quite different from those of previous cosmologies. . . . One would have to remould completely simplistic ideas about the relations between hypothesis and experiment. Indeed, *the hypothesis of the meson was initially an essentially mathematical hypothesis*, and not an image related to experiment. . . . One could just as well call the philosophy of the meson: *from mathematical theories of the nucleus of the atom to aeronautical experiments on cosmic rays'* (my emphasis – D.L.).

to the example of Descartes, that the notion of 'general scientific method' is vacuous, a notion which misses the real motion of knowledge (*savoir*). The texts which are essential in this respect are in *The New Scientific Mind* and in the Speech on 'The Philosophical Problem of Scientific Methods', already referred to. This title is itself significant, since it clearly signals that according to Bachelard there is no *one* method, but *methods*, specific to each science, and even to each determinate epoch of any given science.

What interests Bachelard – and it is more intelligible when one has discovered the function of epistemology – is not the system of concepts in which the scientist thinks the order of his investigation *after the event*; as are all Discourses on Method. But rather the reality of the investigation, with its hesitations, its setbacks, its mistakes; in a word, at its 'summit', in Bachelard's words, i.e., at the level of the difficult formulation of problems.

5. PROBLEMATIC

As early as 1927, Bachelard asserted that the *sense of the problem* was the sinew of scientific progress; in his later work he constantly took this idea further. Its most fully perfected expression is found in *Applied Rationalism*, where Bachelard introduces the new concept of the *problematic* to account in the framework of the new epistemology for what he had already attempted to think in terms of the mathematical metaphor of a *field* (*corps de problèmes*) – just as he had already attempted to think the set of concepts of technical materialism within the metaphor of an 'experimental and definitional field' (*corps d'experience et de précaution*).[9] Benefiting by the relations it maintains with the other concepts of Applied Rationalism, the concept of the problematic is the richer.

9. Allow me to note in this regard that these metaphors borrowed from mathematics are not isolated in the work of Gaston Bachelard. One could even say that the framework of the vocabulary of his philosophy is *scientific in character*. The framework of traditional philosophy is moral, legal or religious in character: noting this fact, I venture to assert that here we have an index of the novelty of Bachelardian philosophy; a philosophy which refuses to be a vehicle for extra-scientific ideological values must start by defending itself against them at the level of the words it uses. This is another reason for the *dépaysement* one feels in reading Bachelard.

It is the positive notion which according to the terminology I have proposed 'stands in elsewhere' for the philosophical idea of data or the 'given'; it resorbs the traditional notion of doubt, which is a correlate of the notion of general method. Let me make this last point clearer: Bachelard opines – against Descartes – that if one admits the existence of a general method of scientific knowledge, the doubt which is its first moment can never achieve specificity. In other words, it is purely formal, it does not allow the production of any rectification, and hence of any knowledge. We may read, for example, in *The Formation of the Scientific Mind*:

Descartes's confidence in the clarity of his image of the sponge is symptomatic indeed of his inability to install his doubt at the level of the details of objective knowledge, to develop a discursive doubt which could unpick every joint of the real and every corner of the image.[10]

We can add that this study has proved that all this depended in the last analysis on the philosophical idea of looking outside knowledge for an object to serve as its foundation.

Bachelard's concept of the problematic takes into account precisely the disqualification of the philosophical notion of object. It could be said to connect the concepts of *given* and *doubt* on another terrain: that of knowledge as a process of objectification. Bachelard writes:

Universal doubt irreversibly pulverizes the given into a heap of heteroclite facts. It corresponds to no real instance of scientific research. Instead of the parade of universal doubt, scientific research demands the setting up of a problematic. Its real starting-point is *a problem*, however ill-posed. The scientific-ego is then a programme of experiments; while the scientific non-ego is already a *constituted problematic*.[11]

Thus for the scientist's work there can be no indeterminate unknown; the indeterminate unknown is of no interest to him; all his effort is on the contrary to specify the unknown. It is at the level of these specifications that the new epistemologist, in pursuit of his constant dual task, must simultaneously defend the scientist from the intrusion of extra-scientific notions, and instruct himself concerning the

10. *La formation de l'esprit scientifique*, p. 79.   11. *Le rationalisme appliqué*, p. 51.

pace of the advance of a given science at a given moment in its history.

6. SCIENTIFIC LOANS

But Bachelard allows us to go further in the – necessarily formal – determination of the structure of all production of scientific concepts. He shows, indeed, especially in *Applied Rationalism*, that the problematics of the different sciences are not wholly independent of one another, but only relatively autonomous, and that zones of partial overlap may appear. What he calls *trans-rationalism*[12] and shows at work with respect to piezo-electricity is of interest insofar as it enables us to pose the elements of a theory of scientific loans.

Bachelard writes that trans-rationalism is established at the end of prolonged theoretical effort, by the intermediary of an algebraic organization. It has nothing to do with some vague correspondence established by an unprincipled empiricism at the *starting-point* of knowledge.[13] On the contrary, it is at the level of a technical organization refined by the determination of ever more precise – and hitherto unnoticed – variables that 'interferences' between domains of rationality can arise.

However, it must be admitted that the principles which Bachelard gives us have not been applied to a large enough number of examples for us to be able to get a precise idea of the mechanisms that govern the details of these scientific loans. But at least, formally, the principles have been laid down and the field cleared. All that is left is to get down to work. . . .

12. ibid., pp. 125 and 129.

13. ibid., p. 133: 'The question is thus no longer posed as one of defining a general rationalism which will collect up the common parts of the regional rationalisms. By such methods one would find no more than the minimum rationalism used in everyday life. The structures would be destroyed. On the contrary, the point is to multiply and refine those structures, which, from the rationalist point of view, must be expressed as an activity of structuration, as a determination of the possibility of multiple axiomatic systems corresponding to the multiplicity of experiments. Integral rationalism can thus be no more than a domination of the different basic axiomatic systems. And it will designate rationalism as a dialectical activity, since the various axiomatics are articulated to one another dialectically.' There is no point here in rehearsing a commentary on this remarkable passage: the whole of this study seems to me to perform this task.

Let me end this exposition of the major concepts of the new epistemology with a point to which Bachelard has accorded the greatest importance ever since *The Formation of the Scientific Mind*: this organization of the production of scientific concepts does not take place in the pure space of disembodied minds. It is materialized in the form of institutions, meetings, colloquia. . . .

As a result there is constituted what Bachelard calls a 'scientific city'; and he constantly draws our attention to the extremely social character of modern science. Bachelard therefore invites us to assess *the cohesion of this city and its effectivity*.

Its *effectivity*: by means of the 'communications' which are made in it and which Bachelard suggests should be considered as a 'mutual pedagogy',[14] theories circulate more rapidly and permit an acceleration of discoveries. Bachelard writes in *The Rationalist Activity*: 'The isolated worker must admit that he could not have made that discovery by himself. . . .'[15]

In return, the city's *cohesion* makes it possible to eliminate every aberration related to the subjective character of any particular research. Modern science is freed from all those reveries which encumbered the science of previous centuries. In this sense, it is more difficult for epistemological obstacles to form – hence, it would appear, the acceleration of scientific time in our days – although their appearance is inevitable, by a necessity of principle which I have demonstrated.

The conclusion: it is the scientific city which creates its own *norms*. It is the city which holds the criteria of objectivity or truth. We can grasp this function, as Bachelard shows, in the technical regions of the city: there one can read *in material form*, the characteristics of the scientific city in general.

14. *L'activité rationaliste de la physique contemporaine*, p. 6. On the same page one may read this passage of anti-philosophical polemic: 'The School – in the sciences – does not hesitate. The School – in the sciences – pulls along. Scientific Culture imposes its tasks, its line of growth. Philosophical utopias can do nothing in this area. Idealism demonstrates nothing. One must go to school, to school as it is, to school as it is becoming, in the social thought that transforms it.'

15. *Le rationalisme appliqué*, p. 23: 'Scientific culture constantly puts a real scientist into the position of a pupil.' Implying: 'The philosopher, on the other hand, is always playing the professor.'

Thus in *Rational Materialism*, Bachelard shows that in contemporary chemistry the 'reagent', a mass-produced item, standardized according to universal norms, is a good illustration of the social character of modern science.[16] He demonstrates the same point with respect to the homogeneity of metals in *Applied Rationalism*.

We conclude, then, that the scientific city stands in for the Reason of the philosophers, but elsewhere; on the other hand, it is strange to see Bachelard attempting in *Applied Rationalism* to found the apodicticity of scientific values in a vocabulary of a psychologistic kind. He attempts – very ingeniously – to show that the social character is first of all an intersubjective character, that this intersubjectivity of objective knowledge produces a *division* within the subject and that the obligation we feel when we come into contact with a scientific value is located in this division.

It is as if Bachelard hoped in this way to resolve a problem whose very terms were forbidden to him from the moment he broke with the conception of a norm-producing Reason as constituted by the philosophical problematic. We must ask if, at the end if his reflections, Bachelard was not suddenly stricken by 'philosophical bad conscience'. These investigations are perhaps an attempt, marginal to his work, to get back to the ground of the Philosophers and to justify himself there.

Thus, as a result of the epistemological work of Gaston Bachelard, we may assert that, to use a different vocabulary, the concept of a theoretical mode of production[17] has been established; in it the formal principles, invariant with respect to every mode of production, are posed and put to the test in the cases of the Physics and Chemistry of the early twentieth century. After seeing by what sort of polemical effort the field of this new concept was cleared, we have now seen what are its internal articulations.

However, it appears that by constructing the concept of the theoretical mode of production, Bachelard had put himself in a position to think the *transition* from one determinate mode of production to another. Even if in his work he never treated this

16. *Le matérialisme rationnel*, p. 78.
17. Louis Althusser has advanced this concept.

problem in all its generality, one can at least see it at work in certain specific notions.

That is how he founds a new concept of the History of the Sciences.

7. THE CONCEPT OF THE HISTORY OF THE SCIENCES

Bachelard thought this concept for itself only in his last works, and at a lecture at the Palais de la Découverte in 1951, but in the *practical* state it is already present in his thesis of 1927: *A Study in the Evolution of a Problem in Physics: the Propagation of Heat in Solids.*

This book begins with these words: 'It is easy to believe that scientific problems follow each other historically in an ascending order of complexity, without always making the effort to move in thought so as to confront the problem as it appeared to the primitive observation.'

The entire novelty of the enterprise is inscribed in this sentence. This novelty is polemically asserted against a positivist 'history', which it explicitly controverts; positively, it is defined as an effort to move back to a previous viewpoint. Or better: this effort is in no sense aesthetic, it is not a question of reliving the past, but of *judging* it, for 'once the solution is found, its clarity lights up the previous data'.

So the first characteristic of this History is its *normativity*: Bachelard repeats this more than once. He maintains it against 'the spontaneous hostility of the historian to every normative judgement'. This leads straight to the second characteristic: the judgement produced will be *recurrent*. It is for this reason, according to Bachelard, that the history of the sciences cannot be a history 'just like all the others'.

The first effect of this double characteristic: a whole type of investigation is disqualified; the work which consists of looking for *precursors* for every scientific discovery. Thus in *Applied Rationalism*, Bachelard attacks those who saw Hegel as a precursor of Maxwell: 'There is nothing in the philosophy of a Schelling or a Hegel to prepare the synthesis of the domains of electricity and optics. . . .

The foundations are established by recurrence. We see the base from the summit.'[18] Similarly, in *The Rationalist Activity* he attacks those who claim that since Raspail proposed a planetary *image* of the atom in 1855, he was a precursor of Rutherford and Bohr.[19]

Bohr and Rutherford did not propose an image, but a concept; it has been shown that there is no possible continuity between the two. The History of the Sciences can make its judgements only when instructed by epistemology.

But where does epistemology itself obtain its instruction? From living science, as we have seen, in the thick of its researches. The consequence immediately follows: recurrence cannot be performed once and for all; it must constantly be performed again. So Bachelard writes in his Lecture: 'Insofar as the historian of the sciences is instructed in the modernity of the science, he will disengage more and more finer and finer nuances within the historicity of the science. . . . It would appear that a luminous History of the sciences cannot be completely contemporaneous with its unfolding.'

It follows that the historian must vigilantly beware of false recurrence – which is what the search for precursors is – that he must proceed with *tact*, as Bachelard puts it, but also that he must affirm the progressive value of the past of the science.

But historical epistemology has already taught us that science progresses by jerks, sudden mutations, re-organizations of its principles: in short, by dialectical slices. It is for this reason that the History of the Sciences must itself be dialectical: it will fasten especially on those 'critical' moments in which the bases of a science are being re-organized.

It will see in the principles which are relinquished the effect on

18. *Le rationalisme appliqué*, p. 153: 'And yet', writes Bachelard, 'Schelling was able to think that the *luminous* aspect of certain *electrical* phenomena was an index of the unity in principle of light and electricity. But it is perfectly obvious that Schelling's comparison is *superficial*.' It is not made in the correct perspective of an *Applied Rationalism*: 'It initiates no constructive thought; it cannot promote any technique.'

19. *L'activité rationaliste de la physique contemporaine*, p. 69. Raspail wrote: 'Imagine a series of railway-trucks moving without one being able to see the locomotive: this motion could just as well be explained by the hypothesis of *traction* as by that of *propulsion*, it being equally possible to suppose the locomotive to be placed in front of or behind the train.' Such is the justification Raspail gave for his 'atomistic astronomy'.

the practice of the science of certain 'epistemological obstacles', which epistemology will teach it to characterize. It is now clear why Bachelard was led to distinguish between two types of critical moment:

– the moment in which at one point at least, in a determinate domain, the tissue of pre-existing ideology is torn and scientificity is installed. This is what he calls the moment of *rupture*;

– the moment after the entry into scientificity when a determinate science reorganizes its bases: this moment is styled *recasting* (*refonte*) or re-organization.

The effect of this distinction is to cut the history of the sciences in two: indeed, moving from re-organization to re-organization one finds on the one hand a clear and rapid History of positivities;[20] on the other, a more slowly moving History of the negative. This is Bachelard's distinction between Ratified History and Lapsed History (*Histoire sanctionnée* and *Histoire périmée*).

But it goes without saying that the task of the historian of the sciences is to pay attention to both, and to be clear that they have reciprocal relations. Indeed, this should be apparent enough to him if he is the epistemologist he should be.

Such, reduced to their logical form, are the characteristics of the new discipline whose principles Bachelard gives us. We have seen how each of these characteristics is the effect of a concept of the new epistemology. We may assert that once it had become historical, in the sense of taking for its object the historicity of the concepts produced by scientific knowledge, epistemology 'enveloped' in a Spinozan manner a new concept of the history of the sciences and a new discipline commanded by that new concept.

20. The history that, in the terms of the *Lecture*, appears as a 'liquidation of the past' and the most regular example of which is the history of mathematics.

Re-working Concepts

Nothing therefore seemed more grotesque to Gaston Bachelard than those philosophers, those professors of philosophy, who spend their lives 'constantly maintaining' a position.[1]

'Such a philosopher', he wrote, probably meaning Meyerson, his favourite target, 'still defends in writing at sixty the thesis he maintained at thirty.' This permanence he saw as immobilism: far from being the token of a firmness in principles, he saw it as the sign of a nullity of thought, or, to use one of his own expressions, of a counter-thought. For – as I have shown – he saw in the *activity* of scientific thought the model for what a progressive thought should be: philosophical rumination he found derisory when he compared it with the audacious procedures of the scientific mind.

Now, it seemed to him that science was constituted by its constant re-organizations. If, by a necessity he had thought theoretically, philosophy accompanies science, it too must constantly resort to 'revisions' of its principles; Bachelard often said 're-aimings' (*revisées*); another way of stating that it must be and remain 'open'. I am therefore justified in taking Bachelard at his word and looking to see if, on contact with the sciences, he really did proceed, as he invited his fellows to do, to the re-working of his concepts.

My task turns out to be facilitated by the fact that, twice in his career, Bachelard dealt with the same problematic. As Georges Canguilhem writes in his article 'Bachelard et les Philosophes', to *Atomistic Intuitions* corresponds *The Rationalist Activity of Contemporary Physics*, to *The Coherent Pluralism of Modern Chemistry* corresponds *Rational Materialism*. It might be objected to this comparison that the sixteen years which separate these books are

1. *Le rationalisme appliqué* p. 43.

not enough to have produced more than minor modifications in the author's thought; but he has taught us precisely that the history of the sciences, so to speak, does not function by the year. It has its own time: its slow years, its lively years, and at the beginning of this study I showed how Bachelard's acute awareness of the enormous acceleration of scientific time in his period had been determinant for his philosophy. Remember, he wrote that one decade of his own period was worth centuries of previous periods. Gaston Bachelard's philosophy cannot but have been transformed by this sprinting evolution.

The project justified, a number of questions remain to be posed, a few observations to be proposed, before entering into the heart of the texts. First observation: it is clear that the judgement: 'One decade of our period *is worth* centuries of previous periods' can only be formulated by a recurrent thought. In dealing with his philosophy, therefore, we have to proceed by recurrence, too.

But it is self-evident that it will be a fragmentary recurrence: to be completely faithful to Bachelard's teaching would force us to examine the period of the history of the sciences which he dealt with in the light of the latest developments in Mathematics, Physics and Chemistry. Obviously, there can be no question of that here, and I shall only be concerned to carry out the recurrence from the 1950s to the 1930s.

Second observation: by a necessity whose theoretical mechanism I believe I have demonstrated, Bachelard's philosophy, anxious to safeguard scientific knowledge from what might stand in its way, is essentially polemical. Remember that in *The Dialectic of Duration* he writes: 'All knowledge at the moment of its construction is a polemical knowledge; it must first destroy to clear a space for its constructions.'[2] It is this *dialectical* movement which he makes it a task of the new epistemology to respect and to ensure respect for. Now Bachelard, highly sensitive to the theoretical conjuncture, knows where the 'points of philosophical sensitivity' are, or else 'which are the fronts on which to fight'. But these fronts *shift*: in 1930, the main front can be said to have been realism-empiricism;

2. *La dialectique de la durée*, p. 14.

in 1950 the threat seemed to come from idealism-existentialism. The attacks on Meyerson give way, in part, to indictments of Sartre, who, as has been recalled, is seen in Bachelard's last work in the ranks of the 'belated alchemists'.

We have seen that a notional analysis could register such variations; but the historical analysis to which I am about to devote myself here and which I conceive as complementary to it must be attentive no longer to the theoretical principle of the variation but to its movement. Hence I shall note that in his last works, Bachelard is more sensitive than he was in 1930 to the idealist variants of the basic 'empiricist' ideology of which he still sees Meyerson as the embodiment. Now, according to the front on which he is struggling, his theses are inflected in one direction or another. To put it in his own way, our only chance to grasp the movement of his philosophy is to look into the dialectic of its rejections.

These general principles posed, I can enter into the very precise – even very technical – details of Bachelard's texts.

In the lecture at the Palais de la Découverte that I have already cited, he stressed how useful it would be to trace the history of the history of the sciences. It was very tempting to apply this suggestion to Bachelard himself, so that I could present a 'History of Bachelardian Histories'. Unfortunately, as we have seen, if it is true that the concept of a History of the Sciences is the object of an extensive elaboration in Bachelard's works, the history of the sciences is rarely practised as such in them. That is why it is preferable to speak of the re-working of concepts, among which appears precisely the concept of a History of the Sciences. It did seem to me nonetheless that at one precise and very restricted point it was possible to attempt to set to work this method of the historics of history. This point is photochemistry.

I. HISTORY OF THE HISTORY OF PHOTO-CHEMISTRY

This is not a matter of giving myself the convenience of a precise example, but of examining a case whose importance Bachelard stressed and to which he returned several times.

He stressed its *importance*: in 1934, he wrote in an article in the *Revue de métaphysique et de morale* entitled 'Light and Substance': 'Photo-chemistry is located at a point of epistemological inflection which ought to attract the attention of the metaphysician anxious to learn from positive science.' I propose to understand by its *site* the mentioned entity which is surely chimerical in Bachelard's eyes: a *metaphysician* who learns from positive science. But no matter.

Let us retain the fact that it is a question of a 'point of epistemological inflection'. The essential, once again, lies in the mathematical metaphor: nothing is more interesting nor more characteristic, in epistemology as in mathematics, than a point of inflection.

Bachelard examines this point in the history of the sciences in four texts: *Light and Substance*, then *Applied Rationalism, Rational Materialism* and *The Rationalist Activity*. That is, one text from 1934 and a group of texts from the 1950s. Our example is a pertinent one.

First observation – which might be an objection – in the article of 1934, the History of Light is much more briefly, much more crudely set out than in the first chapter of *The Rationalist Activity*. This is no doubt related to the fact that in an article one has neither the time nor the wish to develop one's thought so extensively as in a book. But that is secondary, since Bachelard writes: 'The shorter the history, the clearer the demonstration.' Hence we are not to have any scruples about comparing two texts of unequal length.

If we start from the most apparent, and also from the most schematic, we shall note first the stages of the history of light – within which photo-chemistry will find a place – such as they are presented to us in 1934:

(a) the pre-scientific eighteenth century characterized as an epoch of naive realism;

(b) a 'decisive event': Fresnel;

(c) the twentieth century in which, he says, *the problems change their meaning*. There is an epistemological revolution.

In *The Rationalist Activity*: the essential dates are the same. And Fresnel's intervention is judged decisive, just as it was in 1934. We read:

Finally Fresnel appeared and instituted optics on an indestructible basis. . . . Fresnel's work will always retain a culture value which will have to be accepted.[3]

What gives Fresnel a scientific value for ever is the fact that he established in optics the 'government of mathematics'. Here is an assertion which will hardly surprise us. But once he has characterized contemporary optics, Bachelard no longer says that the problems change their meaning. He says we are witnessing a 'historical synthesis'. What he finds interesting is the fact that there can be a synthesis in the discontinuity. However subtle it is, I propose to take this variation in the formulations seriously; to consider it precisely as the index of a re-working of concepts.

Let us say that in 1934 Bachelard felt the need, against Meyerson – the man of continuity – to affirm the radical discontinuity of contemporary optical science. Everything is then clear, as far as I am concerned – which gives a different import to the comment I made a moment ago – once it is realized that in *Light and Substance* Bachelard is really aiming at the metaphysicians. When he affirms that the 'problems change their meaning', we should understand, 'the problems posed by the metaphysician for himself'. In 1950 Bachelard has constituted his epistemology by the disqualification of all existing metaphysics; we have seen that settling accounts with all philosophy is what opened to him the field of his historical epistemology.

Hence when he now speaks of a 're-organization of learning' (*savoir*), it is no longer in the sense of the general problems of knowledge (*connaissance*), but a matter of scientific learning (*savoir*). He now has at his disposal the new concept 'problematic' and conceives the history as a mutation of problematics. Thus we can understand why he is able to designate this instant as a historical synthesis, i.e., as an instant in the process of *rupture* inaugurated by Fresnel. We also understand why in 1934 Bachelard could not designate this instant as a synthesis – rather: *think* it both as a synthesis and as a discontinuity – he could only feel it and affirm it, in a necessary polemic, as a radical discontinuity.

3. *L'activité rationaliste de la physique contemporaine*, p. 44.

In short, in this point we can grasp by recurrence Bachelard's re-working in moving from *the awareness of rupture as a fact* to the *finished concept of rupture as a process*. Hence I think I can propose that in spite of the apparent similarity in the dates, the history in the two texts envisaged is not written in the same way. More precisely, the history is not thought in 1934. In order to think it Bachelard needed the organic system of concepts which was not available to him then and which only the constitution of historical epistemology allowed him to form.

I shall draw from this a confirmation and a conclusion: a confirmation of the fact that the formation of the concept of the History of the Sciences is contemporaneous with *Applied Rationalism*, for the reasons, decisive, I think, suggested elsewhere; a conclusion: in the texts of the 1930s, the presence of certain words, certain expressions, even of certain concepts is the result of the absence as such of other concepts; it is these concepts we must be on the look-out for.

This therefore commits us to a detailed scrutiny of our text. Concerning the eighteenth century the characterizations are, as we have seen, identical in all points: it is a question of naive realism; if the word epistemological obstacle does not appear in the text of 1934, the concept of it is already present: in fact, Bachelard is proposing to show that in the eighteenth century the science of the chemical actions of light – which is to become photo-chemistry – cannot be constituted, and he writes: 'A chemist then could not imagine that a phenomenon might not pertain to a substance.' We recognize here what he was to designate as a substantialist obstacle in the terminology of *The Formation of the Scientific Mind*. In fact, in support of this these, he twice quotes the same text by Macquer: 'The substance proper of light is fixed in all plants, and enters materially into the composition of the only one of their principles that is combustible, i.e., the oily part. . . . Light becomes the cause of all the colours.'[4] This text shows us that it is the image of material absorption, the prerequisite of the substantialist obstacle, which closes the investigation and induces a suspension of thought.

4. Pierre Joseph Macquer, *Dictionnaire de Chymie*, Paris, 1766, vol. II, p. 292.

But another text that Bachelard cites three times – in both our texts and in *Rational Materialism* – allows a number of specifications. This text dates from Year II of the French Revolution (1794), and is by Fourcroy; here are its essential passages:

The colour called blue, or red, is produced in bodies by an absorption of all the other rays, except the blue or red, which are reflected back. . . . If it be true, that bodies exposed to the contact or impulse of light, experience an alteration or change of nature without any other evident cause, it must follow, that light itself is the agent, and produces its effects by a chemical attraction.[5]

In 1934, Bachelard only sees in this text a fine example of 'an argument riveted to immediate sensory experience'. In 1951, he says much more. In *The Rationalist Activity*, he writes:

Given that at the end of the eighteenth century the forces of gravity and the forces of chemical affinity were conceived as identical in nature, Fourcroy is able to conclude that the changes that light makes in chemical substances prove that light is a body and that it produces these phenomena of diffraction by a *chemical attraction*.[6]

It is not a question of the displacement of the commentary onto one particular expression: chemical attraction. What Bachelard is showing us here is the *wherefore* of the substantialist obstacle, at the theoretical level of its insertion into a historically determinate problematic. The 'Fourcroy is able to conclude . . .' should be understood as 'Fourcroy is unable not to conclude . . .' In short, it is a question of another way of writing the History of the Sciences.

If we wanted confirmation of this, we should find it in *Rational Materialism*. Quoting the same text by Fourcroy, Bachelard adds:

This is a very dangerous text for the historian of the sciences unless he forms his judgement in the light of the multiple philosophical nuances capable of separating reasons from facts. One can indeed claim that the formulation 'light acts *chemically* on bodies' corresponds to a *reality* abundantly verified by immediate experience; one can add that this *truth*

5. Antoine François de Fourcroy, *Elements of Chemistry and Natural History*, English translation, 5th edition, Edinburgh, 1800, pp. 141-2.
6. *L'activité rationaliste de la physique contemporaine*, p. 32.

has been ratified during the development of chemistry by a whole science called precisely: photo-chemistry.[7]

Now, the object of his demonstration is later to denounce the faulty character of this reference: precisely because Fourcroy was unable to avoid running into the substantialist obstacle of absorption.

Once again, here by a blank, we grasp the effect of the absence of the concept of problematic in the 1934 text. One more remark remains to be made and we shall, I think, have exhausted the two texts we are considering here: it is about photo-chemical science, which on this occasion is absolutely positive. In *Light and Substance*, Bachelard adheres, certain reservations notwithstanding, to the theory of Perrin, who had proposed the restoration of the concept of *collision* (*choc*) as the cause of photo-chemical reaction. He writes: 'The collision will thus have to be analyzed more or less indirectly in its wave characteristics, and the energy of the collision reduced to the energy of an oscillation. It then seems as if the chemical act will sooner or later have to be analysed in space-time. . . . After that, the idea of a substance entirely based on the absolute separation of space and time will surely have to be profoundly modified.' He admits: 'The details of these correspondences are still difficult to see.' Now, in *The Rationalist Activity*, we read: 'With the notion of collision we are in the presence of a kind of epistemological monstrosity.'[8] There follows a whole attack on *collisionism* (*choquisme*), another form of *thingism* (*chosisme*), another head of the realist hydra. I think that here we can see a fine illustration of an evaluation-re-evaluation of epistemological values: the very task Bachelard assigned to philosophy, as we have seen.

Read pages 116 and 117 of *Applied Rationalism* and you will get an idea of the advantages gained by abandoning the notion of collision. There Bachelard is able to assign different axes of rationality concerning light and colour: that of physics, that of chemistry, of ocular physiology, of the psychology of visual sensation. The distance traversed since the 'vague correspondences' of the 1934 text is clearly visible.

7. *Le matérialisme rationnel*, p. 88.
8. *L'activité rationaliste de la physique contemporaine*, p. 84.

2. RE-WORKING OF THE CONCEPTS
OF THE PROBLEMATIC IN PHYSICS

I shall now examine the re-working of the concepts of the problematic in Physics. A preliminary objection: the two books considered – *Atomistic Intuitions* and *The Rationalist Activity* – correspond to different projects. Does not Bachelard say in the introduction to the former that he sees his task as 'quite simple and quite didactic'?[9] This attempt to classify the classical atomistic doctrines thus seems an unpretentious book for schoolchildren: they may find in it a few of the essential features of atomistic philosophy. But in *The Rationalist Activity*, one can read: 'Physicists must not be made more realist – more traditionally realist – than they are in reality, nor must the atomism of modern science be linked to the atomism of the philosophers, as it seems to be by Meyerson.'[10]

Now we can see what is hidden behind the apparent modesty – one could easily say innocence – of the didactic project of the earlier work. A *polemical* enterprise; Meyerson is declared to be the main enemy here, the symbol of philosophical immobilism, and this should not surprise us; but what is essential is to see that by this classification, Bachelard wants to show us, if I may say so, that the philosophical doctrines concerning the atom are 'classified' (*classées*), i.e., obsolete (*déclassées*), that they must be broken with to reach the concepts of modern atomism, which he then calls 'axiomatic atomism'. Hence we are within our rights in saying that these two books correspond to one another.

The 1930s were for physics years of profound transformations. In 1930, *Dirac* presented his relativist interpretation of wave mechanics, and the hypothesis of the positive electron; in 1931, *Pauli* discovered neutrinos, and in 1932, *Anderson* discovered positrons in cosmic rays. In the same year, the first cyclotron was perfected by *Lawrence*. In 1934, *Chadwick* discovered the neutron; the meson was discovered in 1936. These dates are given as indicators; they concern events which Bachelard has reflected at one point

9. *Intuitions atomistiques*, p. 13.
10. *L'activité rationaliste de la physique contemporaine*, p. 78.

or another in his work. But when, in 1932–3, he wrote *Atomistic Intuitions*, all the particles had not yet been discovered, and he was in no position to conduct a detailed reflection on the implications of the discoveries of those that had.

Hence it would be of little interest for our purposes to proceed to a mere comparison: surveying what does appear in the book of 1933 and what does not. That would be no more than to give a catalogue of the scientific discoveries made between 1930 and 1950; in other words, to repeat myself. All we would find in it would be one more proof of how vigilantly and restlessly Bachelard followed the movement of the science of his time; in its actuality, to adopt a term which often flows from his pen. It is interesting for us to note that in *The Rationalist Activity*, Bachelard devotes two chapters of a general scope to the notion of a particle (chapters 3 and 4), which repeat from scratch, so to speak, the examination of atomism undertaken in *Atomistic Intuitions*. Read the first lines of Chapter 3:

A philosopher who begins studying contemporary physical science is initially embarrassed, like everyone else, by the weight of common knowledges, then, like every person of culture, by the memories of his own culture. Thus, he imagines, following the intuitions of normal life, that a particle is a small body, and he thinks, in traditional homage to the philosophy of Democritus, that the atom is an indivisible, the ultimate element of a division of matter.[11]

It seems remarkable to me to find that while in *Atomistic Intuitions*, he devotes all the first chapter to the weight of common knowledges, under the heading 'The metaphysics of dust', and four of the other five chapters to the weight of Democritean and Epicurean philosophies on recent atomistic theories, in *The Rationalist Activity*, he gives both about four pages: I repeat, these questions are obsolete. We read:

I signal all these echoes of a common-sense-based discussion because it is against them that I believe it is useful to establish a psychoanalysis of objective knowledge. Will a philosopher who claims to defend the continuity of common knowledge and scientific knowledge still accept similar

11. ibid., p. 75.

arguments? To maintain them on the threshold of culture is to accept the sloth of a mind satisfied by quick images. Contemporary science has completely freed itself of the objections of the ignorant.[12]

Thus one might think that if in 1951 Bachelard is more brief on this point, that is because he considers that he has already done the work in *Atomistic Intuitions*. There is more to it, I feel, and this more is more novel: in fact Bachelard has the notion that these objections are now *impossible*; I mean inside the science, for everything is possible for a philosopher. What matters is the fact that in 1951 similar philosophical objections can no longer hinder the progressive advance of the science. Their only remaining interest is to reveal philosophical laziness and, if possible, to make philosophy understand the inanity of its position. Whereas in 1934 such objections still had actuality inside the science and threatened it. Confirmation of this can be found in *The Rationalist Activity*,[13] where Bachelard shows that it is because of the highly social character of contemporary science that it no longer has to fear such philosophical objections, inspired by common sense. There is a scientific city which is able to defend itself from philosophical intrusions. Returning to arguments developed in *Applied Rationalism*, he shows that he who is unwilling to bend to the discipline of this city is compelled to remain at its gate, on the threshold.

It is clear that this scientific city was already constituted in 1930, but:

(a) Bachelard had not yet elaborated the concept of it;

(b) it is possible that the physicists' city, or, more precisely, its nuclear region, did not have the consistency it has since acquired.

I shall now apply myself to the explanation of a rectification which Bachelard makes in the second book, one which he presents to us as such and which therefore deserves all our attention. In *The Rationalist Activity*, in fact, he writes, about Millikan's experiment: 'Since I have assumed the task of determining the philosophical aspects of science, I must stress, against the judgements I have myself made in other circumstances, that Millikan's experiments were produced in a

12. ibid., p. 41.   13. ibid., p. 42.

realist, or even a thingist perspective.'[14] Before going into their description, let me recall that these experiments were carried out in 1925-6, and that their aim was to determine the mass and the elementary charge of the electron. This is what Millikan's experiment consisted of: Darmois, in his book *L'électron*,[15] sums up Millikan's central idea as follows (I choose Darmois because his is a book to which Bachelard refers several times): 'By means of an atomizer, very tiny drops of a non-volatile liquid (oil, mercury) are introduced between the plates of a condensor. These drops are electrified by their passage through the atomizer; in the absence of an electric field in the condensor, they fall slowly; by establishing an electric field, this fall can either be accelerated or decelerated; they can even be made to rise, and in every case their velocities can be measured. On ionizing the air contained between the plates, the velocity of a given drop can be observed to undergo sudden variations from time to time.'

This is interpreted by suggesting that the charge of the drop varies when it meets one of the ions of the gas. A comparison of the measurements shows that the charges captured are multiples of an elementary charge. Now, as the e/m ratio (energy/mass) has been known since 1903, thanks to another experiment of Millikan's, the two terms can now be established.

What did *Atomistic Intuitions* have to say about this?

Bachelard saw this experiment as a fine example of what he was later to call technical determinism. An anti-realist argument. Twenty years later, though, Bachelard corrects himself: 'These experiments were still realist.' A fine example for us of recurrence and re-working. It is up to us to attempt to show why in 1934 he could not see in Millikan's experiment an experiment in the realist style, i.e., a scientifically impure experiment. It is not enough, in fact – though it has some importance – to say that it is the anti-realist polemic which led him to inflect his interpretation in the axiomatic direction. For here it is not a matter merely of an inflection but rather of an about-turn in his views on a point he saw as fundamental.

14. ibid., p. 99.
15. Eugène Darmois: *L'électron*, PUF, Paris, 1947, p. 3.

I propose once again to see in this *about-turn* the effect of the absence of certain scientific and epistemological concepts which can be revealed with the help of recurrence. I venture the following explanation: in 1934, Bachelard did not have at his disposal the main concept of *The Rationalist Activity*: that of electron-cause or particle-cause. He did not yet make the distinction between the chemical atom, which is a substance, and the physical particle, which is a cause. This is, *mutatis mutandis*, the same kind of hesitation in thought that I brought out in discussing Perrin's theory of collision. I shall take as an *index* of it the simple observation that in *The Rationalist Activity* there is hardly any longer any question of atomistics; Bachelard gives the following explanation of this:

Here, moreover, is a philosophical characteristic which distinguishes the particles which concern contemporary Physics. These particles do not present themselves in a properly atomistic intuition. The modern atom is a hypothesis of Chemistry and its true characteristics spring from a combination of different atoms to produce molecules. The modern particle is a hypothesis of Physics.[16]

Hence it is an uncertainty in the distinction of problematics that seems to give *Atomistic Intuitions* the mixed character of a book which very often concerns the chemist more than it does the physicist. Let me add that the distinction could only be rigorously made after the discovery of the particles. From then on, closely examining the 1934 text, we find Bachelard, in the context of a demonstration which tends to prove that modern science is a science of effects – this famous passage is found on the previous page – writing: 'Millikan's apparatus . . . is thought directly as a function of the electron or the atom.' I hold that the crux of the argument lies here: there is at once a blank and an ambiguity, the symptomatic effect of that blank. Bearing in mind what Bachelard himself tells us in 1951 about the realist character of the experiment, the blank is 'as a function of the electron (to be produced)'; the ambiguity is in the 'as a function of', which manages to be valid both in the case of an axiomatic explanation and in that of a realist production.

16. *L'activité rationaliste de la physique contemporaine*, p. 90.

In other words, when Bachelard claims that he presented the experiment in a non-realist light, whereas it now seems to him that it was in fact realist, he ought to add that he was unable to think it as realist then; for he himself was still realist on this point. Let us reflect on this *paradox* which implies that it is an excess of realism which made Bachelard take up an axiomatic position. 'It is because he conceived the particle as a *thing* that he could make it a fixed point for axiomatic *thought*. Surreptitiously, in a very subtle and sophisticated way, it is the philosophical couple abstract/concrete which has been re-introduced here.' Here we have a proof that realism really is the counter-thought I have been discussing; for it to appear as such thought must be purged of it; it must be able to manifest its other; and it can be said that realism is a kind of ever renewed precipitate, always re-precipitated by the conquests of the scientific mind: impossible to see oneself as realist when one is realist; impossible to reveal the realism when one is oneself to some degree trapped in the tissue of its illusions. Impossible for Bachelard to take a correct view of Millikan's experiment in 1934 without thinking the particle as a cause.

I have thus explained why the word atomistics no longer appeared in *The Rationalist Activity*; I still have to show why what is no longer atomistics is not called 'axiomatics'. This is an important point, for the characterization of Physics as axiomatic is not confined to a single work: in 1937, still, in *The Experience of Space in Contemporary Physics*, the term axiomatics provides the title for the last chapter. Now, we have not once found this term in *The Rationalist Activity*, nor in any other work of the period. I propose to understand thereby that at this time, having available the major concepts of *Applied Rationalism*, whose importance I have underlined, Bachelard is now concerned with what, using a new word, he calls: the *labour* (*travail*) of scientific thought. This new word designates a new concept: the concept of the activity of a science as a process of production.[17] More precisely, we find the notion of axiomatics, guilty in his eyes no doubt of opening the way to a formalism, replaced by a

---

17. The word 'production' is henceforth found several times in his writings. Cf. *Le rationalisme appliqué*, p. 62, *L'activité rationaliste de la physique contemporaine*, p. 66.

system of concepts among whose number we can register that of the rational information of experience, and that of the operator, which, as has been seen, play a large part in the later works.

I shall say that what takes the place of what Bachelard surely intended by his notion of axiomatics is the idea that the thought of Contemporary Physics is 'aesthetic and constructive', or, to use an expression from *Applied Rationalism*, that it is marked by an aesthetic of hypotheses.

3. THE RE-WORKING OF THE CONCEPTS OF THE PROBLEMATIC IN CHEMISTRY

In *The Coherent Pluralism of Modern Chemistry*, Bachelard writes:

Since a revolution is already visible [in chemistry], I recognize that the philosophical effort I have made in order to write this book will have to be repeated later on a new basis.

And further on:

But all this new science obliges the philosopher to give his answer on the basis of the development of the concepts of quantum mechanics and wave mechanics. I can only undertake this task incidentally in the present work.[18]

This, with a few minor exceptions, is the business of *Rational Materialism*, which dates from 1953.

I propose to begin with a few reflections on the titles of the two books. In *The Coherent Pluralism*, Bachelard proposes to show that modern Chemistry is simultaneously pluralistic and coherent. The important term here is 'simultaneously' (*à la fois*). His project is to reveal a dialectic between two philosophical ideas in chemists' thought: the pluralism which arises from the multiplication of elementary substances and from the production of numerous heterogeneous compounds; and the idea of a reduction of the plurality which is formed by the scruple of coherence.

Rational Materialism is Bachelard's last great epistemological

18. *Le pluralisme cohérent de la chimie moderne*, pp. 9 and 223.

work, published two years after *The Rationalist Activity*; it might be asked why he did not call it 'The Rationalist Activity of Contemporary Chemistry', particularly given the fact that in the course of the work he happens to use the expression several times. I believe that this can be explained by the polemical import of the two words in alliance: Rational and Materialism. More precisely, there is the materialism of the philosophers which Bachelard characterizes as a 'simple, even a simplistic' philosophy, and then there is a materialism which is a 'science of matter'; in short, to return to a principle which Althusser has recently borrowed from Lenin, it is a question of opposing the philosophical category of matter to the scientific concept of matter. Note on the other hand that neither the word nor the concept of materialism appear as important in *The Coherent Pluralism of Modern Chemistry*. For the essential task he sets himself in that book is to disengage chemistry from the traditionally substantialist character attributed to it.

We read: 'Here is a slightly new characteristic of my own work. I have asked whether this chemical philosophy was necessarily substantialist. I believe I have been able to see that if the substantialist philosophy traditionally recognized as a characteristic of chemistry truly illuminated the first phase of the alternation I discussed earlier [the multiplication of substances], it gave way when the second phase supervened to a philosophy animated by general themes and illuminated by unitary views which are far from satisfying a realism as accentuated as it is usually said to be.'[19]

Much might be said about this text, and certain of the remarks I have made about Physics could be repeated for it. Let it suffice if I add that the general unitary views which Bachelard discusses here have a name: they are what he calls *the idea of the harmony of matter*. A word and a concept present on every page of the book of 1932 and one which provides the title and the theme of its philosophical conclusion. A word and a concept absent, with one exception which I shall analyse shortly, from *Rational Materialism*. I consider this change to be a basic one. And I propose to compare the whole of *The Coherent Pluralism* with the essential chapter which responds

19. ibid., p. 7.

to it in *Rational Materialism*: the one entitled 'The Modern Systematics of Simple Bodies'.

To go straight to the conclusion, it is precisely the concept of systematics which replaces, but on a different terrain, the concept or image of material harmony. But the problem is to account for it according to the method I have applied again and again in this chapter. I am obliged to make a detour: to disengage briefly the major themes of *The Coherent Pluralism*. As might have been expected, one theme is constant: that of the substantialist obstacle as a barrier to the constitution of modern Chemistry. For example, he writes:

Berthelot recalls the disappointing results of certain distillation experiments so often repeated during the eighteenth century. This method allowed a very delicate separation of the most varied essences. However, used for the analysis of organic substances, 'it was recognized, not without surprise' [writes Berthelot in *La Synthèse Chimique*[20]], 'that all vegetable substances subjected to distillation produced the same general principles: water, oil, phlegm, earth, etc. Food and poison give birth to the same general products; . . . in the presence of results so distant from the point of departure, they had to resign themselves to a recognition that the means of analysis set to work had denatured the natural materials.'

Bachelard comments: 'Thus, a method like distillation revealed itself as improper for the isolation of the intermediate substances which would enable us to concretize the different phases of the chemical composition.' And he adds: 'Our surprise at such a failure derives perhaps from a substantialist prejudice which leads us to see in distillation an operation whereby we draw from a complex substance its elementary substances. The intuition of latent substances is at the bottom of every realist doctrine.'[21]

Texts close to this one can be found in *Rational Materialism*; once again it is a matter of denouncing a substantialist prejudice and correctly marking the distance separating Chemistry from Natural Science. But the essential point lies elsewhere: once these first errors

20. Pierre Eugène Marcelin Berthelot, *La synthèse chimique*, Paris, 1876, p. 211.
21. *Le pluralisme coherent de la chimie moderne*, pp. 64–5.

have been criticized, Bachelard transfers his attention to Mendeleev's table, which twenty years later he will again describe as constituting 'one of the most philosophical pages in the History of the Sciences'. Having demonstrated the necessity of replacing the traditional *linear* classifications with a table, i.e., with an intersecting order based on the two general notions of valency and atomic weight, he shows that Mendeleev's genius was to take as a reference a monovalent element acting as a classifier. But what he finds interesting is the fact that, classified in this way, the elements distribute themselves into periods, or, as he repeatedly prefers to put it, into *octaves*. If is from the consideration of these octaves that he gets the idea of a material harmony.

It is interesting to note that it is not so much Mendeleev's table itself that Bachelard sees as deserving to hold the philosopher's attention as its *evolution*: the way in which later discoveries that have been inscribed in it have on several occasions modified its meaning without modifying its *order*; this is what is central to *The Coherent Pluralism*; it is also what is dealt with in *Rational Materialism* under the rubric: 'The Systematics of the Elements'.

In *The Coherent Pluralism*, he writes: 'After so many confirmations, from the very fact that it has survived although even the initial principle which had first constituted it has been shaken, Mendeleev's table thus emerges with a profoundly unitary meaning. It is the *diagram* of the natural order, it is the *summary* of all the experiments which might cast light on an evolution of substances.'[22] Now we have just seen that it is by means of the notion of a chemical *octave* that Mendeleev's table gave Bachelard the idea of a 'material harmony', the central thesis of his book. Such is at least the genesis he himself states for his thought. But examing it more closely, Bachelard only takes as his authority a *single passage* from Mendeleev.

It runs as follows:

And if the properties of atoms are a function of their weight, many ideas which have more or less rooted themselves in chemistry must be developed and worked out in the sense of this deduction. Although at first sight it appears that the chemical elements are perfectly self-existent in their

22. ibid., pp. 152–3.

character, and completely independent of each other, yet this idea of the nature of the elements must now be replaced by the notion of the dependence of their properties upon their mass. . . . Many chemical deductions then acquire a new sense and significance, and a regularity is observed where it would otherwise escape attention. This is particularly apparent in the physical properties.[23]

It has to be admitted, as Bachelard does, that if a 'harmonic preoccupation' can be revealed in this passage, its expression is 'wrapped up'. Now, I repeat, this is the only text cited in support of the thesis. Which amounts to saying that it is not from Mendeleev that Bachelard takes his essential notion; but rather onto him that he projects it. It therefore comes to him *from elsewhere*. Not from a philosophy or metaphysics of harmony: he denies it absolutely in his conclusion; but precisely from the series of reorganizations of the table up to that time.

In this series he observes an *epistemological substitution*. He writes: 'Perhaps I have succeeded in replacing little by little harmony considered as a fact with "harmony considered as a reasoning".'[24] In other words, what interests Bachelard in the notion of harmony is the fact that it can be a reasoning; this is its inductive value; or again the fact that it can serve as a *guide* to successive reorganizations – or rectifications – of knowledge (*savoir*).

But, as always: *inductive value = polemical value*. Harmonic thought is invoked *against* the idea that rationalism must be a philosophy of analysis; against a Neo-Kantianism *à la* Hannequin (attacked in *The Philosophy of No* and *Atomistic Intuitions*); *for* a demonstration that *the law* has priority over *the fact*, that the order of substances is imposed as a rationality; for making it clear that paradoxically – against current philosophical opinion – chemistry, complicated with four elements can become simple and unitary with 92 or with 100. *Against* above all the realism of atomic weights: 'It will perhaps be objected that atomic weights are known by a mere comparison of weighings and that this amounts to a return . . .

---

23. D. Mendeleev, *The Principles of Chemistry*, 3rd English edition, translated by George Kamensky, edited by Thomas H. Pope, Longmans, London, 1905, Vol. II, p. 31.
24. *Le pluralisme cohérent de la chimie moderne*, p. 226.

to the primacy of Physics and even of Mechanics over Chemistry. But . . . the objection loses its force in proportion to the affirmation of the harmonic conception of atoms.'[25] What Bachelard is showing is that in fact the atomic weights contribute a superfluous characteristic to the harmonic classification, since the atomic weights only intervene by their order.

With the modern discovery according to which the hydrogen atom that served Mendeleev as his classificatory element, is itself complex – electrically complex – new problems have arisen, but without casting doubt on the periodic ordering of the table. Bachelard indicates how the justification of the anomalies in Mendeleev's table (inverted places and empty places) opened the way to the concept of *atomic number*, which he describes as 'the principal factor of material harmony'. One of the greatest theoretical conquests of the century, in the sense that this variable might seem eminently artificial since it is a matter of a mere ordinal number which establishes the place of the chemical element in the table. But this number – initially analogous to that of the page of a book – acquires a resolutely experimental meaning with modern discoveries. It has come truly to give the measurement of the chemical reality of the various elements.

Such is the essential thesis of *The Coherent Pluralism*, it is confirmed for us in more precise fashion in the conclusion on the notion of *harmony*. What we are made to see is that an experimental reasoning can be confirmed by a harmony; Bachelard considers that this is an extension of inductive reasoning. The rationality of the science depends more on well-ordered variations of experiment than on a monotonous identity. The chemical substances, understood within a coherent and harmonic pluralism (I propose to read: coherent therefore harmonic or: coherent, i.e., harmonic), suggest possibilities of construction.

Now, I have said: the word harmony only appears once in the work of 1953. Let us see under what conditions it does appear:

In the problem which concerns us, we should realise that clarity is brought by the multiplicity of the periods of Mendeleev's table. Clarity is born

25. ibid., p. 101.

here from the repetition of examples, hence from a multiplicity. The theme appears thanks to its variations. What would we know of the doctrine of simple substances if the list of simple bodies stopped at the end of the first period? This great keyboard with its many octaves was needed before we could grasp this general harmony of simple substances.[26]

So that everything is clear, I think two parts should be distinguished in the sentence:
   – in the first we find the concepts;
   – in the second the images induced by these concepts.

What is conceptual is: 'The clear is born from the repetition of examples'; what is metaphorical is: 'the theme appears thanks to its variations'.

The great keyboard, the octaves and the harmony – too much an image not to arouse our suspicions – are no more than the literary unwinding of the metaphor; old images appear as soon as the imagination is given free rein to cover up the novelty of the concept to the advantage of a word.

Why, then, does the *concept* of harmony disappear completely? I put forward two complementary explanations: Bachelard is giving us the first when on the same page he writes: 'We can *now* see the impossibility which suspended a doctrine of matter when the knowledges had not gathered together documentation about a sufficient number of simple bodies for the intuition of their *totality* to form. It was necessary to pass from several to all. And it was impossible to be certain of having them all before rationally constituting a doctrine of the totality.'[27] Now, a large part of *Rational Materialism* is devoted precisely to an examination of the discovery of the latest elements (technecium, prometheum), but what seems more decisive to me is the following: in a short page from *The Coherent Pluralism* there is a text which seems to me to be the explanation for Bachelard's assertion, recalled at the beginning of this section, according to which he would have to repeat the book on new bases.

This text tells us: the recently discovered complex character of

26. *Le matérialisme rationnel*, p. 97.   27. ibid.

the atom impairs the material harmony in the form in which it was initially promised. It is confirmed by Chapter VI of *Rational Materialism*, entitled 'The Rationalism of Energy in Chemistry', in which we find that it is now energy that has the role of the thing-in-itself. It is now electronic dynamics which makes it possible to explain chemical bonds.

In 1932, Bachelard regards the electron as the unit of matter, or again as 'the veritable atom', a 'perfect concrete unit' in the sense that it is identical everywhere. In short, it is what is counted because it is the only thing that can be counted. It is also what is accountable for the harmonic organization of what he then called *electrical chemistry*. In *Rational Materialism*, on the contrary, what is central to Bachelard's thought is the *duality* of electronic organization and chemical organization. In 1935, taking into account the discoveries of the particles, it is *energy* that is fundamental in Bachelard's eyes. It is a matter of realizing – it is presented to us as an imperative – that it is impossible from now on to say that matter *has* an energy; we must rather insist that it *is* an energy. What is imposed on the investigation is the essentially energic root of chemical phenomena. Energy must be taken as a prime notion, better: as a *primary reality* (understanding this expression in its rectified sense as a realism of second posing, a worked realism). It therefore has to be understood that chemical reactions are in the last instance relations of energy. My insistence simply repeats Bachelard's. It is easy to see the novelty of these theses as compared with the problematic of *The Coherent Pluralism*.

This is one of the basic characteristics of Quantum Chemistry: energy states determine geometrical structures. Energy, quantified, must be included among the number of primary notions. The second basic characteristic of this Chemistry is the fact that – like Contemporary Physics – it no longer *measures*, it *calculates*. This replacement of measurement by calculation is an epistemological fact of the first importance in Gaston Bachelard's eyes. He returns to it constantly in his last three works. That is why he can write about Mendeleev's table, to which we have at last returned, 'Mendeleev's table reorganized at the level of current knowledges accedes to a truly arithmetical rationalism of matter.'[28] I think it is clear that this 'arithmetical rationalism' of matter is the epistemological concept which has replaced the notion of material harmony, about which it can be claimed, by recurrence, that it is no more than an image functioning as an ideological concept in the work of 1932. Which could lead us to suppose already the – poorly specified – multiplicity of the functions it has there.

Reciprocally, I can claim that in 1953 the word harmony *can only* be an image incidentally illustrating a use of the new concept. This demonstration seems to me to confirm what a rapid analysis of the text of *Rational Materialism* had suggested to us. One more proof: Bachelard writes further on: 'Before electronic dynamics the representations of chemical bonds could only be static representations, skeletal outlines.'[29] I believe that he would willingly have included his concept of material harmony among these anachronisms.

The examination I have just undertaken seems to me, in every case, conclusive: Gaston Bachelard, faithful to his own principles, has, like the physicist, never stopped 'remaking his intellectual life'. That is perhaps the most visible characteristic of the novelty of his philosophy; to my mind, it is its most exemplary trait.

28. ibid., p. 96.   29. ibid., p. 181.

Conclusion

What remains at the end of this study?

The hope, of course, that I have been able to demonstrate the historical event that Gaston Bachelard's appearance has constituted in the field of Philosophy. Historical, i.e., a ratified event, ratified for ever.

The ambition that I have proved that he performed the work of an *innovator* in Philosophy because he took it as his motto to 'go to school with the scientists'; and that in so doing he was able to discern the 'truth' of Philosophy, which lies in its *function* as the spokesman of ideologies vis-à-vis the sciences.

The idea that it was his having disengaged scientific practice from the image which philosophy traditionally gave of it, and in which even the scientists thought they could recognize themselves, that opened to him the field of a new philosophy.

The question of what, precisely, justifies such a movement implying that one can, within philosophy, emerge from philosophy. Probably we should theorize the play which we have seen revealed in Bachelardian epistemology on the occasion of its inauguration between the instances that determine it (sciences, morality, religion, etc., . . .) and to ask ourselves whether it is not his having introduced a *shift* (*bougé*) in the order of these instances which gives this special status to Bachelard's Philosophy.

Lastly, an anxiety; for, once the last page of Bachelard's last book has been turned, one does not feel the serenity with which a systematic philosophy will fill you at little cost. One is anxious, but with an anxiety which is not that vague and lazy sentiment in which some existentialist or mystical philosophy might revel. It is an *engaged* anxiety: one is, literally, set in motion. Precise tasks are set on the new territory for which the actual practice of the sciences constitutes the ground and the horizon. One would like to say: 'To work!'

Appendices to Part One

A. BRIEF BIBLIOGRAPHY

1. Epistemological Writings of Gaston Bachelard

Books:

Essai sur la connaissance approchée (Essay on Approximate Knowledge), Librairie Philosophique, J. Vrin, Paris, 1928.

Étude sur l'évolution d'un problème de physique: la propagation thermique dans les solides (A Study of the Development of a Problem of Physics: the propagation of heat in solids), Vrin, Paris, 1928.

La valeur inductive de la Relativité (The Inductive Value of Relativity), Vrin, Paris, 1929.

Le pluralisme cohérent de la chimie moderne (The Coherent Pluralism of Modern Chemistry), Vrin, Paris, 1932.

Les intuitions atomistiques (Atomistic Intuitions), Boivin et Cie, Paris, 1933.

Le nouvel esprit scientifique (The New Scientific Mind), Presses Universitaires de France [PUF], Paris, 1934.

La dialectique de la durée (The Dialectic of Duration), Boivin, Paris, 1936.

L'expérience de l'espace dans la physique contemporaine (The Experience of Space in Contemporary Physics), PUF, Paris, 1937.

La formation de l'esprit scientifique: contribution à une psychanalyse de la connaissance objective (The Formation of the Scientific Mind: a Contribution to a Psychoanalysis of Objective Knowledge), Vrin, Paris, 1938.

La philosophie du non (The Philosophy of No), PUF, Paris, 1940.

Le rationalisme appliqué (Applied Rationalism), PUF, Paris, 1949.

L'activité rationaliste de la physique contemporaine (The Rationalist Activity of Contemporary Physics), PUF, Paris, 1951.

Le matérialisme rationnel (Rational Materialism), PUF, Paris, 1953.

Articles:

'La richesse d'inférence de la physique mathématique' (The inferential wealth of mathematical physics), *Scientia*, Revue Internationale de Synthèse, No. 8,

Bologna, 1928 (reprinted in Gaston Bachelard, *L'engagement rationaliste*, PUF, Paris, 1972).

'Noumène et Microphysique' (Noumenon and Microphysics), *Recherches Philosophiques*, I, Paris, 1931 (reprinted in Gaston Bachelard, *Études*, Vrin, Paris, 1970).

'Le monde comme caprice et miniature' (The World as Caprice and Miniature), *Recherches Philosophiques*, III, 1933 (reprinted in *Études*, op. cit.).

'Idéalisme discursif' (Discursive Idealism), *Recherches Philosophiques*, IV, 1934 (reprinted in *Études*, op. cit.).

'Le surrationalisme' (Surrationalism), *Inquisitions*, No. 1, Éditions Sociales Internationales, Paris, 1936 (reprinted in *L'engagement rationaliste*, op. cit.).

'Lumière et substance' (Light and Substance), *Revue de métaphysique et de morale*, Paris, 1938 (reprinted in *Études*, op. cit.).

'Univers et Réalité' (Universe and Reality), *Travaux de IIᵉ Congrès des Sociétés de Philosophie française et de Langue française, Lyon, 13–15 avril 1939*, Neveu, Paris, 1939 (reprinted in *L'engagement rationaliste*, op. cit.).

'Hommage à Léon Brunschvicg' (In Honour of Léon Brunschvicg), *Revue de métaphysique et de morale*, 1945.

'Le problème philosophique des méthodes scientifiques' (The Philosophical Problem of Scientific Methods), *Discours* au Congrès internationale de Philosophie des Sciences, Paris (October 1949), coll. 'Actualités scientifiques et industrielles', no. 1126, Hermann, Paris, 1951 (reprinted in *L'engagement rationaliste*, op. cit.).

'L'idonéisme ou l'exactitude discursive' (Idoneism or Discursive Accuracy), *Études de philosophie des Sciences* (mélanges Ferdinand Gonseth), Éditions du Griffon, Neuchâtel, 1950.

'L'Actualité de l'histoire des sciences' (The Actuality of the History of the Sciences), Lecture at the Palais de la Découverte, 20 October 1961 (reprinted in *L'engagement rationaliste*, op. cit.).

Translations into English:

The Philosophy of No, Philosophy of the New Scientific Mind, translated by G. C. Waterston, Orion Press, New York, 1968.

2. Studies of Gaston Bachelard's epistemological work

Hommage à Gaston Bachelard (G. Bouligand, G. Canguilhem, P. Costabel, F. Courtès, F. Dagognet, M. Daumas, G. G. Granger, J. Hyppolite, R. Martin, R. Poirier and R. Taton), PUF, Paris, 1957.

'Hommage à Gaston Bachelard', *Annales de l'Université de Paris* (G. Canguilhem, L. Guillermit), January–March 1963.

Georges Canguilhem: 'Sur une épistémologie concordataire', *Hommage à Gaston Bachelard*, 1957, op. cit.

— 'L'histoire des sciences dans l'œuvre épistémologique de Gaston Bachelard', 'Gaston Bachelard et les philosophes', and 'Dialectique et philosophie du non chez Gaston Bachelard', in Georges Canguilhem: *Études d'histoire et de philosophie des sciences*, Vrin, Paris, 1968.

François Dagognet: 'Le matérialisme rationnel de Gaston Bachelard', *Cahiers de l'Institut de Science Économique Appliquée*, Paris, June 1962.

— *Gaston Bachelard*, coll. *Philosophes*, PUF, Paris, 1965.

Gilles-Gaston Granger: 'Visite à Gaston Bachelard', *Paru*, Monaco, 1947.

Jean Hyppolite: 'Gaston Bachelard ou le romantisme de l'intelligence', *Revue Philosophique*, Paris, January–March 1954, reprinted in *Hommage à Gaston Bachelard*, 1957, op. cit.,

— 'L'épistémologie de Gaston Bachelard', *Revue d'Histoire des Sciences*, Paris, January 1964.

3. Bibliography

A complete bibliography of Gaston Bachelard's writings has been established by Jean Rummens and is to be found in the *Revue internationale de philosophie*, Vol. XVII, 1963.

B. INDEX TO THE MAIN CONCEPTS OF BACHELARDIAN EPISTEMOLOGY

I conceive this Index as a *working instrument*: thus it has no pretensions to comprehensivity; in it I indicate the main texts on the basic concepts of historical epistemology as a guide for those who want to study the French texts of Bachelard's work. By that I mean the texts I believe deserve to hold the reader's attention for their *range*, for their strategic *position* in Bachelard's work or for the clarity of their *formulation*. Let me add that it is an index of *concepts*: hence there should be no surprise at the occasional reference to certain passages where the word indicated does not appear. I leave to the reader the trouble of recognizing in those passages the presence of the concept, and of reflecting on the theoretical implications of the absence of the word. Lastly, it is clear that if this index is necessarily incomplete, the choices I have had to make conform to the interpretation proposed in the preceding study.

To simplify, I have adopted the following abbreviations:

Essai   *Essai sur la connaissance approchée*
Étude   *Étude sur l'évolution d'un problème de Physique: la propagation thermique dans les solides*
VIR   *La valeur inductive de la Relativité*
IA   *Les intuitions atomistiques*
PCCM   *Le pluralisme cohérent de la chimie moderne*
NES   *Le nouvel esprit scientifique*
Dial.   *La dialectique de la durée*
Exp.   *L'expérience de l'espace dans la physique contemporaine*
FES   *La formation de l'esprit scientifique*
Non   *La philosophie du non*
RA   *Le rationalisme appliqué*
AR   *L'activité rationaliste de la physique contemporaine*
MR   *Le materialisme rationnel*

precursor (*précurseur*)
  Étude, 123; *RA*, 153; *AR*, 69
problematic (*problématique*)
  Étude, 128; *RA*, 51, 55, 57
recasting (*refonte*)
rectification (*rectification*) (cf. also 'error' and 'dialectic')
  Essai, Ch. II; *VIR*, 30; *NES*, 30; *FES*, beginning and 231
recurrence (*récurrence*)
  Étude, 13; *NES*, 8; *FES*, 109, 235, 251; *RA*, 2; *AR*, 69, 93, 102, 108, 111;
  MR, 75, 97
reorganization (*réorganisation*)
  NES, 175; *RA*, 168, 187; *AR*, 18, 51, 173, 176; *Conférence au Palais de la
  Découverte*
rupture (*rupture*)
  Essai, 270; *VIR*, 7; *Dial*, 75; *AR*, 77, 93
rupture, epistemological (*rupture épistémologique*)
  RA, 104–5
simplicity (*simplicité*)
  Essai, 93, 100–1; *VIR*, 28–9; *PCCM*, 57; *NES*, 138; *AR*, 50–1; *MR*, 73–4, 179

Part Two

Part Two

For a Critique of Epistemology
(Bachelard, Canguilhem, Foucault)

Introduction

The texts you are about to read have a history, and to know it will doubtless help you to appreciate their true import. This history hangs on an *encounter* – that of Marxism and epistemology – which may itself appear as the fruit of a double historical 'accident'.

The first accident is a matter of the peculiar history of epistemology in France: an original 'tradition' has arisen there, famous for the few names you will find in this book: Gaston Bachelard, Georges Canguilhem, Michel Foucault. Doubtless it would be hard to imagine works more dissimilar in their respective objects, aims and echoes. If it is indeed possible to compare the work of Foucault with that of Canguilhem because of their common interest in the history of the biological sciences, it has to be admitted that, for his part, Bachelard, who was exclusively attentive to the physics and chemistry of his time, says not a word about them. It should also be added that Canguilhem's strict specialization is opposed to the 'encyclopædism' of Foucault, who talks about linguistics, political economy, etc., just as much as he does about natural history and biology. On the other hand, if Canguilhem in a certain sense takes up the Bachelardian project of 'giving science the philosophy it deserves', i.e., of struggling, in his special domain, against the encroachments of idealistic philosophies of knowledge, it must be admitted that although this polemic is no less constant in Foucault's work, it has there undergone a remarkable displacement, a veritable 'decentring' with respect to the history of the sciences, to bring it to bear on the most general conditions of 'knowledge' (*savoir*). Lastly, whereas the interest of Bachelardian epistemology was recognized and its originality respected from the very first, the real importance of Canguilhem's works has only been grasped in the last few years, after twenty years of more or less deliberate neglect. As for those of Foucault, they have been the object of a strange misunderstanding, since they have owed a part of their rapid celebrity to the echo they aroused in a camp to which it is clear today that they did not belong, that of 'structuralism'.

For all these reasons, it would be inaccurate to speak of these writers as belonging to an epistemological 'school'. Canguilhem, after all, is a historian of the sciences, and Foucault would correctly refuse to be described as an 'epistemologist': he calls himself an 'archæologist of knowledge' (*savoir*). Under these conditions, is it possible to speak in their case, as I propose to do, of an 'epistemological tradition'? I find this justifiable because of the existence of a common feature which is transmitted to each of these œuvres, despite their apparent diversity. It would be superficial to seek to explain it by the supposed intellectual 'influences' which masters may have exercised on disciples. It is true, of course, that Bachelard was Canguilhem's 'teacher', and Canguilhem Foucault's, but we cannot appeal to psychology as a substitute for historical analysis without immediately renouncing any understanding but an anecdotal one. The common feature I have mentioned is more real and more profound, it constitutes their point of agreement and pertains to their common 'position' in philosophy.

To put it briefly, and provisionally formulating it in a negative form, it lies in their radical and deliberate '*non-positivism*'. This non-positivism, inaugurated by Bachelard, while it seems to me to form the 'cement' of the tradition uniting my three authors, simultaneously distinguishes this tradition from everything practised elsewhere under the name of 'epistemology'. It counterposes it to another tradition, one which does have its 'schools' and its 'institutions', a tradition dominant today and in which converge investigations conducted in the East and the West, at the University of Yale and in the Moscow Academy of Sciences.

I say that this other tradition, despite the internal distinctions that have to be made in it, is massively 'positivist' in that it always, in one way or another, presents itself as an attempt to elaborate a 'science of science' or – the technocratic variant – a 'science of the organization of scientific work'. This is the case with the Anglo-Saxon specialists Bernal and Price who, more than twenty years ago, announced under this title of a 'science of science' the emergence of a new discipline and established under this sign an original institution. The insistent references made to it today by the editors of the philosophical journal of the Moscow Academy of Sciences (*Voprosy Filosofii*) – Kedrov, Mikulinksy and Rodnyi – in order to take up the same project in the same terms, sufficiently prove that they range themselves in the same camp.[1] Although in a quite different form, this is also the case with the 'logical neo-positivist' current which attempts, on the basis of the concepts of the scientific discipline of mathematical logic, to form the categories of what Reichenbach called 'a scientific philosophy',[2] the philosophy of our time, that of the 'age of science', which is to be both a 'science of science' and a scientific critique of philosophy.

Whether epistemology is made into a kind of 'cross-roads' at which a cohort of heteroclite disciplines with scientific pretensions come to conjoin their disparate concepts in order to constitute a general theory of science, or whether a determinate science is made responsible for the provision of its categories, the philosophical presupposition of the undertaking is the same, and it is this presupposition that leads me to describe these attempts as 'positivist'. Truly, this common presupposition could find no better expression than the slogan: 'A science of science is possible.'

The claim I have just ventured may cause some surprise: that 'the science of science' is mortgaged by a *philosophical* presupposition. A paradox, since, precisely, both groups claim to have put an end to the 'philosophical usurpation', restoring to science its most legitimate property and its most precious birthright: itself. However, I continue to state that philosophy is not absent from these efforts. Let me add, to complete the paradox, that *two* philosophical presuppositions are conjoined in it. It is their very conjunction which

---

1. These articles have been translated into French in the series of the *Cahiers du Centre d'Etudes et de Recherches Marxistes* entitled 'Science et production'.
2. The title of Reichenbach's main work is *The Rise of Scientific Philosophy*, University of California Press, Berkeley and Los Angeles, 1951.

constitutes the positivism that I am denouncing. One pertains to the unity claimed for the duplicated singular term 'science'; the other relates to the circle of this duplication within the reflexiveness it attributes to the term with itself: 'science *of* science'.

The first point is well known today: to speak of science in general as one single entity which might itself take itself as an object is to make use – here: double use – of an ideological notion. It is to suppose that the ensemble of scientific practices can be treated as a homogeneous reality, constituting, at least in principle, the unity of an undifferentiated whole. This 'treatment' or this 'point of view' on science is peculiarly philosophical. It even repeats, beneath a modernist and scientistic exterior, one of philosophy's classical procedures. Better, *the* classical procedure of idealist philosophy which, when it speaks of the sciences, is eager for one thing only: to disengage their common 'essence' so as to be able to speak of 'science' in the singular – and then to take the theses produced thereby as a justification for the elaboration of a theory of knowledge. Re-read the history of philosophy: it is easy to establish with what remarkable regularity this procedure has been applied, from Plato to Husserl.

Hence the philosophical presupposition whose presence I therefore detect in the positivist epistemologists is an *idealist* philosophical presupposition. As such it simultaneously conceals and reveals, in the symptomatic mode, a reality which we have momentarily glimpsed: the ensemble of scientific practices. More accurately: by attributing to this ensemble the unity of a whole, the presupposition 'resorbs' – imaginarily annihilates – the reality of these practices, which resides in their *distinctness* – each having its own object, its own theory and its specific experimental protocols – and in their *uneven development* – each having its particular history. I say that it is the very reality of these practices which is thereby masked, for they do not exist outside the system that they constitute. Now this system, far from unfolding beneath the appearance of calm identity which has been foisted onto it, itself only has reality through the different contradictions entertained between the theoretical disciplines which feature in it. It is the intertwining of its contradictions which gives a form to its *history*. Thus we now know what is 'concealed' in the last analysis by the idealist philosophical presupposition here in question: it is the actual history of the sciences.

To say that a science of science is possible is, besides, to claim that 'science' can unveil, by mere reflection on itself, the laws of its constitution, and thus of its functioning as of its formation. It is to claim of 'the scientific discourse' that it has the intrinsic – and exceptional – virtue of being able, by itself, without going outside itself, to state the principles of its own theory. In other words, the 'scientific discourse', sovereignly autonomous, is accountable to no one and constructs itself, without let or hindrance, in the pure space of scientificity instituted, laid out and delimited by itself. Without let or hindrance, since every obstacle is in principle always already located, stated and surmounted in the implicit discourse it is constantly conducting with itself – a quiet murmur in its inmost soul, that in case of trouble need only be made explicit to illuminate everything. An immediate and decisive consequence follows: if it is the laws of scientific discourse itself which determine the space of its own deployment, if in principle it encounters no let or hindrance in that space, then the completion of knowledge (*savoir*) – its end and its perfection – is always in principle possible. All that remains in fact is to level out the few, quite formal difficulties that momentarily block it. A question of technique. Let us translate: there is no real history of the sciences; time has nothing to do with it. Or rather: time can only intervene in the form of *delay* or *anticipation*. The history of 'science' is merely a development, at best: an evolution, which guides knowledge from error to truth; in which all truths are measured against the latest to appear.

Now, once again, we can state that a very old philosophical operation is being repeated in a new form. Did not what are customarily called the 'Great Philosophies' (an *appellation à contrôler*) have as their project – and avowed claim – to state the criteria for all real or possible scientificity? Did they not put themselves, with respect to the existing sciences, in the position here declared of constitutive reflection? As the point is of some importance, I shall resort to a typical illustration: the philosophy of Hegel. In the discourse it conducts on itself, this philosophy, as is well known, takes as its 'foundation', i.e., as its basis and guarantee, the categories which are stated in that strange book entitled *The Science of Logic*. The peculiar status of this book in the Hegelian system deserves a special study for itself alone.[3] For our purposes, we shall only consider one small fact: Hegel declares that to it are consigned the categories of the scientificity of science. Witness the following passage in which the author situates the book with respect to *The Phenomenology of Mind*:

In *The Phenomenology of Mind* I have set forth the movement of consciousness, from the first crude opposition between itself and the object, up to absolute knowledge. This process goes through all the forms of the relation of thought to its object, and reaches the Concept of Science as its result. Thus this concept (apart from the fact that it arises within the boundaries of Logic) needs here no justification, having already received its justification in that place.[4]

For us, this text has a dual interest. It reveals the position of the content of logic with respect to the existing sciences – those that Hegel calls: 'empirical sciences'; it is logic that presents the concept of science; or, better, it is Hegel's book that contains the 'justification', the 'foundation' for the concept of science. In short, Hegel's *Science of Logic* is the philosophical science, the true science, the science of the sciences.

Hegel's philosophy presents itself as 'the philosophy of all philosophies'. Doubtless it would not be illegitimate to take its declarations at their word and see in it in fact, in the position it attributes to itself with respect to the system of the existing sciences, 'the truth', having attained self-consciousness, of what previous philosophies were tacitly practising. It would then be seen that the keystone of this philosophy is a 'science of science'. One step further: it is clear that, according to Hegel's own statements, even the writing of this book – *The Science of Logic* – presupposed that *The Phenomenology of Mind* was complete, and that therefore *history* itself was complete.

3. The best that has been given until now is Hyppolite's in his *Logique et existence, essai sur la Logique de Hegel*, PUF, Paris, 1953.
4. G. W. F. Hegel: *The Science of Logic*, translated by W. H. Johnson and L. G. Struthers, OUP, Oxford, 1929, Vol. I, p. 59.

In these conditions it is obvious that the project of a 'science of science' is merely the *repetition* in a new form of the same peculiarly philosophical operation. An operation whose effect fits in well with the one we have registered vis-à-vis the constitution of the unitary ideological notion of 'science': it annihilates the actual reality of the history of the sciences by placing it beneath the sign of a *teleology*. Now, abstracting from the specific structure taken by this teleology in the Hegelian dialectic, we can say – to return to the terms used at the beginning of this analysis – that the regular effect of the project of a 'science of science' is to reduce the actual history of the sciences to a kind of evolution. In other words: positivism and evolutionism go hand in hand. Or alternatively: evolutionism is the obligatory complement in the history of the sciences to positivism in epistemology.[5]

In these conditions it is hardly surprising that the non-positivism of the epistemological tradition I am discussing begins with and holds to a deliberate rejection of an 'evolutionism'. I shall say that its non-positivism leans on an *anti-evolutionism*. Today everyone knows the prime term for this rejection in Bachelard's work, the notion of epistemological 'rupture', is an injunction against every philosophy of history which would like to bring within its jurisdiction the epistemological categories he works on. Nor is it unknown that Georges Canguilhem, proposing to distinguish between the 'beginnings' of a science and its 'origins', relentlessly denouncing every attempt to seek more or less remote 'precursors' for a 'discovery', shares the same concern. But it is surely Michel Foucault who, analysing the notion of 'discontinuity' at the beginning of *The Archæology of Knowledge*, has best demonstrated the theoretical implications, decisive for the conception that can be held of history, of the anti-evolutionism that all three profess.

I can now give the positive content of the *differentia specifica* of this epistemological tradition, so far stated in a negative and polemical form. Their non-positivism and their anti-evolutionism pertain

5. This assertion could easily be illustrated by a study of a doctrine such as that of Ernst Mach, in which the notion of an 'economy of thought' operates the junction of a resolutely positivist epistemology and a conception of the history of the sciences inspired by Spencerian evolutionism.

to the *link* they recognize between epistemology and the actual practice of the history of the sciences. A link, or, rather, a *unity*, whose theory, as we shall see, each has attempted to outline in his own way. However, these attempts seem to me to have failed up to the present. An inevitable failure, no doubt, for this theory belongs in principle to a discipline which they do not recognize: 'historical materialism', the Marxist science of history. For all that, all epistemological problems undergo a revolutionary displacement from the mere fact of their practice of this unity; and on the other hand, their failure, insofar as it occurs on the basis of a correct practice, is infinitely valuable to us, since it designates to us, caught in its displacement, the site where we have to re-work.

It remains to understand why it was thus possible for this anti-evolutionist non-positivism to arise and be handed down in French philosophy *alongside* and *against* other currents more in accord with the dominant – spiritualist and positivist – tendencies of that philosophy.

This analysis belongs to a history of philosophy which still has to be written. I can only say that in the last analysis this history would be the history of the *unity* I have been discussing: a history of its formation, of its inconsistencies, of its failures, of its struggles and of its successes. To this day I only have at my disposal one factual suggestion on this subject;[6] here it takes the form of a paradox requiring elucidation: it seems that it was really Auguste Comte and his disciples who made this unity possible and inscribed it in French academic institutions, making the history of the sciences a discipline belonging with philosophy. In fact, France since then has been one of the only countries in the world – if not the only one – in which the history of the sciences is practised and taught in philosophy faculties. Thus it is to the founders of positivist philosophy that we should impute the beginnings of a tradition whose major trait is, as we have seen, its non-positivism. . . .

As for the second 'accident', it relates to the history of 'Marxism' in France: by itself it constitutes the *encounter* I mentioned at the

6. I owe it to Georges Canguilhem.

outset. It too might be characterized in a negative and polemical way: Louis Althusser's investigations, which have induced it, situate themselves in fact under the sign of 'theoretical anti-humanism' against an institutionally dominant current, represented in the 1960s by Roger Garaudy, which is theoretically neo-Hegelian and politically revisionist. But this anti-humanism is simply the negative and polemical obverse of a quite positive attempt from which we are still learning lessons: the reaffirmation of the scientific character of Marx's major theoretical work: *Capital*. Everyone knows that to this end Althusser appealed to certain Bachelardian epistemological categories: notably to the now famous notion of an 'epistemological rupture'. No doubt it is easy today to be amused at a Marxist philosopher uncritically borrowing a 'bourgeois' philosophical category, but for all that no one can honestly dispute the fact that, in its time, this loan fulfilled a positive function, allowing what has been called a 're-commencement' of dialectical materialism. After what I have said about it, it is clear on what basis this encounter and this re-commencement were able to occur: on the basis of the materialist elements liberated by the non-positivism and anti-evolutionism of the epistemological tradition in question.

The theoretical and political consequences such a loan has managed to produce are also known. Althusser has been the first to recognize them and to give them a name: 'theoreticism'. All the difficulties crystallized, as it happens, around the status of 'dialectical materialism', of 'Marxist philosophy'. By making this philosophy – making theory – the 'theory of theoretical practice' and by making the scientific character of this discipline, already announced by Marx, depend on the factual existence of 'historical materialism', of the science of history, Althusser was able to think that he could *found* the unity of Epistemology and the History of the Sciences, hitherto only practised and postulated. In reality, by a new paradox which does not seem to have attracted enough attention, the effect of the importation of non-positivist epistemological categories was to re-activate in a new and unexpected form the positivist mirage of a 'science of science', christened with the name of Theory.

Althusser's later works, and notably his *Lenin and Philosophy*, have provided the elements of a rectification of this status of philosophy, bringing back into view, thanks to a careful re-reading of *Materialism and Empirio-Criticism*, a character hitherto absent from the theoretical stage: *politics*. By defining philosophy, following Lenin, as 'a political intervention vis-à-vis (*auprès de*) the sciences', Althusser there suggested two new tasks, unthinkable within the old fabric: that of elaborating a non-philosophical theory of philosophy, and that of elaborating a materialist theory of the history of the sciences. I say 'unthinkable within the old fabric' because, being 'trapped' in 'dialectical materialism' conceived more or less explicitly as a 'science of science', they could not find their proper site, the space in which their specific concepts have to be constituted: 'historical materialism' itself.

This rectification has important consequences. Not least is that it imposes on us a *return* to the epistemology from which it all began, in order to pose to it, with respect to these new disciplines, the question of its claims, and to assign to it a status: was it only an imposture or does it constitute a kind of anticipation, parallel to these disciplines of the future? In the latter case, what is the theoretical mechanism at work in such an anticipation? Such are the questions I have tried to pose. The texts that follow witness to it.

But, to come back to my beginning, these questions also establish the true import of these studies. It is only a matter of a *stage* which leads us to the threshold – only to the threshold – of a labour which, armed with a few new concepts whose construction will have been made possible by this return, will engage us '*on the terrain*' of the history of the sciences. Or more accurately: on that terrain whose contours I hope the reader will begin to discern when he has finished this book: the history of the sciences as a relatively autonomous region of the Science of History: a small country in a vast continent.

Dominique Lecourt
May 1971

From Bachelard to
Historical Materialism

The title of this article[1] will cause some surprise: Gaston Bachelard was not a Marxist, nor even a materialist; as a reminder, the passage from *Applied Rationalism* will be cited where materialism is presented as a 'flat', 'abstract' and 'crude' philosophy; it will be recalled that, 'discursive' as it may have been, Bachelardian epistemology explicitly wished to be idealist; it will be pointed out, lastly, that the most obvious point of agreement in this apparently contradictory – epistemological and 'poetic' – œuvre is precisely a dynamistic conception of thought, which is fundamentally very 'psychologistic'. According to the philosophical camp, two symmetrical and opposed types of objection will be advanced. One group will say: 'You want to reduce Marx's philosophy, "dialectical materialism", to a re-organized Bachelardian epistemology; you are betraying Marx!'; the other: 'Your Bachelard is not ours; you want to steal Bachelard for your own purposes; you are betraying Bachelard!'

The first group can easily be answered by pointing out that the philosophy of Marx, which they invoke, cannot be very familiar to them if they reject in principle any reading of an idealist philosopher which is not purely and simply a destruction. It is precisely Marx and after him Lenin who have taught us what a *materialist reading* of an idealist philosopher is. Re-read the *Philosophical Notebooks*: you will see there how a materialist proceeds when he reads an idealist philosophy *par excellence*, that of Hegel. It is such a type of reading I should like to attempt here with Bachelard.

1. First published in *L'arc* no. 42, Autumn 1970, this article repeats the substance and corrects some of the points of *Gaston Bachelard's Historical Epistemology* (Part One above).

As to the other group, I am willing to agree that my Bachelard is not theirs. However, let me add the following specification: it seems to me that a materialist reading of Bachelard has the advantage that it gives Bachelardian epistemology all its *contemporaneity*. It preserves it from all those philosophical – spiritualist and positivist – vampires against which it was laboriously constituted. Hence it is not impossible that my Bachelard would have been accepted by Bachelard himself more easily than theirs.

Finally, I hope to be able to show that such a reading makes it possible to think the *limits* of Bachelardian epistemology. To *think* them, and not just to observe them, i.e., to determine their necessity, but also how they are to be surpassed. It will thereby provide an understanding of the status of the psychologistic conception of thought that does in fact govern Bachelard's poetics and extends its effects to the very heart of his epistemology.

I. THE MEANING OF POLEMIC

Anyone who knows how to read Bachelard will easily recognize that the most constant feature of his epistemology is that it is *polemical* through and through. Bachelardian epistemology is the offspring of a never ending polemic against the philosophers. From the 'realism' of Meyerson to Sartre's existentialism, no philosophy escaped his sarcasms. This perpetual polemic, far from arising from a personal psychological disposition, has a precise and profound theoretical meaning. It has to be taken seriously. Its principle can be found outside philosophy in the upheavals experienced in the actual history of the sciences at the beginning of this century: the development of non-Euclidean geometries, the theory of Relativity, the beginnings of Micro-physics, etc. The new disciplines then inaugurated seemed 'unprecedented' to Bachelard; his first works are but the reflection of this radical novelty: they take note of a rupture in the actual history of the sciences. They want nothing else, so to speak, than to be its 'self-consciousness'.

In 1934, Bachelard published a book which gives a systematic picture of this 'recasting' of knowledge (*savoir*) which he had witnessed: *The New Scientific Mind*. In it he proposes a novel philo-sophical category – whose function at this stage is still descriptive: the category of 'No' or 'Non-'. This category was formed by a con-trolled extension of the negation which had served to think the disconcerting novelty of the *non-Euclidean* geometries: in the same way, one can speak of 'non-Newtonian' mechanics, 'non-Lavoisier-ian' chemistry, etc. It has a dual function, descriptive and normative, since it has to account for the *fact* of the mutation which occurred during these two 'heavy-weight decades' of the history of the sciences, but also includes the *exigency* for philosophy to reform its most fundamental notions in order to think this novelty.

For from this moment on, Gaston Bachelard had encountered, and run foul of, the philosophy of the philosophers: the discontinuity he registers in *The New Scientific Mind* is opposed to the principle that governed the then dominant philosophy of science, that of Émile Meyerson: *The Inductive Value of Relativity* (1929) is counter-posed to *La Déduction relativiste* (Relativist Deduction), in which Meyerson, with some courage and considerable ingenuity, had undertaken to 'deduce' Einstein from Newton by showing that, at least in its principles, the theory of Relativity was already present 'in germ' in the *Principia* of 1687. Meyerson, convinced of the identity of the human mind in all its manifestations, held that the discon-tinuous was an illusory appearance attributable to the philosophical ignorance of scientists. Hence one must state that Bachelardian epistemology, starting not from a philosophical 'principle' but from a summons addressed to philosophy by the contemporary re-organi-zation of the exact sciences, ran, in the very recognition of its object, into a set of philosophical theses which were obstacles in its way. This collision was first thought by Bachelard as a *delay* (*retard*) of philosophy with respect to science, a delay which was still awaiting its concept.

But the 'encounter' with Meyerson's philosophy had another, still more decisive consequence: in it Bachelard discovered the *solidarity* between a thesis concerning the theory of knowledge: 'realism', and a thesis concerning the history of the sciences: 'continuism'. In it the historical continuity of learning (*savoir*) is supported by the homogeneity of the forms of knowledge (*connaissance*) – ordinary and scientific. An attack on the former could not but ruin the latter: such is the double, historical and epistemological, meaning of the now famous thesis of the 'rupture' as it functions in Bachelard's works. It is clear in what sense this epistemology has to to be called 'historical'; it was so from the very first; from the moment it took as its task to draw the philosophical implications of the 'no' which the new scientific mind addressed to previous science. A task which received its formulation and the beginnings of a realization six years later in *The Philosophy of No*: the question, it says there, is 'to give science the philosophy it deserves'.

Bachelard was to carry out this undertaking during the next ten years: from *The Philosophy of No* (1940) to *Applied Rationalism* (1949). In doing so he steadily acquired the conviction that this philosophy could only be elaborated marginally to all the existing 'theories of knowledge'. Not only 'marginally to' but also *against* them. What he had defined as the 'delay' of philosophy now seemed to him to be a systematic 'displacement' of *every* philosophical theory of knowledge with respect to the scientists' actual work. That is why *Applied Rationalism*, which can be said to realize, but also to rectify in many points, the programme of *The Philosophy of No*, opens with several crucial pages in which Bachelard sets out what I propose to call a 'topology' of philosophy. This topology takes the form of a 'spectrum' in which all the types of theory of knowledge appear dispersed around the reality of the work of production of scientific concepts, in which this topology proves to be a 'typology'. Allow me to reproduce this spectrum (on p. 133) in order to analyse it.

This spectrum has two very remarkable characteristics: (a) every philosophy – to the extent that it contains as a principal component a theory of knowledge – is defined in it by its *place* – its specific 'displacement' – with respect to scientific knowledge; (b) scientific knowledge has the role of an *axis*: that is to say that by a mere 'fold' around this axis it is possible to make the various typical forms of philosophy coincide. Three conclusions can be drawn from these two characteristics: (a) what is given as the *content* of philosophy is none other than the hallucinatory materialization of its peculiar *dispersion* (*écart*) from science; (b) the always possible coincidence of symmetrical and opposed typical forms of philosophy is the index of a fundamental identity: each form is merely the 'inverted' but identical form of an opposite form; (c) the essence of philosophy can only be determined from the point of view of the axis, i.e., from a non-philosophical point of view.

Idealism

↑

Conventionalism

↑

Formalism

↑

(philosophy of the production of scientific knowledges: applied rationalism and technical materialism)

↓

Positivism

↓

Empiricism

↓

Realism

This 'identity in inversion' that I have just emphasized is analysed at length in Bachelard's last works. He there remarks that it is supported by a certain number of philosophical *couples*, each term of which can by turns be dominant or dominated. These categorial couples form the apparent 'content' of the philosophical theories of knowledge. Stated as such in *Applied Rationalism*, they are as follows: subject-object, abstract-concrete, given-construct, etc.; they are interchangeable and complementary. They all have as *correlate* and *cement* the philosophical category of *truth* which presents itself as the concept of their *accord* and *closes* the space of philosophy. Now this last category, implying that the completion of the process of knowledge is always possible in principle or realized, makes inconceivable the actual history of scientific knowledge: its ruptures, its reorganizations, its failures, its contradictions, its risks. . . . That is why an epistemology which is historical will pay more attention to *error*, to *failure*, to *hesitations* than to truth: its space will thus be *open*, and *non-systematic*.

If what I have just said is correct, the 'philosophy of no' turns out to be a 'non-philosophy', and thereby delivers, in a free state, the elements of a non-philosophical theory of philosophy. *For us*, this is one of the most precious gains of Gaston Bachelard's epistemology.

But the Bachelardian polemic has an even more profound import: this is based on another statement, more serious than the previous one. Make no mistake, in fact: to wish to 'give science the philosophy it deserves' is not to undertake to renovate philosophy for its own salvation; nor is it the luxury of a homage offered to science by one of its worshippers on the solemn occasion of one of its 'revolutions'. The 'delay' or displacement of philosophy with respect to the 'activity' of the contemporary sciences would not have had any seriousness for Bachelard had he not quickly been convinced that it rebounded on scientific work itself.

Once he had established that in respect of the 'essential progressiveness of scientific knowledge' the philosophers – lazy by nature and function – had 'seceded', Bachelard turned to the scientists to ask them the following naive question: 'What then is the philosophy of your practice?' But he realized, not without astonishment, that this question obtained *the same* answers – a few terminological variations apart – as those the philosophers themselves might have given it. Even in *The Philosophy of No*, he could write, slightly disabused: 'The scientists do not always even profess the philosophy of their own science.' That is to say, the philosophy of the scientists is contradictory: to use an expression of Bachelard's, it mixes together a 'diurnal philosophy', the clear philosophy of the science, and a 'nocturnal philosophy', the philosophy of the philosophers to which the scientists inevitably turn when they reflect on their own practice. I shall say that the scientist maintains an *imaginary relationship* to his own practice and that the philosophy of the philosophers plays its part in the constitution of this relationship. It remains to go beyond this descriptive level and think the *wherefore* of this intervention of the philosophy of the philosophers in that of the scientists. Bachelardian epistemology sets out a whole system of concepts for this purpose.

II. OBSTACLE AND RUPTURE

The first concept to be constructed, the one which sustains the whole edifice, is the concept of 'epistemological obstacle'; it designates the effects on the scientist's practice of the imaginary relationship he maintains with this practice. This concept is still famous thanks to the many and often terrifying illustrations Bachelard gave of it in *The Formation of the Scientific Mind* (1938). It must be said that, preoccupied with what was most urgent, he concerned himself less with its mechanism than with its effects. Or rather with its unique effect; for, although 'polymorphous', the obstacle functions in a single direction: going back on the 'no', it closes the rupture between ordinary knowledge and scientific knowledge and re-establishes the continuity threatened by the advance of scientific knowledge.

It may arise at the moment of the constitution of the knowledge, in the form of a 'counter-thought', or at a later phase in its development as a 'suspension of thought' (*arrêt de pensée*). Whatever the case, the obstacle reveals 'a *resistance* of thought to thought'. More precisely: assuming that scientific thought only advances by its own reorganizations, it can be said that the epistemological obstacle appears whenever – but only then – an existing organization of thought – whether it is already scientific or not – is in danger. Let me add that it appears *at the point* at which the rupture threatens – which other efforts than those of Bachelard have been able to show to be the site of an 'overdetermination', of an accumulation of contradictions. Localized in its appearance, the obstacle is solidary with a determinate structure of thought which will later appear, by recurrence, as a 'tissue of tenacious errors'. The status Bachelard attributes to the 'philosophy of the philosophers' is now clearer: it is the *vehicle* and *support* of the epistemological obstacles, since it is what structures the relationship of the scientist to his scientific practice. It registers scientific ruptures and reorganizations by inversions in its spectrum; and, in the closed field of its basic categories, it thereby assimilates the advances of scientific knowledge and lives by their exploitation. It is easy to observe its action, to describe it, even to foresee it: Bachelard, for provocative reasons – in order to shake the philosophers out of their 'torpor' – more than once tried this out. But one question about the epistemological obstacles remains unanswered: once their effects and the mechanism of their intervention in scientific practices have been described, that of their *formation* remains to be thought. Rather: what necessity is there in the fact that epistemological obstacles are always being formed and reformed? We shall find that this question reveals the *limits* of Bachelardian epistemology.

First we must examine the positive categories released by the recognition of the obstacles as such and by the respect for ruptures and re-organizations. We can say that all these categories are ordered according to an unprecedented conception of the *dialectic*. In Bachelard this category designates the reality of scientific work: the process of mutual *adjustment* of theory and experiment. Now, given the rejection of every fixed point – through an initial and polemical rejection of the subject-object couplet – this adjustment has to be thought not as a formal adequation but as a *historical* process. In a history which implies no certainty, no fate destines theory always to find the means of its realization. The risk is that at a given moment the language of the physicist and that of the mathematician, for example, should become contradictory. Philosophy will hasten to see in this a 'crisis' of science.[2] For the mathematicians and physicists, it will be the opportunity for some work: the former will revise their theories, formulate other hypotheses, the latter will refine their experiments, check their instruments. Neither the former nor the latter will hesitate to reconstruct the edifice of their science 'from top to bottom' if need be. Georges Canguilhem has shown that this category of the dialectic cannot be assimilated to any classical conception of the dialectic: this is readily understandable once the meaning and implications of Bachelard's anti-philosophical polemic have been grasped. The *dialectic* that emerges is the 'spontaneous' dialectic of scientific practice: it affirms – against philosophical scepticism – the *existence* of the objects of science and

2. This is what happened early in this century with the beginnings of Micro-physics.

proceeds by a reorganization of learning (*savoir*) 'from top to bottom'. It seems to me that this is most precisely what Lenin in *Materialism and Empirio-Criticism* called the spontaneous 'dialectical materialism' of the scientists. Lenin and Bachelard coincide at this point even at the level of vocabulary: both claim that knowledge is a *'historical production'*.

III. TECHNIQUE AND EXPERIENCE

Bachelard's polemic against the philosophical theories of knowledge has one last effect: it demands a rectification of the philosophical category of *experience* by a correct appreciation of the function of *instruments* in the production of scientific concepts.

Everyone knows Bachelard's thesis that scientific instruments are 'materialized theories'; but it is essential to add the following counter-point: the 'materialization' of theory is not for him an accessory phenomenon. On the contrary, he ceaselessly stressed that it is one of the most characteristic features of the contemporary sciences that they are 'artificialist', that they contain as one of their essential components a technique for the production of phenomena; what, in parody fashion, he has called a 'phenomeno-technics', and which is the object of that new discipline programmatically adopted by *Applied Rationalism*: 'technical materialism'.

The notion of phenomeno-technics has to be taken seriously: it enables us to understand in what sense the word 'production' is to be understood: not only the 'theoretical' production of concepts, but indissociably the *material* production of the object of theoretical labour; of what can no longer be called its 'data' or 'givens' (*données*), but rather its 'material'. The philosophy of the philosophers, when it is confronted with this material intervention of instruments in the production of concepts can only think it as an inessential 'mediation', and leave it to fall within the general and vague category of 'experimental method', a specification 'for the use of the scientist' of the philosophical category of experience. According to Bachelard, this general category, ignoring the specificity of the *cases* in which instruments function, gives no real knowledge of what takes place in scientific practice.[3] It is unable to explain the new fact that a concept must from now on integrate into its constitution as a concept the technical conditions of its realization. Ultimately this is because the notion of 'method' and the philosophical category of experience are solidary with the conceptual couplet 'abstract-concrete'. Now, the practice of phenomeno-technics consists precisely of proceeding to *couplings* (*couplages*) between the abstract and the concrete by the expedient of the setting up of theoretically defined instruments and systems of apparatus according to programmes of rational realization. Thus the 'objects' of science, far from being poor abstractions drawn from the wealth of the concrete, are the theoretically normed and materially ordered products of a labour which endows them with all the wealth of determinations of the concept and with all the sensitivity of experimental specifications. It can thus be said, following Bachelard, that these objects are 'concrete-abstracts'.

The dual status of scientific instruments has the additional interest of revealing – materially – the 'eminently social' character of contemporary science. Bachelard's last epistemological work, on chemistry, *Rational Materialism* (1953), is particularly instructive in this regard. In it he systematically opposes what the chemist calls a 'substance' to what the philosopher means by substance. Among the essential characteristics of a chemical substance is 'purity'. Here is what Bachelard writes about it:

It can be said that there is no purity without purification. And nothing better proves the eminently social character of contemporary science than the techniques of purification. Indeed, purification processes can only be developed by the utilization of a whole set of reagents whose purity has obtained a kind of social guarantee.[4]

Elsewhere, as is well known, Bachelard could write that only 'society can send electricity along a wire'.[5] In short, he reveals the need, in order to think the history of a science, to take into account the state of the 'technological city' (*cité technicienne*). But that state is quite

3. Cf. 'Le problème philosophique des méthodes scientifiques', in *L'engagement rationaliste*, PUF, Paris, 1972.
4. *Le matérialisme rationnel*, p. 77.
5. *L'activité rationaliste de la physique contemporaine*, p. 222.

clearly linked to the history of the techniques of production; i.e., to the city as such. What type of determination is there between the history of production techniques and that of scientific instruments, between that of scientific instruments and that of concepts? These questions remain unanswered. Here too we see the *limits* of Gaston Bachelard's epistemology.

IV. THE LIMITS OF BACHELARDIAN EPISTEMOLOGY

At two points in our route we have found that Bachelard's epistemology left unanswered a question it had helped to pose. I believe that these two points in principle designate the same difficulty, the same conceptual lacuna.

In the case of the status of 'scientific instruments', what is missing from Bachelard's analysis is a concept that would enable him to think together several histories with different statuses; in short, the concept of a *differential history*. When it is a matter of the formation of epistemological obstacles, the same lack is felt, but the consequences, as we shall see, are much more serious. Once the *rupture* between ordinary knowledge and scientific knowledge has been registered, it is indeed a matter of determining the constitution of that 'tissue of tenacious errors' with which science 'breaks'. At the same time, this is also to account for the necessarily imaginary nature of the relationship the scientist maintains with his own practice.

Bachelard attempted this in two directions, unevenly explored in his work. The first, evoked above all in *The Formation of the Scientific Mind*, consists of casting doubt on scientific education, which, both in its lessons and in its 'practical work', displaces the true interests of science behind the mask of pedagogy: the constant appeal to the images and experiences of everyday life made in physics courses seems to him particularly damaging. The philosophy class is also incriminated, but for a different although complementary reason: it diffuses an undeserved valorization of 'general culture' to the disadvantage of the scientific specializations, which are, however, the only motor of the advance of the sciences. Thus, by means of educational institutions, the conditions of the reproduction of scientific knowledges have their effects on the forms of their production.

The second direction is intended to be more profound, and it is more minutely analysed by Bachelard; it constitutes the object of the new discipline he believed he had founded: the *'psychoanalysis of objective knowledge'*. It must be candidly stated: all that enables Bachelard to think the necessity of the 'epistemological obstacles' is a certain conception of the human soul which roots the 'imaginary relationship' in the imaginary of the images produced by the imagination. The pages – and they are numerous – in which Bachelard describes this inhibitory intervention of images in scientific practice are still famous. But their crucial theoretical status must be understood: they attempt to elaborate a system of concepts which will make it possible to think the intrication of *two histories*: that of the scientific and that of the non-scientific in the practice of the scientists. Hence it is not surprising that this historical epistemology culminates, in *The Rationalist Affectivity of Contemporary Physics* (1951), with the project of an epistemological history which is presented as a dual history: a 'ratified history' (or history of the scientific in scientific practice) and a 'lapsed history' (or history of the interventions of the non-scientific in scientific practice).

But if we turn to the realizations of this double history, we find that the only example of a *ratified history* that he elaborated – in *Applied Rationalism* – he elaborated vis-à-vis the history of mathematics, whose very special character was stressed by Bachelard himself, following Cavaillès, for mathematics immediately manifests the existence of what he calls a 'logical time', a *continuous identity*, which is not found as such in the other sciences. As for *lapsed history*, illustrations of it will be sought in vain: it is thought very precisely as a non-history: as a *'museum* of horrors' or an 'unformed *magma*'. Given this, the conjunction of the two histories and their mutual determination remain obscure.

His resort to the *libido* of the scientists to explain the constitution of epistemological obstacles here at once reveals all its meaning: it compensates for Bachelard's inability to think the differential history of what *I* shall call sciences and ideologies. By that very fact, all Bachelard's epistemological concepts are haunted by psychologism: in the term 'scientific mind' it is the term *mind* that tends to become dominant; the notion of scientific *labour* and, correspondingly, philosophical *laziness*, take on a subjective connotation; the ⹁*application* of 'applied rationalism' threatens to capsize into psychopedagogy; *obstacles*, finally, can be understood as mere difficulties, whereas the *scientific city* is conceived as an 'inter-subjectivity'. It has to be admitted that many pages of Bachelard are open to such an interpretation.

But if the notion of an 'imaginary relationship' is referred, not to a psychology of the imaginary, but to the scientific concept of ideology as it features in 'historical materialism', in the science of history, and which designates precisely the 'imaginary relationship of men to their material conditions of existence', it is clear what is designated, but not thought, by Bachelard: the necessity, in order to construct the concept of a history of the sciences, to refer it to a theory of ideologies and of their history.

Such a reading really does allow us to assign limits to Bachelard's epistemology since it reveals the 'psychologism' that sustains his 'poetics' as a *point of retreat*, better as a 'return of philosophy', if it is true that, unable to think the relation scientific non-scientific as a differential history, Bachelard based it on the repetitive permanence of great themes, myths or complexes in an eternal unconscious. In short, paradoxically, he turns to the analogue of a theory of knowledge. Hence it has to be said that Gaston Bachelard's historical epistemology remains a non-philosophy *in* philosophy. Nevertheless, by its respect for the spontaneous dialectical materialism of scientific practice, it provides us with precious elements for a theory of philosophy and of its history, and on condition that we know how to read it, precisely where it is inconsistent it reveals the ways to supplement it so as to construct a materialist theory of the history of the sciences.

Epistemology and Poetics
(a Study of the Reduction of
Metaphors in Gaston Bachelard)

'To separate oneself from images one must act
on the real' (*Le matérialisme rationnel*, p. 57)
'Look out, Pretty Wave, there is a swarm of photons
under your skirt' (*L'activité rationaliste*, p. 192)

'Which Bachelard?'[1]

Are there two? Two in one: prodigious duplication or disturbing duplicity. Should we celebrate the achievement of a rare all-rounder? Or rather be disturbed by such an acute contradiction: could one really, without loss, divide one's interests to such an extent?

Let me admit straight away that I am not much concerned to know whether Gaston Bachelard was the last representative of a tradition of balance and harmony in which a certain humanism, in slight disarray today, has sought, by going beyond the Renaissance back to Classical Antiquity, to rediscover the original innocence of its wry features; or whether, on the contrary, behind the twinkling eyes of the philosopher from Champagne there was not a silent and undecided battle being fought out between two unreconcilable 'passions': the disparate writings being then the 'natural' product of a subject 'divided' in itself. I think that we can – and therefore must – break with this normal run of the mill of questions raised by the double range of Bachelard's books. Whichever solution it is given, that solution seems to me to share the same terrain, derive from the same presuppositions: both seek more or less explicitly in the psychology of the man for the ultimate explanation of the constitution of the work. Since Michel Foucault we have known what a ballast of

1. This text reproduces, in slightly modified form, a paper presented to Jacques Derrida's seminar in 1970.

ideological implications is carried by the notion of an *author*. Hence I shall not seek here for any line of descent, any genesis, any itinerary leading us from Bachelard's works to his 'secret'.

I shall take the œuvre as it is, in its *duality*, and pose the question of the *co-existence* of two heterogeneous systems of concepts. More accurately: if it is true that 'co-existence' is not mere 'juxtaposition', but always presupposes, in one form or another, a *unity* in the duality, be it only in the form of a 'recognition', I shall ask what type of unity we are dealing with here. To put it plainly: I shall attempt to discern what in Bachelard's epistemological work 'called for' the constructions of his poetics. Not that I presuppose between the two sides of the œuvre an 'echoing' or 'complementary' relationship that would leave them face to face, in a boundless externality, but because I believe that I have registered in the very functioning of the episte-mological categories the site of an *omission* which is the opening for the 'poetics': a theory of the imaginary that has no other reality than to fill imaginarily a located absence. Or, to express myself in a differ-ent vocabulary: an imaginary solution to a real contradiction by a theory of the *imaginary*.

Hence it is insofar as it constitutes a bias – the best bias in my opinion – by which to grasp the originality – i.e., the unity of this contradiction and its solution – of Bachelard's epistemology that I propose to study the question of the treatment reserved for meta-phors in it. We shall find that the question is not so simple as my title might suggest: images and metaphors do not have the status of mere unseasonable dross, parasites, that the epistemologist, kibitzer or watch-dog of scientific activity, is supposed to recognize, identify and chase away. Of course, they do have to be 'reduced'; but we shall find that this 'reduction', of necessity, cannot be a destruction pure and simple. Of necessity, because there is a *scientific* use of images and metaphors. As is borne out by the following program-matic and prudent text from *The Rationalist Activity*:

Images, like the tongues cooked by Aesop, are good and bad, indispensable and harmful, by turns. One has to know how to use them moderately when they are good and to get rid of them as soon as they become useless.[2]

2. *L'activité rationaliste de la physique contemporaine*, p. 68.

Hence in Bachelard there is an attempt, suggested on several occasions, to elaborate a theory of the use – of the good use – of images. This theory was required by the starting-point of his epistemology: Micro-physics. Given that work was being done '*below*' space with 'non-figurative' hypotheses, the inevitable inadequacy of images (figurative in essence) posed a delicate problem. It can be said that the question of the use of images is raised by the 'devalorization' of geometrism in the new doctrines. At a stroke, the scientific language which, according to Bachelard, had registered both in its vocabulary and in its syntax the primacy of the geometrical, found itself in the situation of a 'geometrical metaphor'. That is why there is in this epistemology, under the name of 'bilingualism', an attempt at a theory of scientific language; this, too, of necessity.

The obverse of this attempt is better known: the disqualification of images and metaphors in *The Formation of the Scientific Mind*. However, the object of that book can only be understood once one has recognized the necessity for the intervention of images in scientific practice as well as that of the contradictions for which they are both the indices and the agents: images and metaphors are, for this epistemology of discontinuity, the constant threat of a restoration of continuism. The safest *alibi* of the theories of knowledge, which in their *wish* – which should be psychoanalyzed – to *found* 'science' imagine it as a given. Here, in one particular point, we return to a polemic in which all Bachelard's enterprise is engaged: its novelty and its difficulties.

I. SCIENTIFIC IMAGE AND THE LANGUAGE OF SCIENCE

The variants of the 'No' function

As is well known, in his first works Bachelard registers the radical novelty of contemporary scientific disciplines in the category 'no' or 'non-' formed by the extension-generalization of the 'non-' which Lobachevsky, Bólyai and Riemann had attached to Euclidean geometry. However, it should be noted that the contradiction which it designates is not strictly isomorphous in the case of the new geometries and that of the new physics. There is novelty and novelty. Bachelard dealt with this point himself in a book published in 1932: *The Coherent Pluralism of Modern Chemistry*. This is how he thinks the respective statuses of the non-Euclidean geometries and of what he proposes to call 'non-Maxwellian mechanics' in regard to the classical disciplines: recalling that the principle of this new mechanics consists of the admission that an electron, in describing a fixed orbit, can have no radiation, he adds: this is a 'physical postulate as heavy in consequences and as audacious as the postulate whereby Lobachevsky's geometry contradicted Euclid's geometry. However, there is one difference: whereas in geometry the domain of *a priori* definition opens equally easily onto two perspectives of divergent construction, in physics the two terms of the dilemma act neither at the same level, nor on the same type of reality. In physics it is the infinitely small that contradicts ordinary experience, it is the spontaneous that demands special laws plainly diverging from the phenomena recorded by our instruments.'[3] An example of this specific contradiction: the absence of radiation from the electron in its orbit contradicts the confirmed results of Rowland's experiment, according to which a rotational movement given to a wheel, one of whose sectors has been charged with electricity, produces induction phenomena in a neighbouring circuit. This contradiction by derogation, typical of Micro-physics, enables us to understand how the problem of the scientific use of images and the special status of the language of physical science is posed for Bachelard from then on. Let us note straight away, before returning to it at greater length, that if the electron does not radiate in its 'orbit' it is surely because the electron's *orbit* does not have the geometrical consistency that the image suggests. In a general way, as *The Formation of the Scientific Mind* has it,

Little by little one feels the need to work *beneath* space, so to speak, at the level of the essential relations which sustain space and phenomena. Scientific thought is then led towards constructions more metaphorical

3. *Le pluralisme cohérent de la chimie moderne*, p. 186.

than real, towards 'configurational spaces' of which sensory space is after all no more than one poor example.[4]

Now, it should be remembered that the construction of 'configurational spaces' represents for Bachelard the very type of the new forms of intervention of mathematics in physics. He devoted a chapter to them in a book published in 1937: *The Experience of Space in Contemporary Physics*. Their principle consists of 'describing the movements of a system of points in the very forms of the movement of a single point.'[5] In real three-dimensional space, to register a point with respect to a system of axes three variables are required, a system of n points therefore requiring 3n variables. If one dimension is made to correspond to each of these 3n variables, one can choose to say: either that the system is represented by n points in a three-dimensional space; or that the entire system is represented by a single point in a 3n-dimensional space. It turns out that the second solution – that of the 'configurational spaces' – greatly facilitates the calculations. Hence what Bachelard designates as the 'metaphoricalness' of the constructions of the new physics is clear; it is, with the intrusion of the infinitely small, the effect of the new type of bond instituted between mathematics and physics. In the same passage from *The Formation of the Scientific Mind*, he writes: 'Mathematicism is no longer descriptive, but formative.'

The Metaphorical and the artificial

It could easily follow that the 'constructions' of Micro-physics are *artificial procedures*, more or less adequate reproductions of a supposedly given reality which is to be discovered by indirect routes. Bachelard ceaselessly fought against such a viewpoint. Thus, in *The New Scientific Mind*, after showing that the *images* of waves and particles are only clear if they are isolated, he points out that wave mechanics, by associating them, obliges us to take them for mere *illustrations*. Illustrations of a mathematical law and not representations of an external reality. He writes: 'With recent theories,

---

4. *La formation de l'esprit scientifique*, p. 5.
5. *L'expérience de l'espace dans la physique contemporaine*, p. 116.

waves are interpreted as probabilities of the presence of particles. The wave is then clearly presented as a mathematical expression extending normally to *configurational spaces* in which the number of dimensions is greater than the three that are characteristic of intuitive space.' This is no reason for considering these spaces as *factitious*; on the contrary, he adds, these spaces are 'quasi-natural spaces for probability studies'. A note recalls the opinion on this point of the physicist Jeans, according to whom, 'a ten-dimensional space is neither more nor less real than our three-dimensional space'.[6] An inversion of the notion of the *real* is taking place here, or, in Bachelardian terminology, a 'transmutation of realist values' which obliges us to give an essentially polemical value to the passage from *The Formation of the Scientific Mind* evoked above: it is in respect of a certain representation of the 'real' that the images of physics are said to be 'metaphorical', it is against the idea that they might be the *reflection-images*, more or less accurate according to the approximation obtained, of a reality offered to investigation. In short, it is with respect to the real of 'realism' that these images are called 'metaphorical'.[7] This is hardly surprising at the beginning of a book entirely devoted to the anti-realist polemic. Nor is it surprising that he could write in *Noumenon and Micro-physics* that it is the

6. *Le nouvel esprit scientifique*, pp. 95–6 and 96n.

7. Which of course rules out any anti-materialist interpretation of these texts: as we have seen, Bachelard stands firm on the fundamental gnoseological question – the question of the relation between being and thought. He maintains that the sciences enable us to know objective reality, he denounces those who consider them to be 'artificial' or 'symbolic' constructions. Thus he writes of Ostwald, the founder of 'energeticism' and the ally of Mach, who taught Bogdanov, Lenin's opponent in *Materialism and Empirio-Criticism*: 'The rationalism of energy relinquishes any possibility of an idealist interpretation. If it tried to develop a subjective interpretation, it would fall victim to the seduction of the beautiful images of activism. The fate of the rationalism of energy is quite different when it is considered in the immense success of quantum energeticism, of discontinuous energeticism. This rationalism is now a rationalism with a real object, a rationalism which informs the major realistic character. Energy is reality itself, as they already said at the end of the nineteenth century. The chemist Ostwald loved to repeat that it is not Scapinus's staff but its kinetic *energy* that is real. But the energeticism of the twentieth century has a quite different import. It is not a mere description of phenomena. It casts light on the production of phenomena' (*L'activité rationaliste de la physique contemporaine*, p. 139). What is at issue in these texts is thus something of quite a different order: it is a matter of the support realism can obtain from a misinterpretation of the 'images' which function as illustrations of mathematical laws in physics.

objects 'which are represented by the metaphors and their organization which appears as the reality': meaning that it is their *mathematical* organization which *is* their reality. If this is taken into account,
this inversion of the attribute 'metaphorical' which we have just
witnessed reveals the originality of the position of Bachelard's
epistemology: on the one hand, it refuses to see in the schemata
of physics a copy of reality, it breaks with realism; on the other,
in contrast to formalism, it puts the accent on their reality.

Applied rationalism

To put it in a word, we see here at work the 'applied rationalism'
whose field Bachelard laboriously defined in his polemic against the
philosophers. For the reality of these constructions, which are only
metaphorical in the eyes of the real of realism – i.e., of philosophy – is
not observed, it is proved, *put to the proof* in the precision of a technically refined experimentation. This experimentation is not, is no
longer, something mounted subsequently to validate or invalidate a
previously constituted theory; it is, for Bachelard, an integral part of
the constitution of the theory itself, for, in a typical expression from
The Formation of the Scientific Mind, a 'concept must from now on
integrate in its constitution the real conditions of its application'.
Such a situation, which I repeat pertains to the new form of intervention of mathematics in physics, makes null and void every theory
of knowledge which would perpetuate the abstract-concrete opposition instead of recognizing the process of the concretization of the
abstract which distinguishes the new disciplines. It is more than a
hyphen that is established between the abstract and the concrete, it
is a real 'transaction', which Bachelard proposes to represent by a
double arrow (abst. $\leftrightharpoons$ concr.). Everyone knows the famous pages
of *Applied Rationalism* which are a commentary on this 'coupling'.
For the moment I shall only note what touches on our concerns.
Every image which is not a representation of the transaction, which
does not receive a double information from mathematical structure
and from technical realization should be rejected. Every image
which is given as the reflection of a being, or the being of a reflec-

tion, is rejected straight away.[8] In this way there is in Bachelard the outline of a theory of the scientific use of images; a theory which allows him to write in *The Rationalist Activity* that images 'like the tongues cooked by Aesop are good and bad . . . by turns'.[9]

The scientific use of images

The scientific use of images, as will already have been guessed, is governed by the transactional structure of concrete-abstract relations; every scientific image is merely the metaphor for the double arrow. That is to say, every image has a date, it intervenes in the *historical process* of the concretization of the abstract which constitutes the production of scientific concepts according to Bachelard. That is why an image may be good or bad by turns; that is also why 'to separate oneself from images one must act on the real'.[10] Thus every image must be 'on the point of reduction'. Here is a text which clearly establishes this *historical* status: in *Rational Materialism*, Bachelard writes on the tetrahedral constitution of the carbon atom:

In modern science, one schema follows on another; it is put forward as *better* than another, as more adequate and, simultaneously, as more suggestive. It seems that the oscillations between rational schemata and empirical knowledges come closer and closer to a common centre at which theoreticians and experimentalists approach unison.

Quoting Édouard Grimaux (*Introduction à l'étude de la chimie*), he adds:

To take these representations for immutable 'would be to reveal philosophical small-mindedness, to ignore the continual transformation of theories, those necessary instruments of science, constantly modified by new discoveries'.[11]

This passage has a dual interest: it stresses the historicity of scientific schemata, but also what Bachelard elsewhere calls their 'socialization' in contemporary science. The latter should be taken to mean the *control*, the *guarantee of objectivity* they receive from the 'scientific

8. Cf. note 7 here, too.   9. *L'activité rationalise de la physique contemporaine*, p. 68. 10. *Le matérialisme rationnel*, p. 57.   11. ibid., pp. 121–2.

city' or again from 'the union of labourers of the proof'. This means that the *imagination* of the investigator turns out to be strictly limited by rational and collective constraints; in short that those vesaniae of which there were so many examples in the eighteenth century and whose only source is the individual fantasy of some particular scientist, can no longer gain currency; literally, they no longer have 'civil rights'. Hence it must be said that the image, to be capable of a scientific use, must first be *de-psychologized*.

A 'suspension of metaphorical imagery'

I shall no doubt be criticized for having assimilated image and 'schema' in the previous example. I believe I can do so, because the essential of Bachelard's reflections on the scientific use of images focuses precisely on the constitution of the atom. One episode particularly holds his attention: the planetary representation of the atom by Niels Bohr. In *The Rationalist Activity*, he characterizes this image as a 'suspension of metaphorical imagery'. This enigmatic expression takes its meaning from the double opposition that pertains between this model and two types of assimilation of the atom to a solar system.

The one is practised by continuist historians of the sciences who make Raspail a *precursor* of Bohr on the pretext that in 1855 he had proposed the name 'atomistic astronomy' for his conception of the atom as a little sun. When we read in Raspail that under these conditions the motion of the electron is comparable to that of a line of railway trucks and is animated by a 'rotatory compression', it is not difficult, adds Bachelard, to perceive the abyss separating Raspail from Bohr. For the former it really is a matter of metaphorical imagery, for the latter the image is rationally ordered, mathematically structured, it intervenes as one element of discussion in an experimentally controlled theoretical effort. The other undue assimilation: that of the 'pedagogue' or 'vulgarizer'. The type is provided by Whitehead who overburdens the mathematical law with an absurd image, expecting thereby to make himself easier to understand: 'How is a mind eager for instruction helped by the page where Whitehead tells us that the classical electron is a horse freely galloping in the meadow, while Bohr's electron is a trolley-bus, running along a wire? What could be educational about this image of an atom of hydrogen constituted by a central nucleus to which is attached a circular tramway?' asks Bachelard.[12] In fact, he recalls, it is not to the starry heavens that Bohr is referring, but to the laws of rational mechanics which govern the motion of the stars. In reality, the situation is more complex: a planetary model, based entirely on rational mechanics, had been proposed by Rutherford, but it had the serious disadvantage that it was contradictory: according to Lorentz's theories, the planetary electrons should constantly radiate energy, which implied the instability of the atomic fabric. Bohr therefore proposed to transform Rutherford's atom by applying quantum theory to it. He could thus claim that an electron had several possible orbits; that it could gravitate along an orbit without emitting any energy; but that if for some reason it passed from one orbit to another, it then emitted or on the contrary absorbed a certain quantum of energy. Let me add that this made possible the rediscovery of precisely the formulae produced by Balmer in spectroscopy. It is clear, despite the schematism of these explanations, why Bachelard could write in *Applied Rationalism*: 'The image of an atom organized like the planetary system cannot impose itself by its *realistic* aspects. It simply refers to a mathematical organization. It has to be read mathematically, without abandoning the dominant meaning of mathematical formulae.'[13]

But the planetary atom has not yet yielded all its lessons: the discovery in 1925 by the Dutchmen Uhlenbeck and Goudsmit of the *spin* of the electron is itself very instructive: I cannot go into the details of Bachelard's analyses (it would be necessary to refer to the chapter of *The Rationalist Activity* on 'Spin and the Magneton'). This is what he writes:

In the planetary atom organized according to quantum theory by Niels Bohr, spectral phenomena are released when an electron jumps from one quantified orbit to another quantified orbit. The play of the integral

12. *L'activité rationaliste de la physique contemporaine*, pp. 68–9.
13. *Le rationalise appliqué*, p. 180.

quantum numbers characterizing the orbits constitutes the spectral terms whose differences specify the spectrum lines. But this astronomy which simultaneously poses the perdurability of the orbits and the jumping character of the electron gives a slightly inaccurate balance of energy. Here and there a half-quantum has to be added, and all the integral-number arithmetic of the first quantum theory has to be corrected by this half-quantum. In 1925, Uhlenbeck and Goudsmit proposed to complete the planetary character of the electron. The electron had its year of revolution, it would have its day of rotation: the electron planet turns on itself, the electron has a kinetic motion of its own. This top-like motion is the *spin*, from the English children's expression, to spin a top.[14]

This completion of the planetary image seems to contradict the Bachelardian injunction that images should not be *completed*. It would seem here that the metaphorical imagery was not suspended and that it made possible a wholly positive discovery. These conclusions are a little too hastily drawn: – firstly, because in the same year, 1925, Heisenberg's formulation of the uncertainty principle was to make it impossible to give a geometric and kinetic reality to this *rotation* of the electron; then, because, once formulated, the orbital kinetic moment, with its quantum character, went against the classical notion of a kinetic moment. Bachelard concludes from this that we are faced with a *reduced* image from the start.[15] In it we have the *illustration* of an algebraic function.

The imagination under torture

It must be admitted that Bachelard's developments on the question remain at the level of the empirical and polemical description of a usage. He does tell us why the images of the new mechanics are to be maintained in a state of permanent reduction. It is clear how the primacy of energetics, of probabilism over the geometrical confers on them a contradictory status. But when the question arises of why in these conditions it is impossible to avoid resorting to images which are known to be necessarily inadequate; when the question arises of the persistence of a dangerous usage, Bachelard leaves us

14. ibid., p. 164.   15. ibid., p. 165.

unsatisfied. Nevertheless, the answers he gives, however disappointing they may be, should be taken seriously in their very insufficiency. Here is one example:

It is comprehensible that it should be *natural*, so to speak, to return from these algebraic spaces to ordinary space, which in the new thought must no longer be taken for anything more than a means of illustration, a propitious site for our images, but never possibly the adequate canvas for the complete relations.[16]

The invocation of the natural – which I have emphasized – is not accidental: on several occasions a kind of 'spontaneous geometrism', rooted in ordinary everyday life, is invoked as an explanation for the use of illustration-images. The world of classical mechanics is presented as *the* natural world, in which the images of our imagination – 'our' images – may unfold. Hence it is not surprising to find Bachelard asserting about nuclear physics that in it the imagination is 'under torture'. The greatest possible attention should be paid to this expression, for it conceals our prey. This theory of the tortures of the imagination is, on closer examination, only the inverted form of the theory of the 'happiness of the imagination' which governs Bachelard's 'poetics'.[17] It is its inverted and complementary form: the suffering felt at the rational constraint has as a counterpart the pleasure provided unreservedly by the transports of literary oneirism. In other words: here Bachelard's psychologism comes to the surface: in this debate between imagination and scientific 'mind' we find on the epistemological side, by the action of its obverse, the dynamic psychology avowed in his poetics. To be quite fair, it should be added that this dynamicist thesis is never developed for itself in *The Rationalist Activity*, for example, and that the question most often remains unanswered. Thus, still on Bohr, he cautiously writes:

To know whether the planetary model is an illustration, a scaffolding, a means of expression, such is the question that should be resolved by an attentive and nuanced philosophy of the sciences. . . .[18]

16. *Le nouvel esprit scientifique*, pp. 95–6.   17. *Le matérialisme rationnel*, p. 18.
18. *L'activité rationaliste de la physique contemporaine*, p. 142.

The bilanguage

The same is true for the outline of a theory of scientific language which is offered to us. Before coming on to a fundamental passage from *Applied Rationalism*, let me return to the image of the 'planetary atom'. There is no doubt that if the orbit is not an orbit, if the rotation is not a rotation, a 'reform of vocabulary' is required; and this is indeed what Bachelard wants. The vocabulary should be 'disintuitionized, de-geometrized, psychoanalysed'. E.g.: the word 'shell' will designate a basic energy characteristic. It will be kept to designate the *set* of electrons having the same principal quantum number in an atom. The electrons with the same azimuthal quantum number will be said to be in the same *state*, etc.

In *Applied Rationalism*, Bachelard is more explicit: discussing the algebra–geometry correspondence in Hilbertian spaces, he puts forward the idea of a *bi-language*:

Thus a special language has been instituted, a kind of bi-language which speaks in double meanings. A *surpassed intuition* is lit up in the mind of the algebraist who studies Hilbertian spaces, which formulates, in the style of geometry, truths that only have meaning in the style of algebra.[19]

He proposed to extend these considerations to the case of the physics–algebra correspondence. That is how, in an apparently enigmatic passage he can write that 'filters' in radionics eliminate both *vibrations* in the apparatuses and *solutions* in the equations. A passage of pure provocation for philosophers, which has no other meaning than to show *in actu* what is the *abstract-concrete* – the coupling of mathematical formulae with highly rationalized technique. In *Rational Materialism*, he is more precise:

Sometimes the continuistic epistemologist is fooled, when he is judging contemporary science, by a kind of continuity of images and words. When it was necessary to imagine the unimaginable domain of the atomic nucleus, images and verbal formulae were proposed which are entirely relative to theoretical science. Naturally, these formulae should not be taken literally and given a direct meaning. A constant transposition of

19. *Le rationalisme appliqué*, p. 158.

language thus breaks the continuity of ordinary thought and scientific thought.

Bachelard continues his demonstration vis-à-vis the notion of temperature: there is nothing in common between the 'temperature' of the nucleus and the temperature of the laboratory. Hence a strange theory of quotation-marks as a mark of the metaphor; as an automatic dis-intuition of the terms of scientific language.

If attention was paid to this often masked translation activity, it would thus be seen that there are in the language of science a great many terms in quotation-marks.[20]

We shall soon see what justifies this attentiveness to the problem of the language of science in Bachelardian epistemology; but it has to be said that this theory of 'masked translation', of a 'bilanguage in quotation-marks' rests on a wholly psychologistic conception of the natural – ordinary – language rooted in the geometry of everyday life. Here, too, it may be said that Bachelard poses more problems than he resolves. Meanwhile, is not the last word of his reflection an imaginary question: 'What poet will teach us the metaphors of this new language?'[21]

The insistence with which Bachelard returns to this problem of the images of science is in itself enough to justify my having spent so much time examining these arid and apparently disappointing texts. In reality, another reason drove me to it: as we shall soon see, the problem of language brings into question the *status* of this epistemology, as well as the use we can make of it.

2. THE METAPHOR: MARK OF A SUBSTITUTE

If the *function* assigned to them by Bachelard is not grasped, the famous texts of *The Formation of the Scientific Mind* may well prove even more disappointing. At best: a garrulous book in which elements of the history of the sciences, 'epistemological' readings of pre-scientific books, delicate psychological notes and debased

20. *Le matérialisme rationnel*, pp. 215–16.
21. *Le nouvel esprit scientifique*, p. 75.

psycho-analytical interpretations are mingled together will leave the reader perplexed. I believe that to stop at such an impressionistic reading does not allow one to understand the import of this text, which I can see might irritate rigorous minds, precisely because of its contradictory character.

A first, terminological, point: four years after *The New Scientific Mind*, Bachelard returns to the locution 'scientific mind'. It has perhaps not been sufficiently noted that the identity of the expression masks a duality in meaning. Perhaps it would be better to say a 'variation' on the meaning of the word *mind*, for of course, the repetition of the same expression in the two cases is not fortuitous. Let me say straight away: it is the sign of a 'blind' contradiction which affects the entire epistemology. When Bachelard speaks of the 'new scientific mind' he is designating the philosophy 'secreted' by the new disciplines, the 'philosophy of no' that he attempted to thematize in 1940.

When he gives *The Formation of the Scientific Mind* as the title of the work which concerns us here, the word 'mind' takes on an individual psychological significance which it did not so plainly have in the first case. That is because, second point, it is a question of an essentially *pedagogic* work: in it Bachelard follows up the pedagogic implications of *The New Scientific Mind*. As it turns out, he then runs up against *the very same philosophy*, the one which misrecognized the philosophy of no. This philosophy bears a name: it is *Realism*, and its typical figure remains Émile Meyerson, but in the work we are discussing it has been promoted to the rank of the 'sole innate philosophy'.

The viewpoint then swings: it is no longer a question of confronting this philosophy with scientific practice at work, but of relating it to what, in the 'Preliminary Discourse', Bachelard calls its 'affective basis'.[22] That is why he develops a whole theory of the *fetishism* of the real.[23] Images and metaphors constitute in pedagogic and pre-scientific discourses the purchase of this analysis of 'fetishism'. They are the royal road which leads to the 'affective basis'. They designate the site at which a non-scientific system of thought is grafted onto the scientific or pedagogic discourse. He writes: 'The danger of immediate metaphors for the formation of the scientific mind is that they are not always passing images; they press on towards an autonomous thought.'[24] But it must be realized that this autonomous thought is always already there, ordered-systematized by a more or less hierarchized set of *values* which have non-scientific *interests* as their supports.

The description of these values is fairly desultory in the book: sometimes we are referred to ideological values whose social origin is not concealed: thus realism appears, very insistently, as a miser's philosophy; sometimes, in a rather loose way, we are referred to a hypothetical *libido* of the teacher or the disciple. But Bachelard's purpose is not to present a completed, systematic theory. It is rather to proceed to an 'essay in psychoanalysis', in the words of the sub-title. Thus, simultaneously with its theory of the 'fetishism' of the real, the book presents us with an essay in the *therapeutics*, in actu, of the scientific mind, in which realism and its variants (thingism, substantialism, collisionism, etc.) appear as 'infantile disorders'. In *Rational Materialism*, fifteen years later, Bachelard characterizes his attempt as an 'automatic psychoanalysis': in it cure is produced by the 'superimposition of *overcharged images*', he writes. Hence the constant recourse made there to the 'worldly, frivolous, curious' science of the eighteenth century, a recourse which should not be taken for an essay in the history of the sciences, but rather for an element of the treatment. For in the eighteenth century, the *scientific city*, the instance of objective control, was not as firmly constituted as it is today: the interests did not then undergo the *censorship* whose object they now are. In the eighteenth century, 'the id chattered' at its leisure. Today, 'the id still chatters', but as a subterranean discourse, latent because it is energetically repressed, which opposes a sharp resistance to investigation. For that 'putter in quotation-marks', the epistemologist, the texts of the eighteenth century thus have the value of a curative example, curative because easier. (Does not Bachelard say in his introduction that he is concerned *on principle* that his book should be *easy* – a remarkable

24. ibid., p. 81.

derogation from the difficulty which he makes the mark of productive epistemological and scientific work?) He therefore counts on a multiform repetition to lead the images back to their bases. Hence there is nothing surprising about the desultoriness, nor about the remarkable invitation made to us in the same introduction to skip pages once we have understood the principle: it is because the therapeutic effect will have been obtained. It is therefore useless to undertake an exegesis of the texts on the sponge, on gold or on coagulation: I shall skip many pages – all the pages even – to ponder this principle. For what is most important *for us is the project*, stated on several occasions, to '*displace the interests*' (according to the expression of the 'Preliminary Discourse'). I shall therefore pose the following question: what is the *sense* of this displacement? or again: to *where* is one displaced? by what interest or interests are the displaced interests to be *replaced*? Really the answer raises no difficulties: the displacement of the displaced interests makes way for the dialectic – abstract-concrete – which is the dialectic of scientific labour. In other words, science is charged to be for itself its own interest. The scientific mind is trusted to be the motor of the mind which wishes to become scientific. It is enough to displace the imaginary interests for the torture of the imagination to find its compensations in the delights of *scientific abstraction*. Or again: the 'lived' and its mirages are replaced by a *different life*, a 'mental life' which is the life of science proper. I am not saying this, Bachelard is, in the Preliminary Discourse: 'The love of science must be an autogenous psychic dynamism.'[25] It seems that we have here a confirmation of the thesis I put forward about the scientific use of images: Bachelard's epistemology is psychologistic through and through. Epistemology and poetics are homologous and complementary; they find their unity in a conception of psychic dynamism which, although it has a double face, is nonetheless unique and unitary. Several cynical questions might then be asked of Bachelard: is it not astonishing to see the epistemology which has made scientific *application* a specific feature of contemporary science make 'disinterestedness' the motor of scientific activity? Is this not a

25. ibid., p. 10.

strange denegation? If it is really true that the *application* of the natural sciences to production – a double application: to the improvement of the instruments of labour and to the organization of production – is characteristic of the capitalist mode of production, does not this denegation or blindness have a very precise political meaning? Is the psychologism innocent *politically*? To my mind, these are real and serious questions. They have to be in one's head for one to be able to read Gaston Bachelard. They should give warning that ultimately what takes place with Gaston Bachelard's epistemology is only an *aggiornamento* of philosophy. But the process of this *aggiornamento*, the elements which it brings into play, must also be taken seriously. For in this process it is the very mechanism of the philosophical operation vis-à-vis the sciences that emerges. That is how Bachelard's epistemology, with all the reservations I have just expressed about it, gives us with its critique of philosophical theories of knowledge – in mystified-disguised-displaced forms – elements for a materialist theory of philosophy. Here I shall appeal to Lenin who, in the *Philosophical Notebooks*, extolled – from a materialist point of view – all the criticisms that Hegel made of Kant: in taking a process of *aggiornamento* of philosophy seriously, he brought to light the elements of the philosophical *intervention*.

Now what is going on in Bachelardian epistemology? It encounters a *delay* in philosophy with respect to the history of the sciences made in the 1920s. This delay, registered first as a blindness or laziness peculiar to philosophy, is then attributed to the typical *dispersion* of every theory of knowledge from the process of production of scientific concepts. The fullness of the theories of knowledge appears in the spectrum of *Applied Rationalism* as no more than the imaginarily closed void of this dispersion. Nothing but that. This is one achievement of Bachelard's epistemology.

A second, corresponding point: the process of production of scientific concepts is thought as a historical *dialectic* of the concretization of the abstract. Or better: *described* rather than thought; Bachelard observes and describes the spontaneously dialectical materialism of the natural sciences. This too is an achievement. It gives us a material useful for the constitution of a theory of the

history of the production of scientific concepts as a relatively autonomous region of historical materialism.

It will still be objected: how can you proceed to such *isolations*?
For either one thing or the other: either this epistemology is
psychologistic and reactionary – and there is nothing to be got from
it – or it is materialist. Answer: it is this isolation, this unshelling –
that constitutes the materialist reading of an idealist work. Hence
I shall cast aside the psychologism as Lenin 'cast aside' God, the
Absolute and the Idea in Hegel. And to show that I am nobody's
dupe, here is one last point, even more surprising than the others.
Everything ultimately depends on the observation that in the contemporary sciences the main philosophical couple abstract-concrete
has to be replaced by a '*coupling*' of the two terms. Now Bachelard
happens to declare incidentally in *Rational Materialism*, 'I use
"coupling" in the electro-dynamic sense.'[26] This is a precious
remark, for it reveals – it 'betrays' – the profound contradiction
affecting the status of this epistemology. On reading this suggestion,
there can be no doubt, in fact, but that the epistemological category
of coupling is in a metaphorical situation with respect to the scientific
concept to which it is referred. From a precise scientific concept
with its own extension and a comprehension specified in the field of
a given scientific discipline, and, incidentally, solidary with determinate experimental protocols, Bachelard expects to make by
transposition and generalization a category which accounts ab-
stractly for every process of scientific work.[27] A typical and revealing
procedure: it makes science itself responsible for the provision of the
philosophical categories which have simultaneously to reflect and to
illuminate its own activity. In doing so it dismisses all constituted
philosophy and builds an epistemology which, in order not to be 'the
pleonasm of science' can only be its . . . *metaphor*. But what Bachelard remains blind to is the fact that this metaphoricalness, far from

26. Here is one among a number of passages illustrating the point: 'Physics has two
philosophical poles. It is a true *thought field*, specified by mathematics and experiments
and at its highest tension in the conjunction of mathematics and experiments. Physics
determines, as an eminent synthesis, an *abstract-concrete* mentality' (*Le rationalisme
appliqué*, p. 1).

27. The same demonstration could be made vis-à-vis the notion of *discontinuity*, which
Bachelard shows was suggested to him by quantum mechanics.

leaving the epistemological category in a space pure of all philosophy, immediately inscribes it in a highly determinate philosophy. The blindness, the misunderstanding, here takes the surprising form of a *play on words*: the coupling – a concept of electro-*dynamics* – is re-inscribed, epistemologically metaphoricized, in the field of a *dynamistic* psychology.

This is where the inconsistency of the *aggiornamento* I have been discussing comes to the fore: just when one wants to bring to light the pure philosophy which is created secretly in scientific work; just when, in the name of this clear and pure philosophy, one is announcing the end of the other philosophy, the philosophy of the philosophers. Hence just when one is leaving the sciences the trouble of themselves stating their own philosophy, the purity of this philosophy has already been adulterated: it compromises its language with that of psychology. Even Gaston Bachelard's 'achievements' are caught in what must really be called 'his philosophy'. The proof that one cannot so easily get rid of philosophy. In other words, if what I have said is correct, of politics. For my part, in the 'coupling' I shall drop the metaphor – the index of a substitute for a theory of knowledge – and retain the dialectic. . . .

June 1970

Georges Canguilhem's
Epistemological History

The Normal and the Pathological, Georges Canguilhem's first book, was published in 1943. Since that date, the book has been enriched by 'new reflections'. In particular: the œuvre inaugurated by its appearance has had the unique fate that everyone today looks on it as one of those which have most strongly stimulated what is alive in contemporary French philosophy, after remaining unknown, if not deliberately ignored, for a long time. It would be easy to measure this influence – a few names would suffice – as it would be to explain this misrecognition – corpses then occupied the forefront of the philosophical stage. My aim will be different: I should like to cast light on the apparent paradox of the encounter that has taken place here between strictly specialized works in the history of the sciences and the theoretical preoccupations of the Marxist-Leninist philosophers grouped around Louis Althusser.

Let me say straight away: to remove this paradox is to admit a truly inestimable theoretical debt, since the history of the sciences as practised by Georges Canguilhem for the last twenty years was undoubtedly the most testing employment of the epistemological categories whose application to historical materialism – to the Marxist science of history – made possible the well-known reading of *Capital*. It seems to me today that historical materialism, thus disengaged from its neo-Hegelian dross, can turn back to epistemology from the history of the sciences and, rectifying its own concepts where necessary, enrich these two disciplines with the fruit of its recent re-entry into the light. More precisely: the time has come when epistemology and the history of the sciences are going to find their places in the field of the science of history. But the 'revolution' which will follow in these disciplines, long left fallow, will owe its possibility

entirely to the existence of *works* such as those of Georges Canguilhem.

Therefore, let there be no mistake: if points of disagreement
appear, which had previously remained in the shade, they can only
be secondary ones. They are anyway provisional, since each year
they are subject to revision through the development of our respective efforts. I shall be happy if I can by these few lines enable the
reader to take part in this discussion: it is not the least homage I
might offer Georges Canguilhem to say that he has always kept it
firmly *open*.

I. A NEW PRACTICE OF THE HISTORY OF THE SCIENCES

A. The Bachelardian Descent

Canguilhem's texts are undoubtedly disconcerting. The tightly-knit
style with its sentences entirely mustered around the concepts which
give them their order, leaving no room for the slightest rhetorical
'play', is rarely reminiscent of what is customary for philosophical
discourse. It does not invite reverie, it does not even urge meditation:
it *demands* of the reader that he set himself to work. Nor is there any
doubt that the precision of the references and dates, the profusion of
proper names, disappoint the expectations of the 'enlightened
amateur', half absent-minded, half dilettante, that the philosopher
reading a book by one of his peers imagines himself to be, in function
if not by right.

There will be more readiness to applaud the erudition than to
reflect on the theoretical import of this superabundance of precision.
For my part, I see in it the plainest index of a true rupture in philosophical practice. I should like to add, in the provocative mode, 'here
someone knows *what* he is talking about'. In other words, in this
work philosophical discourse has an original relation to its object.

Georges Canguilhem never fails to recall that he gets this original-
ity from his predecessor at the head of the Institute d'Histoire des
Sciences at the University of Paris, Gaston Bachelard. In fact,
Bachelard was the first to recognize that *historicity* is essential to the

object of what was then called the 'philosophy of the sciences'; he had conceived this object – the articulated system of scientific practices – as a set of historically determinate relations of *production* of concepts, and had accepted as an epistemologist the rule of respecting the work of scientists.

Such a 'respect', unfailingly applied for thirty years to the contemporary physico-chemical sciences, enabled Bachelard to state the following simple proposition, which is pregnant with a philosophical revolution: every particular science produces at each moment of its history its own norms of truth. In this Gaston Bachelard was making an almost unprecedented[1] rupture in the history of philosophy and putting into place the elements of a 'non-philosophical' theory of philosophy. It seemed indeed that for this historically determinate production of always specific norms, these theories substituted as their 'object' the repetitive identity of a single question, that of 'The Truth'. A category universal and absolute by decree, casting a shadow which circumscribes the – necessarily closed – field of the theories which it supports. By invalidating the absolute category of Truth in the name of the actual practice of the sciences that it was its mission to 'found', Bachelard denied philosophy the right to tell the truth of the sciences and accepted it as his duty to tell the truth about The Truth of the philosophers.

This truth is as follows:

– the essential determination of all philosophy insofar as it contains as a master component a 'theory of knowledge' is the specific relation it has with the sciences;

– this specific relation, although capable of taking diverse or even opposite forms (idealism or empiricism), is always a relation of the 'displacement', of the 'dispersion' or the 'secession' of the philosophy of the philosophers with respect to the actual *work* of the scientists.

The key notion of this *œuvre*, that of 'epistemological obstacle', clearly explains this situation: the philosophy of the philosophers has no *object* in the sense in which the sciences have objects, it lives in the *imaginary*; or, to put it better, it lives *on* the imaginary, which

1. I say '*almost*' unprecedented, because Spinoza and Marx had, each in his own way, gone before him on this path.

makes it take the emptiness of its dispersions from scientific practice for the fullness of an object with all the consistency of the 'real'. Bachelard relates this obstinate mistake to the permanent ascendancy of great imaginary themes over the human soul. That is why he thought he had founded a new discipline: the 'psychoanalysis of objective knowledge', a kind of 'catharsis' for scientists with the function of defending them against philosophical mirages and helping them to state the clear philosophy of their real practice.

It does not much matter here that this attempt was not followed up. On the other hand, it is very important to state that Bachelard thereby made the philosophy of the sciences undergo a revolutionary *displacement*. He pointed out for it a place which had never had an occupant: an empty site, but one recognized as such, at the junction of each scientific practice and the ideologies that intervene in it under philosophical cover. At the same stroke, he assigned it a dual task, indissociably *polemical and historical*: polemical because the disentanglement of the philosophical and the non-philosophical is a *struggle* – a struggle of one philosophy against another, a liberation struggle against the imperialism of the philosophy of the philosophers; historical, because this disentanglement can only be conceived with reference to the internal history of the discipline considered and to that of the ideologies which lay siege to it from within.

Georges Canguilhem, drawing attention to this situation, was able to write, in an article on Bachelard: 'It is really essential to grasp the originality of Bachelard's position with respect to the history of the sciences. In one sense he never did anything in this respect. In another sense, he was constantly doing so. If the history of the sciences consists of counting the variants in the successive editions of a Treatise, Bachelard is not a historian of the sciences. If the history of the sciences consists of making appreciable – and simultaneously intelligible – the difficult, thwarted, repeated and rectified edification of knowledge (*savoir*), then Bachelard's epistemology is always *in actu* a history of the sciences.'[2] There is probably

2. *Études d'histoire et de philosophie des sciences*, p. 178 (for full bibliographical details of Canguilhem's works, see the Appendix to Part Two).

no better definition of the history of the sciences as it is conceived and practised by Georges Canguilhem himself; it is here that it seems completely justified to make him Bachelard's heir. Recognition of the historicity of the object of epistemology imposes a new conception of the history of the sciences. Gaston Bachelard's epistemology was historical; Georges Canguilhem's history of the sciences is epistemological. Two ways to state the revolutionary *unity* that both institute between epistemology and history of the sciences.

For I must add: his history of the sciences is only epistemological because his epistemology is itself historical. The proof: at the moment in *Knowledge of Life* in which he is examining the properly epistemological question of experimentation in biology, it is the history of that science which appears in a polemical form. In a lesson on muscular contraction, he explains, notably, the teacher is quite happy to have established a *fact* when he has performed the classical experiment which consists of isolating a muscle in a beaker of water and demonstrating that under the action of an electrical stimulation, the muscle contracts without altering the level of the liquid. From this 'fact' he will conclude: contraction is a modification of the form of the muscle without any change in its volume. Canguilhem comments as follows: 'It is an epistemological fact that an experimental fact taught in this way has no biological meaning. That's just how it is.'[3] To give such a meaning to this fact, we have to go back to the first person who thought of an experiment of this kind, i.e., to Swammerdam (1637–80): he was concerned to show, against the then dominant theories of Galenian and Stoic origin, that no substance was added to a muscle in contraction. Isolated from this dispute, congealed into a history-less pedagogy, this so-called 'fact' loses its real, in truth *historical*, meaning, to take its place in the dreary dissertations on the 'experimental method' which are the mainstay of a certain dogmatic epistemology. One might say that if epistemology is the description of the general procedures, the methods and results, of 'Science' or 'Reason in the Sciences', Canguilhem never produces any. On the contrary, if epistemology consists of disengaging – discovering and analysing – the problems

3. *La connaissance de la vie* (2nd edn), p. 18.

as they are posed – or eluded – resolved or dissolved in the actual practice of scientists, then he is constantly doing so. Take care: the reversal that I have made in the formula he applied to Bachelard's work in relation to him is not a mere trick; it simply translates the unity whose importance I have just stressed and which has not yet yielded us its last lesson.

The practice of the history of the sciences inaugurated by Georges Canguilhem thus sets to work, develops and rectifies Bachelardian epistemological categories in its own proper field. It has the same specific relationship to its object, and, installing itself in the space uncovered by the Bachelardian break-through in philosophy, it pursues and deepens the polemic against the philosophy of the philosophers. Having taken seriously a certain form of *writing* (*écriture*) has enabled me to restore a line of *descent*. This line of descent enables me to give a *meaning* and a price to the novelty of the concepts introduced by Georges Canguilhem. It is hardly surprising that this novelty in its turn takes a polemical form.

B. *Epistemological Propositions*

The history of the sciences is not a chronicle. Georges Canguilhem attacks a *tradition* in the history of the sciences which can itself be said to reflect on itself in the form of *tradition*: the transmission (from one scientist to another or from one period to another) of truths acquired and problems unsolved along the thread of a linear and homogeneous time whose only virtue is to pass (or to be past). This history of the sciences delights in detailed biographies, spicy anecdotes and edifying commemorations. All of us know the grey sands of these conceptual deserts, having at least once gone astray in them. But nothing is more seductive than the investigation of what is perhaps its chosen object: the 'precursor'. Nothing at any rate better equips us to grasp its tacit philosophical assumptions. I shall therefore not hesitate to re-transcribe the following recently written (1968) page in which Canguilhem analyses this 'virus of the precursor':

Strictly speaking, if precursors existed the History of the Sciences would be meaningless, since science itself would only apparently have a historical dimension. . . . A precursor is supposed to be a thinker, an investigator who once made a few steps on the road more recently completed by another. The willingness to search for, to find and to celebrate precursors is the clearest symptom of an inaptitude for epistemological criticism. Before putting two distances on a road end to end, it is advisable to be sure that it really is the same road. In a coherent knowledge (*savoir*) one concept is related to all the others. His having imagined the hypothesis of helio-centrism does not make Aristarchus of Samos a precursor of Copernicus, even though the latter referred to him as an authority. To change the centre of reference of the heavenly motions is to relativize high and low, it is to change the dimensions of the universe, in short, it is to compose a system. Now Copernicus criticized all theories of astronomy before his own for not being rational systems. A precursor is supposed to be a thinker of several periods, of his own and of those assigned to him as his continuators; as the executors of his uncompleted undertaking. Hence the precursor is a thinker whom the historian believes he can extract from his cultural frame in order to insert him into another, which amounts to considering concepts, discourses and speculative or experimental acts as capable of displacement or replacement in an intellectual space in which reversibility of relations has been obtained by forgetting the historical aspect of the object dealt with in it.[4]

This passage shows the critical advantage the history of the sciences can gain by taking into account epistemologically the historicity of the production of scientific concepts. Each science has its own movement, its rhythm, and, to put it better, its specific temporality: its history is neither the 'lateral fibre' of a so-called 'general run of time' nor the development of a germ – in which lies 'preformed' the still un-filled-in outline of its present state; it proceeds by re-organizations, ruptures and mutations; it turns around 'critical' points: points at which the tempo is more lively or, on the contrary, more ponderous; it experiences sudden accelerations and sudden retreats. Lastly, it is undoubtedly relatively autonomous, but the existence of a pure 'intellectual space' in which it deploys its concepts sovereignly is a matter of fiction: a science can only artificially be isolated from what Canguilhem here calls its 'cultural frame', i.e., from the set of

4. *Études d'histoire et de philosophie des sciences*, pp. 20–1.

relations and ideological values of the social formation in which it is inscribed.

The 'virus of the precursor' which animates the 'chronicle-history' of the sciences has as its unseasonable corollary an epidemic of *accidents*. When the object of the history of the sciences is denied all real historicity, anything can indeed happen, at any time, as the effect of any cause. Analysis then gives way to astonishment: several historians are constantly celebrating those so-called 'accidents' which, conjoining the 'miracles of technology' with the 'wonders of science', cannot fail, so they say, to give a certain idea of the human adventure. . . . The history of the sciences then becomes a pure adventure novel. Georges Canguilhem takes the opposite position to this conception.

Hence the second epistemological proposition, which I shall state as follows: the history of the sciences is not the story of a series of accidents. Perhaps there is no better illustration of this than the article he has written on *The Pathology and Physiology of the Thyroid in the Nineteenth Century*.[5] The object of this article might seem a mere quibble if one were unaware of the theoretical intention underlying it. Abstracting from the real interest of the question for the history of physiology, that intention is as follows: to refute the 'contingent' conception of the history of the sciences on its own terrain. The history of the pathology of the thyroid does indeed seem to be governed by a *double accident*: the accident of the discovery of iodine; the accident of the importation of iodine into therapeutics. Georges Canguilhem shows that neither of these accidents is accidental.

The discovery of iodine presents itself in the form of an *encounter*. That of a Parisian manufacturer of saltpetre, Bernard Courtois, who, wishing to obtain soda in large quantities from seaweed ash, was surprised to produce an additional substance whose effect, as unexpected as it was lamentable, was to produce extensive corrosion in his metallic apparatuses, and of two chemists, Clément and Desormes, to whom he went for advice. That is how iodine was

5. 'Pathologie et physiologie de la thyroïde au XIXᵉ siècle', *Thalès*, IX, 1959; reprinted in *Études d'histoire et de philosophie des sciences*, pp. 274–94.

discovered in 1812. A typical example of a theoretical re-organization proceeding from a technical *failure*, this discovery seems completely fortuitous. However, adds Canguilhem, if we remember that at this period chemistry was generally orientated towards the investigation and identification of the active substances present in organic compounds, and that this orientation was a response to a demand from industry, the conclusion can be drawn that 'in a certain sense the discovery of iodine occurred non-accidentally in a theoretical and technical context which would at any rate have called on it by other roads'.[6] The proof: in less than thirty years, as a result of the same solicitation, morphine, strychnine, quinine, alizarin and codeine were all isolated.

As for the importation of iodine into clinical medicine, it depended on a mutation in the history of the latter. A mutation familiar to us since Michel Foucault's *Birth of Clinical Medicine* which is marked by the relinquishing of expectant medicine of the Hippocratic type and the emergence of what Claude Bernard was to call 'empirical' medicine. This was not yet 'experimental' medicine, but like it it regarded diseases not as essences to be described and classified but as the objects of a *positive action* to restore health. Hence the idea of producing rationally controllable chemical reactions that was introduced into pharmacology and replaced the blind faith held hitherto in the 'essential virtues' of the substances patients were made to ingest. It is therefore no accident that the Genevan doctor Jean-François Coindet should in 1821 have had the idea of treating hypothyroidism with iodine.

Georges Canguilhem goes further: he shows how the 'chronicle-history' and the 'contingency-history' have one and the same origin; one and the same thing is wrong with them: they both depend, explicitly or implicitly, on a certain philosophy of history. No doubt this philosophy of history is capable of taking a variety of forms, but it has an invariant *effect*: that of measuring against the latest scientific theory to appear the validity of those that have preceded it. Such that the history of the sciences, even if strewn with those few

6. ibid., p. 283.

comforting thunderbolts, the 'strokes of genius' of the fortunate 'precursors', is no more than the museum of the errors of human reason. In that case, explains Canguilhem, 'for the scientist, the history of the sciences is not worth an hour of his trouble, for, from this point of view, the history of the sciences is history, but not of the sciences'. He goes on: 'Such an attitude presupposes a dogmatic conception of science and, if I may say so, a dogmatic conception of scientific criticism, a conception of the "progress of the human mind" which is that of the *Aufklärung*, of Condorcet and of Comte. What hangs over this conception is the mirage of a definitive state of learning (*savoir*). . . . The epistemological postulate which governs it is that "chronological priority is a logical inferiority".'[7] One might say that the philosophy of history – whether or not it is presented in the form of a body of doctrine in the field of a given philosophy – has as its function to *denegate* the specifically philosophical annihilation of the actual historicity of learning (*savoir*). It is the *guarantee* which every theory of knowledge provides itself in order to erase-efface the historical conditions of its own emergence. It is the imaginary *substitute* for the repressed unity of Epistemology and History of the Sciences. Or again: it dilutes the historical transition from non-learning to learning (*savoir*) with the logic of true and false, atemporal by decree.

C. The History of Concepts

The rejection of every philosophy of history of this type leads Georges Canguilhem to concern himself more with the descent of *concepts* than with the concatenation of *theories*. In the introduction to his thesis on *The Formation of the Concept of the Reflex in the Seventeenth and Eighteenth Centuries* (1955), Georges Canguilhem has given the clearest account of this reversal of viewpoints. Once again I shall allow him to speak for himself: 'I personally think that in matters of the history of the sciences the rights of logic should not give in to the rights of the logic of history. Such that before

7. *La connaissance de la vie*, pp. 43–4.

arranging the succession of theories according to the logic of their conformity and the homogeneity of their inspiration, one must first be certain, in the presence of a given theory in which one is attempting to reveal some implicit or explicit concept, that the idea one has of it is not one from which every concern for internal consistency is absent. . . . The theory in question, although almost nothing is left of it today in the order of principles, can nevertheless be called false only by reason of a judgement made of the principles, according to their link with assessed consequences, which implies that the parts of the doctrine are supposed to be adjusted to one another other than by inconsistency and the concepts to be combined together other than by juxtaposition. This leads one to look for conceptual lines of descent in a different direction. Instead of asking which is the author whose theory of involuntary motion prefigures the theory of the reflex current in the nineteenth century, one is led rather to wonder what a theory of muscular motion and of the action of the nerves must contain for a notion such as that of reflex motion, concealing the assimilation of a biological phenomenon with an optical phenomenon, to find in it a sense of truth, i.e., first of all a sense of logical consistency with a set of other concepts.'[8] These deliberately polemical lines are simultaneously the statement of an injunction against any 'logical' conception of history and the formulation of a programme – better, the indication or prescription of a *direction* for historical analysis: to move from the concept to the theory and not vice versa. That is because, for Georges Canguilhem, to define a concept is to formulate a *problem*. Now the formulation of a problem requires simultaneously the rationally organized presence of a certain number of other concepts which are not necessarily those that will appear in the theory which provides the solution. In other words, as Pierre Macherey pointed out in an already old article on 'Georges Canguilhem's Philosophy of Science', 'the constant presence of a concept throughout the diachronic line that constitutes its history is evidence of the permanence of a single problem. The important thing then is to recognize in the sequence

8. *La formation du concept de réflexe aux XVIIᵉ et XVIIIᵉ siècles*, pp. 5–6.

of theories "the persistance of the problem within a solution that is supposed to have been given it" '.[9]

It is understandable that Georges Canguilhem should have concentrated his attention on the conditions of *appearance* of concepts, i.e., ultimately on the conditions which make problems *formulatable*. The theories in which they function only appear after the event. On this path a new obstacle appears, a new task suggests itself: it is essential to know how to distinguish between the presence of the *word* and that of the *concept*. Georges Canguilhem often reminds us: a word is not a concept. Echoing theses of Bachelard's, he shows that there is no possibility of any mechanical deduction from the presence of the word to that of the concept. What is more: one and the same word can conceal different concepts; that is why the *language* of scientific works has to be closely scrutinized. The metaphors and analogies must be analysed and taken back to the terrain of their origin. In the case of the reflex, we have just seen that the optical metaphor, ignored by historians, directly incites his interrogation. Inversely, the absence of the word is not necessarily the index of the absence of the concept: if the concept is essentially 'problematic' it may be that the formulation of the problem has been achieved before the word has been invented, or imported from another theoretical domain. Indeed, it must be added that the word is the most constant, though often the least conscious, vehicle of 'theoretical loans': the loan from one scientific domain to another, or what often has more and graver consequences, the importation of non-scientific ideological values into the scientific. On this point, re-read the study of 'cellular theory' and see how the term 'cell' may be the vehicle of different sociological and political values according to the period considered: see also what it may cost science and philosophy.

Thus on Oken (1779–1851): 'The organism is conceived by Oken in the image of society, but this society is not the association of individuals as it was conceived by the political philosophy of the *Aufklärung*, but the community as it was conceived by the political

9. 'La philosophie de la science de Georges Canguilhem', *La Pensée* no. 113, January–February 1964, p. 66.

philosophy of romanticism.'[10] And in a more general fashion: 'The history of the concept of the cell is inseparable from the history of the concept of the individual. This has already been my justification for claiming that social and affective values preside over the development of cellular theory.'[11] In this way Canguilhem explains the obstacles the 'vitalist' current represented by the Montpellier School encountered in France. He notes that the basic conceptions of German romantic physiology accepted by this current provided nourishment and justification for a political thought profoundly foreign to the French ideals of the period; if the opposition was so open and sharp on the medical terrain, it was because 'just at the time when French political thought was proposing to the European mind the social contract and universal suffrage, the vitalist school of French medicine suggested to it an image of life transcending the analytical understanding.'[12]

When one has to explain the persistent hostility of Auguste Comte to the cellular theory – another example – one should certainly remember the respect he had for the work of Bichat, who regarded *tissue* as the ultimate element at which analysis had to stop: tissue – Bichat obtained this dogma from Barthez and the Montpellier School – is the 'cloth from which living beings are cut, a sufficient image of the continuity of the vital fact, demanded by the vitalist exigency';[13] but one should also understand that this fidelity to Bichat had other motives than strictly biological ones: for Comte, 'just as in sociology the individual is an abstraction, so in biology the "organic monads", as Comte said speaking of cells, are abstractions'. Here, obviously, the word is the point of insertion of ideology – of theoretical and practical ideologies – in scientific practice.

To complete this analysis I must invoke the studies on the notions of *environment, organism* and *evolution*; in doing so I should follow by the bias of language, as I have done briefly with the notion of 'cell', the transformations-distortions of the concept from the moment of its 'birth' – the absolute beginning at which a determinate

10. *La connaissance de la vie*, p. 61.   11. ibid., p. 62.
12. ibid., p. 63.   13. ibid., p. 64.

problem can be formulated: transformations-distortions which are, in the last analysis, no more than an index of the constant reformulation of the problem in different theoretical fields, as the effect of diverse, even contradictory, ideological determinations.

Thus: to speak of the 'object' of a science is, for Georges Canguilhem, to speak of a problem to be posed and then resolved; to speak of the history of a science is to show how – for what theoretical or practical motives – a science 'has gone about it' to pose and resolve this problem. Thus with him the history of a science takes the form of a *struggle* or dispute: the struggle of the man who wishes, in Marx's expression, to 'appropriate the world in the mode of thought', a struggle for scientific experimentation. The function of the historian is to analyse its phases, and, far from restricting himself to drawing up the balance-sheet of victories and defeats, he must be capable of giving a rational account of the sudden changes of terrain, unforseen withdrawals and surprise attacks. In short, he must be up to analysing the sequence of theoretical and practical *conjunctures* which 'constitute' that history.

D. The History of History

The history of the sciences conceived in this way as a 'History of Concepts' reveals unexpected lines of descent, establishes new periodizations, disinters forgotten names, throws into disorder the traditional and official chronology. In short, it draws up a 'parallel history' which has the speciality of constantly crossing-colliding with the calm discourse of the dogmatic historians. A new question is then posed: what is the status of this strange discourse – always and solemnly repeated – which pretends to trace 'objectively' the thread of time? If it is true that this discourse does not explain the actual history of the sciences that it pretends to trace, how are we to explain the persistence of such a blindness? What *other* reality does it translate? Better: what interests then drive the scientists themselves to recognize the history of their discipline in a fictional narrative? What are the aims and the mechanisms of this fiction?

It is these questions that are answered vis-à-vis one particular point by the extraordinary second part of *The Formation of the Concept of the Reflex*. In the first part, Canguilhem establishes that, contrary to universally accepted opinion, the concept of the reflex did not emerge in the field of a physiological theory of the *mechanistic* type. He shows that Descartes, to whom paternity of the concept is generally attributed, *could not* have formed it:

The formation of the concept of the reflex found its main obstacle in Cartesian physiology in the region of the theories relating to the motion of the spirits in the nerve and muscle. Because, according to him, the spirits only play a part in the centrifugal phase of the determination of involuntary motion, because their movement from the brain towards the muscle is a one-way movement, Descartes could not imagine that the transport of some influx from the periphery towards the centre might be returned or reflected towards its starting-point.[14]

In fact, by a close analysis of Descartes's texts, Canguilhem shows that at no moment is such a movement thought, and, in addition, that the word reflex never appears.

Where then does the concept appear? In a truly fantastic doctrine – and one completely ignored by the historians; in a theory of a *vitalist* type which alone, by assimilating life to *light*, made it possible to conceive of the movement of *reflection*. In this way re-emerged from a secular oblivion the names of Thomas Willis (1621–75), Professor of Natural Philosophy at Oxford and of medicine at London, and of Georg Prochaska (1749–1820), Professor of Anatomy and Ophthalmology at the University of Prague. It is because Willis dared to think life integrally as light that in order to describe motion he resorted to the optical laws of reflection, thus realizing the link between two domains that Descartes had missed.[15] And yet Willis and Prochaska have been 'forgotten' by the historians. How are we to explain such an oblivion? Or rather, how are we to explain the *substitution* of Descartes for Willis? No doubt we must invoke the epistemological prejudice that a concept must necessarily appear in the field of a theory homogeneous with the one in which it is later

14. *La formation du concept de réflexe aux XVIIe et XVIIIe siècles*, p. 51.
15. ibid., p. 66.

to find its regular functioning. In the present case: only a mechanistic theory could, from this point of view, fulfil this condition. It was enough that a few passages from Descartes, and also a few diagrams, might suggest an analogy for there to be a rush to see in them what was not there. But the persistent and tenacious effectivity of this prejudice, and of the silence about the essential contribution of the Czech scientist, still have to be understood.

It is here that Georges Canguilhem opens up, beneath the placid dogmatism of the official history, a whole world of bitter controversies in which it turns out that politics plays a determinant part. For example, we find Du Bois Reymond (1818–96), holder of the chair of Physiology at the University of Berlin, putting Descartes forward in order to conjure Prochaska away. And it appears that he did so in order to assert the nationalist supremacy of a 'strong' science over the science of a dominated nationality embodied in this case by Prochaska. . . . The motives for the fiction thus come out into the open: they are not at all fictional in themselves; on the contrary, they are quite real, and reveal what is inadmissible in the supposedly objective discourse of the historians. Only an epistemological history could carry out such a 'critical' undertaking. The history of the reflex concept will remain a model of a genre which ought to have other realizations with respect to other objects in other domains.

The general epistemological theses I have just summarized are not stated for themselves *in abstracto*. They have been elaborated and pertinently rectified on the basis of precise and concrete works dealing with the history of the biological sciences. They are strictly solidary with them. This solidarity is, as we shall see, both the strongest and the weakest link in Canguilhem's enterprise, indissociably. The strongest because it is these works that confer on them both their substance and their fruitfulness; the weakest, too, insofar as this solidarity presents itself, in its *factuality*, for its own theory. Hence it is this solidarity that I shall take as the object of my analyses, and, finally, of my questions.

2. THE EPISTEMOLOGICAL HISTORY
OF THE BIOLOGICAL SCIENCES

Where it is a matter of the history of the biological sciences, Georges Canguilhem's work is governed by a dual preoccupation: to bring out the *specificity* of their object and to define precisely, in the particular case of medicine – that 'art at the crossroads of a number of sciences' – the actual relations instituted in it between techniques and theoretical knowledges. A reading of the book on *The Normal and the Pathological* shows as well as might be that the two questions go side by side. The first explains the insistance with which Georges Canguilhem returns to the so-called question of 'vitalism'. The second makes comprehensible the status he accords the notion of 'norm'. Both govern the privileged interest he grants to several major figures in the history of the biological sciences and of biological philosophy: the Montpellier School, Bichat, Auguste Comte and Claude Bernard. . . .

A. Vitalism

The study of the 'formation of the concept of reflex' that I have just evoked at some length thus led Georges Canguilhem to re-evaluate the role of the vitalist current in the history of the study of the nervous system. This circumstance is far from being accidental: it derives from a kind of *theoretical challenge*, since it was a matter, ultimately, of confronting 'mechanicism' on the terrain in which it seemed most certain of its success and in which its authority could, in addition, take advantage of that of Cartesian philosophy. No doubt the works of Bethe, von Weiszäcker, Goldstein – following those of 'the illustrious Sherrington' – had shaken the dogma of the biological reality of the elementary reflex arc, no doubt Merleau-Ponty's books had broadcast their results widely among the French philosophical public; but on the one hand, the mechanistic theory of the reflex, dominating the manuals of secondary education, remained nonetheless the chosen terrain of many physiologists; Cartesian philosophy, on the other hand, had no lack of scrupulous guardians who were not disposed to see the integrity of the Master's work infringed, even in a matter which they were hardly accustomed to bother with. Georges Canguilhem insists, against the tradition, on the fact that *vitalism* was the only current in biology which took the specificity of the living seriously, which cut short any encroachment of metaphysics on biology, whatever the appearances.

Here again, it depends just what is meant by 'vitalism'. Canguilhem defines it precisely by a double rejection, a double dismissal of two metaphysical doctrines, opposed but solitary in their misrecognition of the proper object of biology. This is what he writes in *Knowledge of Life*:

It will be necessary . . . to give up the accusation of metaphysics and hence of fantasy, to say the least, which pursues the vitalist biologists of the eighteenth century. In fact, . . . vitalism is the rejection of two metaphysical interpretations of the causes of organic phenomena, animism and mechanicism. All the vitalists of the eighteenth century were Newtonians, men who refused to frame hypotheses on the essence of phenomena and who only thought they had to describe and co-ordinate, directly and without pre-judgement, the effects as they perceived them. Vitalism is merely the recognition of the originality of the vital fact.[16]

As a counter-example I could invoke the end of the chapter devoted to Descartes in *The Formation of the Concept of the Reflex*, where Canguilhem, after showing that in Cartesian theory the incomprehensible fracture instituted between man and animal refers men to the wisdom of God, concludes in the following terms: 'I shall say that only a metaphysician can, without risking initially the absurdity he has to reveal finally, formulate the principle of a mechanistic biology.'[17]

Thus over and above the challenge it represents, Georges Canguilhem links himself to vitalism because he sees in it the real and *specific* philosophy animating the progressive investigations in the biological sciences. In Bachelardian terms: vitalism represents the 'diurnal' philosophy of the biologists. A philosophy which is, as such, constantly besieged by the philosophy of the philosophers and

16. *La connaissance de la vie*, p. 156.
17. *La formation du concept de réflexe aux XVIIᵉ et XVIIIᵉ siècles*, p. 56.

by the 'nocturnal' philosophy of the scientists that is but one of its avatars. A philosophy which, on the other hand, is constantly subject to transformations correlating with those undergone by advancing biological science. In short, a philosophy which works in the scientific practice and whose categories, far from being – or calling themselves – eternal, are constantly enriched by re-adjusting themselves to their 'object'. That is why, with Georges Canguilhem as with Bachelard, concepts are always re-worked in the light of the revolutionary actuality of contemporary science. Here again the 'New Investigations' in *The Normal and the Pathological* are a fine example.

Once one has grasped the theoretical import of his interest in vitalism, there is no longer anything paradoxical in the sight of this historian, resolutely anti-positivist as he is, devoting himself on more than one occasion to the analysis of the philosophy of Auguste Comte. It is not so much as a historian of science that Comte fascinates him, if I may say so, but as 'the most illustrious representative of the Montpellier School in biological philosophy, if not in biology';[18] as the admirer of Bichat and the disciple of Barthez. As the man who constantly fought for the autonomy of biology against the 'cosmological usurpation', i.e., the ambitions of the physicochemical sciences to provide biology with its explanatory principles. As the man who opposed Cartesian mechanicism in all the forms in which he thought he could espy it (witness his mistrust of Lamarck's theories). This is what Canguilhem writes in a commentary on Comte:

The concept of the organic molecule or of the component animalcule in a complex living being carries with it a dangerous analogy between chemistry and biology. Life is necessarily the property of a whole.... It is definitely the spirit of Barthez that inspires this declaration of Comte's in which as many prohibitions are pre-echoed as scruples revealed: Any organism constitutes, by its nature, a necessarily indivisible whole which we decompose, by a mere intellectual device, to improve our knowledge, and always bearing in mind an eventual recomposition.[19]

18. *Études d'histoire et de philosophie des sciences*, p. 80.
19. ibid., p. 79.

Here we should be able to re-transcribe in full the passages in which Canguilhem analyses the function of the notion of 'consensus' in Auguste Comte, as well as those in which he reveals the extension given in them to the concept of *environment*.

It is in the same interest – but reinforced by an intention of episte-mological polemic – that his analysis returns on a number of occasions to Claude Bernard's decisive contribution to the history of physiology. First he is concerned to break with a certain traditional interpretation, still very widespread in France today, of the *Introduction to the Study of Experimental Medicine*: according to this interpretation, still dominant in secondary if not in higher education, this book is the rational and elegant codification of a universally valid method which Claude Bernard was able to 'apply' to physiology. Such a reading justifies itself by the general developments that are actually to be found in the first part of the book. Georges Canguilhem takes the opposite standpoint and shows that 'Claude Bernard's teaching is that method is not susceptible to formulation separately from the investigations from which it has emerged.'[20] In consequence of this he proposes to read the *Introduction* in the opposite direction: only in the light of the investigations set out in the latter two parts is it possible to grasp the real significance of the abstract considerations with which it opens. It will be seen that they are in solidarity with the formation by Claude Bernard of the concept of the *internal environment*.

Now it is precisely this concept that at last enables physiology to be a deterministic science, on the same basis as physics, without giving in to the fascination of the model proposed by physics. Thus we have returned to Canguilhem's main preoccupation. The formation of the biological concept of the 'internal environment', arising from the discovery of the glycogenic function of the liver, and correlating with the notion of 'internal secretion', enabled Claude Bernard to break with the mechanicism he had inherited from his teacher Magendie: the 'internal environment', writes Canguilhem, 'solidarizes the parts in a whole everywhere immediately present to every one of them. The radicals of the organism do not live in the

20. ibid., p. 147.

metrical space in which we represent their arrangement. There is something more. The existence of the internal environment guarantees the living being, called higher because it has it, an "obvious independence", a "protective mechanism", an "elasticity".' Canguilhem adds that it is certainly because he is and knows he is a non-mechanist that Claude Bernard insists so much on his determinism, that he rejects any assimilation of his doctrine to a theory of life that seeks its specificity in the exception to physico-chemical laws. It is still the same fight. If the Bernardian revolution in physiology seems so instructive to Canguilhem it is because it presents in typical fashion the double polemic against two metaphysics, opposed but solidary in their misrecognition of the real philosophy of investigation in biology.

What I have chosen to expound vis-à-vis two authors – whose centrality is already suggested in *The Normal and the Pathological* – might be illustrated by a mere selection of articles written by Canguilhem and collected in his *Studies in the History and Philosophy of the Sciences*: 'The Role of Analogies and Models in Biological Discovery', 'The Whole and the Part in Biological Thought', etc.; or again in *Knowledge of Life*: 'Machine and Organism' and 'The Living and its Environment'. I have said enough to give an understanding of the precise function that the author's 'vitalism' has in them: to bring out, in Bachelardian style but on the specific terrain of biology, the philosophical categories which are at work in an actual scientific practice.

B. Technique and Science: the Notion of 'Norm'

The second question which traverses this 'epistemological history' and is announced in *The Normal and the Pathological* is that of the relations existing between sciences and techniques. A question which takes the following form: what relations are there between the history of therapeutics and the history of physiology? Does this history proceed according to the logical schema which holds that physiology governs medicine via the intermediary of pathology? Or again, in a more general way: what kind of line of descent is there between the living and its own concept? As we shall see, the answer to this last question, posed all over again a little while ago on the occasion of the 'revolution' in biology constituted by the discovery of DNA, gives Georges Canguilhem's vitalism a new dimension.

The answer to the first question is established via the elaboration of the concept of the 'normal'. For, in fact, 'without the concepts of normal and pathological, the thought and activity of medicine are incomprehensible'.[21] Therapeutics is always presented as an attempt to restore the 'normal'. Now, against the positivist idea that the normal is a statistical mean, Canguilhem, in the name of the vitalism he defends, points out that this conception amounts to treating the living as a system of laws instead of seeing in it an 'order of specific properties'. An *order* in the dual sense of the term, since for Canguilhem the essential feature of the normal is to be 'normative', i.e., to be institutive of norms and capable of changing the norms that it has instituted. Anticipating by several years the title of a book by the Nobel Prize winner Lwoff, Canguilhem thus speaks of a 'biological order' which has to be understood as an *exigency* of the living as well. It is this exigency that gives rise to the medical practice whose failures as well as its successes solicit the elaboration of a biological science. This primacy of medical practice is the object of a constant reminder. It is essential to see that it ultimately depends on the idea that life, a polarized activity, points out the paths not only for the restoration of its normal state, but also for its own conceptualization.

This peculiarly philosophical position, always present but 'withheld' in Canguilhem's work, has found 'support' in the latest developments of macro-molecular biology and appears as such in one of his most recently published articles: *Concept and Life*.[22] I believe that it gives the vitalism maintained in it a new meaning. That is why this text should be closely analysed.

The question is presented as follows:

In the knowledge of life do we proceed from understanding to life or

21. *La connaissance de la vie*, p. 155.
22. 'Le concept et la vie', *Revue philosophique de Louvain*, LXIV, May 1966; reprinted in *Études d'histoire et de philosophie des sciences*, pp. 335–64.

rather from life to understanding? In the first case, how does understanding encounter life? In the second, how can it miss life?[23]

One instance is not a usage: let us leap straight to the conclusions which emphasize the actuality of the question:

> To say that biological heredity is a communication of information . . . is to admit that there is a *logos* inscribed, preserved and transmitted in the living. . . . To define life as a meaning inscribed in matter is to admit the existence of an objective *a priori*, of a peculiarly material and no longer purely formal *a priori*.[24]

Allow me to translate this position in the form of an equation: *life* = code = information = concept of life = *concept*.

The vitalism becomes, in Canguilhem's own terms, a 'philosophy of life' as well as a theory of knowledge. In striking pages Canguilhem shows how this question of the relationship between *concept* and *life* haunts the whole history of philosophy. It is Aristotle and Hegel rather than Kant and Bergson whose theses turn out to be sanctioned here: the discovery of DNA by Watson and Crick in 1953 is 'a kind of confirmation of Aristotelianism' which saw – by means of the notion of 'form' – the concept of the living in the living itself.[25] A confirmation also of Hegel, who saw in life the 'immediate unity of the concept with its reality, without that concept being distinguished in it'. Canguilhem concludes in the following terms: 'Today the question can be posed as to whether what biologists know and teach about the structure, reproduction and heredity of living matter, on the cellular and macro–molecular scale, might not justify a conception of the relations between life and the concept closer to that of Hegel than to that of Kant and, at any rate, than to that of Bergson.'[26] I refer the reader to the text for the penetrating

23. *Études d'histoire et de philosophie des sciences*, p. 335.
24. ibid., p. 362.
25. 'If the function of reproduction has such an eminent role in Aristotelian classification it is because the perpetuation of structural type and hence of behaviour, in the ethological sense, is the clearest sign of purpose and of nature. This nature of the living, for Aristotle, is a soul. And this soul is also the form of the living. It is simultaneously its reality, *ousia*, and its definition, *logos*. The concept of the living is thus finally, according to Aristotle, the living itself' (ibid., p. 336).
26. ibid., pp. 347–8.

analyses of Kant and Bergson. Let it suffice to say that for me they are unequalled. But if I am convinced by the recurrent division made in the history of philosophy, I am less so as to the validity of the conclusions drawn therefrom. I do not have the same assessment of the 'philosophical import' of the 'new' biology.

To put it plainly: it seems to me that the equation suggested above, far from being the solution to the question repeated by philosophy, institutes what I would willingly call a theoretical 'short-circuit' to which I cannot subscribe. The line of descent from life to the concept by the mediation of the concept of life does not seem to me at all legitimized by the actual material existence of DNA. Is it not necessary on the contrary to continue to 'withhold' what is withheld in the mere affirmation of the polarity of the living, which previously constituted 'vitalism'? In other words: does not the step taken on the discovery of DNA cancel all the advantages of the polemical content of the earlier vitalism? By short-circuiting life and concept in the name of this material *a priori* does one not return too much into Aristotle's camp; does one not take up a position in the camp of *empiricist* theories of knowledge? A *speculative* empiricism no doubt, since it is the *logos* which has to account both for itself and for its conception, but an empiricism nonetheless, with the danger only too clearly stated here of letting slip the 'objective source of knowledge'. All these questions are questions which Georges Canguilhem *alone* enables us to formulate. They should be and are the object of discussions. For myself, I should propose to adopt the following position with respect to the discovery of DNA: to *preserve* towards and against everyone the polemical aspect of the old vitalism: to retain the aspect in which it is a *prohibition* vis-à-vis every theory of knowledge and to think the new concepts *within* this prohibition. This would make possible the simultaneous affirmation, confirmed, repeated and rectified by the material existence of the genetic code, of the idea that there is a 'polarity' or a 'dialectic' inscribed in the living. To be precise: is not the correct position to hold these two theses *simultaneously*, in their apparent incompatibility. The first having the unique action of 'cutting short' the propensity of the second to grow into a theory? One day we shall have to inquire into this propensity which is spontaneous only in appearance. In other words, one day we shall have to settle the irritating question of the 'dialectics of nature', whose theoretical urgency is revealed to us by the last questions posed by a text like *Concept and Life*. Perhaps the regulated functioning of the two vitalisms I have just outlined contains the elements of the solution in the field proper to the sciences of the living?

It is time to close by returning to my initial question: how are we to explain our theoretical 'meeting' with Georges Canguilhem's history of the sciences? I have already provided the elements of an answer in passing: it is the *unity* which he institutes between the history of the sciences and epistemology that brings him close to historical materialism and dialectical materialism – to their specific unity – that is why I have been able to maintain that this unity was 'revolutionary'. We have seen that it was Gaston Bachelard's work that first disengaged this unity. But it seems to me that in Bachelard, this recognized and practised unity did not find its concept.

Georges Canguilhem stresses it himself: Bachelard's psychologism, which is supposed to found the unity, is not very convincing. It is the weakest link in this epistemology. Canguilhem's attempt is even more interesting: he thinks he can found this unity between epistemology and history of the sciences on another unity which he finds at the end of his labours, that of *concept* and *life*. I confess that I cannot follow him on this road which, as Pierre Macherey emphasized some time ago,[27] often leads him to a 'biologistic' conception of history itself. But I add the following essential specification: the necessarily idealist effects of such a conception are always-already erased, countered, in his work by the polemical import of his vitalism. That is why I can say without reservation that our route is a common one.

December 1970

---

27. 'La philosophie de la science de Georges Canguilhem', op. cit.

On Archæology and Knowledge
(Michel Foucault)

Much was written about *The Order of Things*; Foucault's latest book, *The Archæology of Knowledge*, has far from aroused the same zeal among the critics.[1]

This discretion is no doubt attributable to the strangeness of a work which is all too likely to leave its reader with an uneasy feeling. Some in fact will turn the last page disillusioned, with the secret feeling that they have been tricked. 'Still the same old story, despite the verbal innovations,' they will say, 'was it really necessary to write a whole book for a change in vocabulary?' A legitimate reaction, for certainly, at first reading, if the thick growth of new words attracts the attention and makes the landscape somewhat unfamiliar, it is not long before the untiring attacks on the 'subject' and its doubles, repeated one-hundred-fold here, make one feel at home; or rather, at Foucault's. Others having finished reading will suspend their judgement and await the sequel: 'It is all new,' they will say, 'we can no longer find our way in it; but nothing has been done: let us wait until we have seen this battery of new concepts working before making any pronouncement.' They will not be wrong either, since the author warns us several times that the elaboration of the new categories threatens the old fabric, that profound rectifications have to be made: the category of 'experience' as it functioned in *Madness and Civilization* is invalidated by its surreptitious restoration of an 'anonymous and general subject of history',[2] the decisive notion of the 'medical gaze', around which *The Birth of Clinical Medicine*

1. The following chapter is a slightly modified version of a text which first appeared in *La Pensée* no. 152, July–August 1970.

2. *The Archæology of Knowledge* (English translation), p. 16 (for full bibliographical details of Foucault's works see the Appendix to Part Two).

revolved, is itself repudiated.[3] Hence anyone who restricts himself to what is most apparent, to the explicit itself, cannot fail to suspect a real novelty of the concepts behind the renewed luxuriance of the style, even if he finds it somewhat difficult to support this suspicion since no new analyses appear and the old ones are only allusively invoked.

It will have been realized that these two contradictory reactions posed the same question: why this book? What necessity was there to write it? It is from this question that it seems to me I should start. Strictly speaking, Michel Foucault does not leave us without an answer. According to him, this book is a methodical and controlled review of what had previously been done 'blindly'. Indeed, as we have seen, the references do not leave the circle of the previous works. Besides this the book abounds in methodological norms, and entire chapters are presented as attempts to codify certain rules which were, we are to believe, tacitly accepted and chaotically practised in the past.

However, it seems to me that this answer obstinately suggested by the author is inadequate: *The Archæology* has a different import and the problematic it sets up is of a real and radical novelty. Here I shall take as an index of this novelty a very remarkable *absence*:[4] that of the notion of the *episteme*, the cornerstone of the previous work, and the prop of all the 'structuralist' interpretations of Foucault. It will no doubt be granted me that such an absence cannot be accidental. I shall therefore propose to take seriously the *paradox* of a book which claims it is a methodical 'review' of previous works and yet 'lets slip' their principal component. This paradox constitutes the whole interest of the undertaking; it poses two questions: what is the meaning of the *insistence* on stressing a continuity which is, manifestly, not without flaws? what *novelty* has been introduced which makes it obligatory to abandon the central notion of the episteme?

3. ibid., p. 54n.
4. I am well aware that the *term* episteme *does* reappear at the end of the book and that its role there is strictly speaking a decisive one, but en route it has undergone such a transformation, such a development and such a rectification that I think I am justified in speaking of a *relinquishment* of the old notion of episteme.

These two questions can, I believe, be given a single answer: it is the abandonment which accounts for the insistence. To be explicit: Foucault feels the necessity to leave behind one of the essential categories of his philosophy, but this relinquishment should not be understood as his rallying to the camp of his enemies; better, the category of the episteme had profound polemical effects against every 'humanist' or 'anthropologistic' theory of knowledge and history. He is concerned to retain them. And yet, the notion of the episteme which described the 'configurations of *savoir*' or knowledge as great layers obedient to specific structural laws made it impossible to think the *history* of ideological formations other than as brusque 'mutations', enigmatic 'ruptures', sudden 'breakthroughs'. It is with this type of history – for reasons I shall have to examine in detail – that Foucault now wants to break. *The Archæology* registers this divorce. The reader will already have guessed: it is the 'structuralist' aspects of the episteme that Foucault wants to cast off here, without for all that resaddling himself with the old trappings of the humanism which he has always fought. The operation is a dangerous one and really needed a whole book; its complexity easily explains the reader's unease and gives a meaning to the critics' discretion: in *The Archæology* they do not rediscover *their* Foucault, the prudent prospector of epistemic structures. Worse: they see History appear; not *their* history but a strange history which refuses both the *continuity* of the subject and the structural *discontinuity* of 'ruptures'!

For my part, I think the critics are well-advised; they are not wrong to tremble, for the concept of history which functions in *The Archæology* has many consonances with another concept of history which they have good reason to hate: the scientific concept of history as it appears in historical materialism. The concept of a history which is also presented as a process without a subject structured by a system of laws. A concept which, on this basis, is also radically anti-anthropologistic, anti-humanist and anti-structuralist.

Thus for me *The Archæology of Knowledge* represents a decisive turning-point in Foucault's work; I should like to show that his new position in philosophy has led him, even in this work, to carry out a certain number of analyses of an astonishing value *from the standpoint of historical materialism*; that, in his own language, he reproduces – but in displacement – concepts which function in the Marxist science of history; finally that the difficulties he encounters as well as his eventual relative failure will find neither solution nor issue except in the field of historical materialism.

FROM ARCHÆOLOGY TO 'SAVOIR'

Against the 'subject'

It may be said that all the 'critical' part of *The Archæology of Knowledge* is inscribed in continuity with the previous work. No doubt Foucault no longer has the same allies, yet he still has the same enemies. But the polemics have grown richer, more profound here, and they reveal conceptual solidarities which had hitherto remained hidden. Thus the attacks on the category of the subject are now coupled with attacks on *continuism* in history.

Here is his reply to his humanist neo-Hegelian critics on the question of *The Order of Things*: 'What is being bewailed with such vehemence is not the disappearance of history, but the eclipse of that form of history that was secretly, but entirely, related to the synthetic activity of the subject.'[5] A favourite point because the perfect alibi for anthropologism: how indeed better fight history than by raising its banner?

For example: *The Archæology* is the site of a vigorous polemic against a discipline currently in favour: 'the history of ideas'. Foucault shows that it rests on an anthropologistic postulate which obliges it to be openly or shame-facedly continuistic. The 'history of ideas' has, according to him, two roles: on the one hand it 'recounts the by-ways and margins of history. Not the history of the sciences, but that of the imperfect, ill-based knowledges, which could never in the whole of their long persistent life attain the form of scientificity.' The examples follow: alchemy, phrenology, atomistic theories.

5. *The Archæology of Knowledge*, p. 14.

. . . In short, 'it is the discipline of fluctuating languages, of shapeless works, of unrelated themes.'[6] But on the other it sets itself the task of traversing the existing disciplines, dealing with them and re-interpreting them. It describes the diffusion of scientific *savoir* from science to philosophy, even to literature. In this sense its postulates are 'genesis, continuity, totalization'.[7] *Genesis*: all the 'regions' of *savoir* are referred for their origin to the unity of an individual or collective subject. *Continuity*: unity of origin has as a necessary correlate continuity of development. *Totalization*: unity of origin has as a necessary correlate homogeneity of parts. Everything fits together, but it cannot, says Foucault, give rise to a true history.

A new front of attack: every theory of *reflection* insofar as it sees in 'discourse' 'the surface of the symbolic projection of events or processes that are situated elsewhere,' in that it seeks to 'rediscover a causal sequence that might be described point by point, and which would make it possible to connect together a discovery and an event, or a concept and a social structure', every theory of 'reflection', fundamentally 'empiricist' or 'sensualist', must take as its 'fixed point' a category of subjects and thus turns out to be immediately open to the charge of anthropologism.[8] More surprising still: the category of *author* itself, however 'concrete' and obvious, is rejected. The author is never anything other than the literary, philosophical or scientific designation of a 'subject' taken to be 'creative'. Hence the 'book' is a naively and arbitrarily separated unit which is im-posed on us in an unreflected immediacy by the appearances of geometry, the rules of printing and a suspect literary tradition. The 'book' must therefore be considered not as the literal and more or less rationalized projection of a subject bearing and installing its meaning, but as a 'node within a network'. Its real existence – not its immediate appearance – lies only 'in a system of references' which acquire consistency in it. 'And this play of references is not the same in the case of a mathematical treatise, a textual commentary, a historical account, and an episode in a novel cycle.'[9]

6. ibid., pp. 136–7.   7. ibid., p. 138.   8. ibid., p. 164.   9. ibid., p. 23.

Against the 'object'

Take care: here, via the detour of an example, appears what is most novel in *The Archæology of Knowledge*: the old polemic turned completely against the 'subject' takes a new twist in turning against the correlative category, the *object*.

That is how meaning is acquired by the – oft repeated – rectifications of certain themes of Bachelardian epistemology. In the latter, everything is concentrated around the notions of epistemological 'rupture', 'obstacle', 'act'. Foucault reveals the solidarity between the philosophical category of the 'object' and the descriptive viewpoint of the *'rupture'* in history: it is because a science is compared to an ideology from the point of view of their *objects* that a rupture (or break) is observed between them, but this point of view is strictly descriptive and explains nothing. Worse: as one might have expected, the category of the object brings with it its correlate: the subject. Bachelardian epistemology is once again a good example: the notion of epistemological rupture demands that what is broken with is thought as an epistemological 'obstacle'. But how does Bachelard propose to think the obstacles? As interventions of *images* into scientific practice. Foucault can thus claim that the object-rupture couple is only the inverted, but fundamentally identical, form of the subject-continuity couple; Bachelard's epistemology is thus a shame-faced anthropology. The 'psychoanalysis of objective knowledge' marks the *limits* of this epistemology, its point of inconsistency: the point at which other principles are required to account for what it describes: of course – it is greatly to Bachelard's credit that he understood it – a science is only established by a rupture with a *'tissue* of tenacious errors' which precede it and are an obstacle to it, but to refer to the scientist's 'libido' to account for the formation of this tissue is to hold to a notion of the 'subject', it is even, at the limit, to let it be understood that scientificity might be established by a voluntary decision of the scientist (or scientists). For Foucault, it is essential to *start from* what Bachelard described, to leave the point of view of the object and to pose the problem of the 'rupture' on new bases. To be quite precise, to examine this tissue which Bachelard did not succeed in 'thinking', in particular the 'false sciences' which precede science, the 'positivities' that the sciences, once constituted, allow us by recurrence to define as 'ideological'. On this point, as we shall see, *The Archæology of Knowledge* makes a considerable contribution.

THE INSTANCE OF 'SAVOIR'

Institutional materiality

We now know to what exigencies the basic categories of *The Archæology of Knowledge* are responding: it is a matter of thinking the laws that govern the differential history of the sciences and the non-sciences, with reference neither to a 'subject' nor to an 'object', outside the false 'continuity-discontinuity' alternative.

The first notion which responds to these exigencies is that of the 'discursive event'. Foucault writes:

Once these immediate forms of continuity are suspended, an entire domain is set free. A vast domain, but one that can be defined nonetheless: this domain is constituted by the set of all actual statements (whether spoken or written), in their dispersion as events and in the instance that is proper to each of them. Before approaching, with certainty, a science, or novels, or political speeches, or the œuvre of an author, or even a single book, the material with which one is dealing in its raw neutrality is a population of events in the space of discourse in general.[10]

Here questions will be accumulating: what is this 'space of discourse'? Is it not the object of linguistics? No, because the 'field of discursive events is the *always finite* and currently limited set of the *only* linguistic sequences that have been formulated'. Is it not quite simply 'thought' which is designated by these esoteric words? No, for it is not a question of referring what is said to an intention, to a silent discourse which orders it from within; the only question posed is: 'What, then is the unique existence which comes to light in what is said and nowhere else?'[11] Let us follow Foucault further

10. ibid., pp. 26–7.   11. ibid., pp. 27–8.

in order to discover the specificity of the category he is constructing and which I shall later allow myself to give a different name. It is really by the advantages he expects to gain from it that Foucault specifies the status of what he calls a 'discursive event'. This notion enables him to determine 'the connexions of statements one to another' – without any reference to the consciousness of one or more authors; or 'connexions between statements or groups of statements and events of a quite different kind (technical, economic, social, political)'.[12]

It is clear that the essential thing here is the notion of *connexion* (*relation*). What Foucault understands by a connexion is a set of relations of 'coexistence, succession, mutual functioning, reciprocal determination, independent or correlative transformation'.[13] But Foucault feels that the determination of such connexions is still inadequate to designate the instance of 'discursive events': if by such a combinatory one may, in a sense, hope to explain the 'discursive', it is impossible to understand what he calls a discursive *event*, it leaves us at the level of the *episteme*. Let me put it in a nut-shell: such an analysis cannot account for the 'material' and 'historical' existence of the discursive event. A decisive question haunts all these pages, which might seem long and redundant: the necessity, which Foucault recognizes, to define 'the regime of materiality' of what he calls discourse, the correlative necessity to elaborate a new – materialist – category of 'discourse' and finally the necessity to think the history of this 'discourse' in its materiality. Such is the triple task which *The Archæology of Knowledge* attempts to carry out; and it is this task which, as we shall see, explains its relative failure.

The proof: turning to the 'objects' of psychopathology, Foucault asks questions of the type: 'Is it possible to know according to what non-deductive sytem these objects could be juxtaposed and placed in succession to form the fragmented field – showing at certain points great gaps, at others a plethora of information – of psychopathology? What has been the regime of their existence as objects of discourse?'[14] Even more sharply: the attempt to characterize the

12. ibid., p. 29.   13. ibid.; cf. notably p. 42 and p. 29.   14. ibid., p. 41.

elementary unit of the discursive event – the unit-event as it were – leads Foucault to propose the notion of the 'statement' (*énoncé*). Now what does he recognize as the precondition for a statement? 'For a sequence of linguistic elements to be regarded and analysed as a statement, . . . it must have a *material existence*.'[15] The materiality is not just one precondition among others, it is constitutive: 'It is not simply a principle of variation, a modification of the criterion of recognition, or a determination of linguistic sub-sets. It is constitutive of the statement itself: a statement must have a substance, a support, a site, and a date.'[16] Without anticipating too much, it can be said that the investigation of the 'regime of materiality' of the statement will be directed more towards the substance and the support than towards the site and the date. 'The regime of materiality that statements necessarily obey is therefore of the order of the institution rather than of the spatio-temporal localization.'[17] What Foucault discovers is in reality that 'spatio-temporal localization' may be *deduced* from the 'connexions' or 'relations' between statements or groups of statements once one has understood that these relations must be recognized to have a material existence, once one has grasped that these relations do not exist outside certain material supports in which they are embodied, produced and reproduced. At the point we have reached, the situation might thus be summed up as follows: it is clearly necessary to think the history of discursive events as structured by material relations embodying themselves in institutions.

Discourse as 'practice'

It will be clear why Foucault is led to give a unique definition of 'discourse': 'Discourse is something quite different from the site at which objects supposedly installed in advance are deposited and superimposed as in a mere surface of inscription.'[18] Indeed, if what has been said of the 'material regime of the statement' is correct, discourse is not susceptible to definition outside the relations which

15. ibid., p. 131.   16. ibid., p. 101.   17. ibid., p. 103.   18. ibid., pp. 42–3.

we have seen to be constitutive of it; in this sense the terms 'discursive connexions' or 'discursive regularities' will be used rather than 'discourse'. In the last analysis this is because this discourse is a *practice*. The category of 'discursive practice' as proposed here by Foucault is the index of the basically materialist theoretical innovation which consists of not taking any 'discourse' outside the system of material relations that structure and constitute it. This new category establishes a decisive dividing line between *The Archæology of Knowledge* and *The Order of Things*. But we must know how to understand it: the word 'practice' does not imply the activity of a subject, it designates the objective and material existence of certain rules to which the subject is subject once it takes part in 'discourse'. The effects of this subjection of the subject are analysed under the heading: 'positions of the subject'; I shall return to this. For the moment, here is the positive definition of discourse according to *The Archæology*: discursive connexions are not *internal* to discourse, they are not the links found between concepts or words, sentences or propositions; but neither are they external to it, they are not the external 'circumstances' which are supposed to constrain discourse; on the contrary, 'they determine the bundle of relations that discourse must establish in order to be able to speak of this or that object, in order to be able to deal with them, name them, analyse them, classify them, explain them', etc.; and Foucault concludes: 'These connexions characterize not the language used by discourse, nor the circumstances in which it is deployed, but *discourse itself as a practice*.'[19] Hence the notion of discursive *rule* or discursive *regularity* to designate the norms of this practice. Hence the definition already alluded to of the 'objects' of this practice as 'effects' of the rules or as a 'bundle of relations': indeed, it is necessary 'to define these *objects* without reference to the ground of things, but by relating them to the set of rules that enable them to be formed as objects of a discourse and thus constitute the conditions of their historical appearance.'[20]

19. ibid., p. 46.   20. ibid., pp. 47–8.

The instance of savoir*

That is how the notion of '*savoir*', the peculiar object of the archæo-logy, is constructed. What is a *savoir*? It is precisely 'that of which one can speak in a discursive practice, which is thereby specified: the domain constituted by the different objects that will or will not acquire a scientific status.'[21] 'A *savoir* is also the field of co-ordination and subordination of statements in which concepts appear, and are defined, applied and transformed.'[22] That is why, unlike epistemo-logy, archæology explores 'the discursive-practice/*savoir*/science axis'.[23] The notion of *epistemological rupture* here acquires a new status. The peculiarity of epistemology, according to Foucault, is to elude the instance of '*savoir*', the instance of the regulated relations whose material existence constitutes the basis on which a scientific knowledge (*connaissance*) is installed. For him, what has to be de-monstrated is 'how a science is inscribed and functions in the element of *savoir*'. There is a 'space' in which, by an *interplay within* the relations that constitute it, a given science forms its object: 'science, without being identified with *savoir*, but without either effacing or excluding it, is localized in it, structures certain of its objects, systematizes certain of its enunciations, formalizes certain of its concepts and strategies.'[24]

I shall have occasion to return to this 'interplay' as Foucault conceives it; in particular vis-à-vis one example in particular, that of the relationship between Marx and Ricardo. It is enough to have demonstrated the principles of the analysis and their effects on existing 'disciplines'.

The archæology's point of retreat

Let us go back to Foucault's procedure in its principles: this

* *Translator's note: savoir* and *connaissance*. Both these words can be translated into English as 'knowledge'; however, the first leans more in the direction of 'know-how', the second more towards the philosophical term 'cognition'. The author gives Foucault's definition of his own use of *savoir*, so it has been left untranslated in this chapter, where 'knowledge' translates *connaissance* unless specified otherwise. Elsewhere the context indicates the particular use of 'knowledge' sufficiently adequately to require no further distinction.

21. ibid., p. 182.   22. ibid., pp. 182–3.   23. ibid., p. 183.   24. ibid., p. 185.

procedure seems to me to mark very correctly the limits of epistemology and to prove the necessity of elaborating a theory of what he
calls 'discursive relations'; a theory of the laws of every 'discursive
formation'. Now it is here that the limits of the 'archæology' appear
in their turn. If my interpretation is correct, the task of the 'archæology' is in fact to constitute the theory of the 'discursive' instance
insofar as it is structured by relations invested in institutions and
historically determinate regulations. This task is only carried out by
Foucault in the form of a description; he says so himself: 'the time
for theory has not yet arrived,' he writes in the chapter entitled
'The Description of Statements'. For my part, I think that the time
for theory was inaugurated by Marx, at least in its most general
principles, a long time ago; but that it will not come for Foucault
unless he resolves to recognize the principles of the theory he is
praying for. These principles are those of the science of history.
For ultimately the most positive thing about *The Archæology of
Knowledge* is the attempt made in it to install, under the name
'discursive formation', a materialist and historical theory of ideological relations and of the formation of ideological objects. But on
what in the last analysis is this incipient theory based? On a tacitly
accepted, ever present, never theorized distinction between 'discursive practices' and 'non-discursive practices'. All his analyses are
built on this distinction; I shall say that it is practised *blindly*; that
the last effort of 'mastery' still to be made is to theorize it. I have no
doubt that, as he foresees himself, Foucault would then find himself
on another terrain.

This distinction is ever present: Foucault, having produced the
category of 'discursive practice', has to recognize that this 'practice'
is not autonomous; that the transformation and change of the relations that constitute it are not produced by the action of a pure
combinatory, but that in order to understand them it is necessary
to refer to other practices of another kind. We have already seen that
from the outset Foucault proposes to determine the connexions
between statements, but also 'between statements and events of
a quite different kind (technical, economic, social, political)'.[25]

25. ibid., p. 29.

Furthermore, to follow the order of the book, *a strange distinction* appears in the definition of discourse as a practice. 'Discursive' connexions are said to be *secondary* with respect to certain connexions said to be 'primary' which, 'independently of all discourse or all objects of discourse, may be described between institutions, techniques, social forms, etc.'.[26] A few pages later we read:

The determination of the theoretical choices that were actually made also derives from another instance. This instance is characterized first by the *function* that the discourse under study must carry out in a *field of non-discursive practices*.[27]

Many other examples might be cited, all of which would prove that Michel Foucault needs this distinction but that he practises it in the form of *juxtaposition*. In particular, it is clearly this distinction that is functioning in the analysis of the relations between Ricardo and Marx. It is the point at which Michel Foucault's 'system of references' reveals its inconsistency. Let us change terrain.

'SAVOIR' AND IDEOLOGY

The third section of the chapter 'Science and *Savoir*' is entitled '*Savoir* and Ideology'. The confrontation of the two titles suggests what is at stake: a critical examination of the theses put forward in already old books by Althusser about the relations between science and ideology. These theses, which undeniably had a revolutionary theoretical value and political importance in their day, used for their own purposes a basically Bachelardian notion of 'break' (*coupure*) or 'rupture'. As we have seen, in *The Archæology*, Foucault proposes a system of categories to re-think – and rectify – this conception of the break (or rupture). He stresses its narrowly descriptive value and its anthropologistic connotations. Hence it is understandable that in response the science-ideology distinction has to be re-organized; this is what he undertakes to do by analysing the relationship between

26. ibid., p. 45.   27. ibid., pp. 67–8.

science and '*savoir*' as the latter concept has been elaborated through-out the book. He is obliged by that very fact to think the difference between what he calls '*savoir*' and what Althusser called 'ideology'. It is precisely this last analysis that concludes *The Archæology*. In it Foucault uses three arguments corresponding to determinations of the new concept of '*savoir*':

(a) If *savoir* is constituted by a set of practices – discursive and non-discursive practices – the definition of ideology as it functioned in Althusser is too narrow. 'Theoretical contradictions,' writes Foucault, 'lacunae, defects may indicate the ideological functioning of a science (or of a discourse with scientific pretensions); they may enable us to determine at what point in the fabric this functioning takes effect. But the analysis of this functioning must be made at the level of the positivity of the relations between the rules of formation and the structures of scientificity.'[28] In short, what is under attack is any conception of ideology as non-science pure and simple. For Foucault, such a definition of ideology misses what is its mark; if you like, it is itself ideological. It is limited to a mechanistic and ulti-mately anti-dialectical statement of the effects of the insertion of science in *savoir*. But the analysis must be *displaced*, it is not enough to fasten one's eyes on science and make ideology the mere inverse of science, its pure absence, as certain unilateral pages by Althusser may have suggested. On the contrary, in order to grasp what is called the 'rupture' it is essential to analyse the network of relations which constitutes '*savoir*', and *on the basis* of which science emerges.

(b) If *savoir* is invested in certain practices – discursive and non-discursive practices – the emergence of a science does not, as if by magic, put an end to those practices. On the contrary, they survive and co-exist – more or less peacefully – with the science. Hence:

Ideology is not exclusive of scientificity. . . . By correcting itself, by recti-fying its errors, by tightening its formalizations, a discourse does not necessarily undo its relations with ideology for all that. The role of ideo-logy does not diminish as rigour increases and error is dissipated.[29]

In other words, if what is intended by the word 'ideology' is really

28. ibid., p. 186.   29. ibid.

'*savoir*', it has to be recognized that its reality, the materiality of its existence in a given social formation is such that it cannot be dissipated as an illusion from one day to the next; on the contrary, it continues to function and, literally, to besiege science throughout the endless process of its constitution.

(c) The history of a science can from then on only be conceived in its relationship with the history of '*savoir*', i.e., with the history of the practices – the discursive and non-discursive practices – of which it consists; it is a matter of thinking the mutations of these practices: each mutation will have the effect of modifying the form of insertion of scientificity into *savoir*, of establishing a new type of science/*savoir* relationship. 'In short, the question of ideology that is asked of science is not the question of the situations or practices that it reflects more or less consciously; nor is it the question of its possible use or of the misuses to which it could be put; it is the question of its existence as a discursive practice and of its functioning among other practices.'[30]

It seems to me that the unadmitted but determinant 'system of references' which is masked by the constant, and here paradoxical self-reference of the author to his own work, has now come right out into the open. I was quite right to suspect the remarkable 'trick' Foucault plays on himself – and on us: to give as constitutive of his work a system of references whose elements he has himself invalidated. What is clear, in fact, at the end of these analyses (precisely at the *end*, as I have noted) is that the system of the 'archæology' is entirely constructed to compensate for the inadequacy of the science-ideology couple when it comes to thinking those 'false sciences', those 'positivities' which are Foucault's particular object. *The Archæology of Knowledge* is constructed on the assertation of an absence. Hence two roads – and two only – were open to Foucault: to attempt to resolve the difficulty by his own means or to trust himself to historical materialism, to the science of history, and to see if it reduced the science/ideology opposition to the one previously stated – provisionally and of necessity so – by Althusser. To be quite precise: if the basic concepts of historical materialism did not make

30. ibid., p. 185.

it possible to disengage a theory of ideology such that the difficulty encountered was already resolved. Michel Foucault has chosen – some would say courageously – the first road. As a conclusion I shall attempt to give a non-psychologist reason for this choice. For the moment we should examine its consequences. Putting my cards on the table and anticipating slightly my results, let me say that the nature of ideology is such that one cannot with impunity maintain a discourse constantly paralleling a constituted and living science. A moment comes when the contradiction re-appears, when the 'displacement' makes itself felt by its effects, when the initially eluded choice re-imposes itself more urgently than ever. This is what I am about to demonstrate.

The parallel discourse: having recognized a real difficulty, whose terms and solution belong by right – and in fact – to historical materialism, Foucault proposes a certain number of homologous, though displaced, concepts. For whoever is able to understand them, he states in their formulation the conditions of their own rectification.

As we have seen, everything turns on the use of the concept of 'practice'. In its literal sense, it admits that at this point the distinction between historical materialism and the 'archæology' is at a minimum; examination will prove, without paradox, that it is also at this point that it is at a maximum. It really is in fact the category of practice – so foreign to Foucault's earlier works – that defines the field of the 'archæology': neither language, nor thought, as we have seen, but what he calls the 'pre-conceptual'. 'The "pre-conceptual" level that we have uncovered', he writes, 'refers neither to a horizon of ideality nor to an empirical genesis of abstractions.'[31] In fact, what is sought is not the ideal structures of the concept but the 'locus of emergence of concepts'; nor is there any attempt to account for ideal structures by the series of empirical operations which is supposed to have given rise to them; what is described is a set of anonymous historically determinate rules imposed on every speaking subject, rules which are not universally valid but always have a specified domain of validity. The main determination of the archæological category of 'practice' is 'rule', 'regularity'. It is *regularity* that

31. ibid., p. 62.

structures discursive practice, it is the rule that orders every discursive 'formation'.[32] The 'rule' can easily be assigned its function: with it Foucault is attempting to think at once – I mean in their *unity* – the *relations* that structure discursive practice, their *effect* of subjection on the speaking 'subjects', and what he calls rather enigmatically the *interlocking* (*embrayage*) of one practice with another.

I have already analysed the first point; all I need add is the specification that 'regularity' is not opposed to 'irregularity': if regularity really is the essential determination of practice, the regularity/ irregularity opposition is not a pertinent one. One cannot, for example, say that in a discursive formation an 'invention' or a 'discovery' escape regularity: 'A discovery is no less regular, from the enunciative point of view, than the text that repeats and diffuses it; regularity is no less operant, no less effective and active, in a banality than in an unprecedented formation.'[33] Irregularity is thus an appearance exploited by the historians of 'strokes of genius' who, loyal worshippers of the 'subject' (or at least of some brilliant subjects), are, as we have seen, fundamentally continuist. This appearance is produced when a modification occurs at a determinate point in the discursive formation, hence *within* and *beneath* the regularity established at that given moment of history. According to the point it bears on, it will be more or less tangible, have greater and smaller effects (some will say: it will display more or less 'genius'). This reveals a new determination of the 'discursive formation': it is structured *hierarchically*. In fact there are 'governing statements' which set bounds on the field of possible objects and trace the dividing-line between the 'visible' and the 'invisible', the 'thinkable' and the 'unthinkable' or rather (in 'archæological' terms): between the statable and the unstatable; which designate what a given discursive formation includes by what it excludes. The apparent irregularity is thus no more than the effect of a modification of 'governorship' Here we should really give a lengthy commentary on the remarkable passage in which the analysis is carried out on the example of Natural History (cf. pp. 192–3 of the English edition).

32. ibid., p. 46.   33. ibid., p. 145.

The second point: this hierarchical regularity is imposed on every 'subject'. This is what Foucault writes about clinical medicine:

The positions of the subject are also defined by the situation that it is possible for it to occupy in relation to the various domains or groups of objects: it is a questioning subject according to a certain grid of explicit or implicit interrogations, and a listening subject according to a certain programme of information; it is a looking subject according to a table of characteristic features and an observing subject according to a descriptive type. . . . , [etc.].

Further on:

The various situations that the subject of medical discourse can occupy were defined at the beginning of the nineteenth century with the organization of a quite different perceptual field.[34]

The third point is crucial; all the contradictions of the 'archæological' enterprise accumulate in it; here the Foucauldian category of practice reveals its inadequacy: it does not enable us to think the *unity* of what it designates except as a *juxtaposition*. I shall show that this is because of its lack of a principle of determination. Now, if what I have said is correct, this absence is only the *effect* of the road chosen by Foucault. Hence it marks the point at which the other road makes its necessity felt, at which rectification can begin.

Foucault has accepted the obligation to think what constitutes the regularity of the rule, what orders its hierarchical structure, what produces its mutations, what confers on it its imperative character for every subject. But on each of these points he runs into *the same difficulty*. That it is the same difficulty is of some interest: it means that Foucault sees the need to refer the whole of this complex process to *one and the same* principle. However, this one principle may be everywhere present and designated, but it is never thought. That is because it exceeds the limits of the category of practice as it functions here. We have already discovered this principle: it is the articulation of discursive practices to non-discursive practices.

I shall be told: all this effort to get here, i.e., to the same enigmatic

34. ibid., pp. 52–3.

point at which the last section came to a halt! Certainly, and it is quite natural, since, once past this point, we are outside Foucault; but take care: I have advanced in my apparent circle, I have now determined the means whereby to escape from the 'archæological' circle. By thinking the point of retreat as such, I have found the road by which to leave without evasion. In fact, I can now say what the distinction discursive-practice/non-discursive-practice is a response to: an attempt to re-think the science/ideology distinction. Better: an attempt to think in their differential unity two histories: that of the sciences and that of ideology or ideologies. No longer to stress uni-laterally the *autonomy* of the history of the sciences, but to mark at the same time the *relativity* of that autonomy. Now, committed to this road, Foucault must recognize (and this is his greatest merit) that ideology (thought within the category of '*savoir*' as a hier-archically structured system of relations invested in practices) in its turn is not autonomous. Its autonomy too is no more than *relative*. But he well knows the danger threatening him: to think '*savoir*' as purely and simply the effect – or 'reflection' – of a social structure. In short, while trying to escape transcendental idealism, to fall into a mechanistic materialism which is no more than an inverted form of the transcendental idealism. Hence his extreme embarrassment and the metaphysical vagueness of the categories he proposes.

Let me take these developments for what they are: the necessarily misrecognizant 'recognition' of a theoretical weakness in the 'archæological' fabric. First recognition: the role of *institutions* in the 'interlocking'. Returning to the analyses in *The Birth of Clinical Medicine*, Foucault writes two remarkable pages on the subject.[35] I shall be content to quote passages from them, underlining certain *words* which illustrate the analyses I have just proposed:

First question: who is speaking? Who, in the set of all speaking individuals, is established as using this sort of language? Who is *qualified* to do so? Who derives from it his own special quality, his prestige, and from whom, in return, does he receive if not the assurance, at least the presumption that what he says is true? What is the *status* of the individuals who – alone – have the *right*, sanctioned by law or tradition, *juridically* defined or

35. ibid., pp. 50–1.

spontaneously accepted, to proffer such a discourse? The status of doctor involves criteria of competence and *savoir*; pedagogic *institutions, systems, norms*; *legal* conditions that give the *right* – though not without laying down certain *limitations* – to practice and to the experimentation of *savoir*.

And further on:

The existence (of) medical speech cannot be dissociated from the statutorily defined person who has the *right* to articulate it, and to claim for it the *power* to overcome suffering and death. But we also know that this status in Western Civilization was profoundly modified at the end of the eighteenth century and the beginning of the nineteenth century when the health of the population became one of the economic *norms* required by industrial societies.

'We also know . . .': let us admit that Foucault hardly gives us the means to pass from this hearsay knowledge to a rational knowledge of the process of modification. Still the same riddle: that of the 'interlocking'. But this text is exceptional in that it makes it possible to specify – in all its richness – the functioning of the category of 'rule' in Foucault: it is solidary with the notions of *status, norms* and *power*. To be quite precise: *status* is defined by a non-discursive instance – *I* can say by part of the State apparatus; it embodies, realizes a certain number of *norms* defined as a function of economic imperatives. This status, literally, makes the profession a body and this body invests the discourse conducted in it – and hence the individuals who conduct it – with a *power*. It is clear that this latter power, which has no existence except in the discursive practice of doctors – insofar as it is no stranger to the State apparatus – has some relation, unspecified by Foucault, with State power. Let us leave this analysis here in order to confront the same problem elsewhere.

On several occasions in the analysis, it becomes perplexed and confused: thus on p. 45, describing the formation of an object of *savoir* as a 'complex bundle of relations', Foucault resorts to an unprincipled amalgam: 'These connexions are established between institutions, economic and social processes, forms of behaviour, systems of norms, techniques, types of classification, modes of characterization; and these connexions are not present in the object.'

Other passages just as rhapsodic as this could be cited (notably p. 74).

It is time to call things by their name and to see why, having taken the wrong road, Foucault had necessarily to come a cropper. If I group together the elements we have picked up *en route*, here is the type of analysis I can propose: starting from a critique of the old – and too narrow – Althusserian notion of ideology, Foucault has elaborated his own category of '*savoir*' and supported it with a poorly built concept of 'practice'. Poorly built since for it to fulfil its function it is palpably necessary to split it without it being possible to give any reason for this split. But, taking advantage of the fact that his critique has found its mark, he reproduces, though in displacement, the determinations of the scientific concept of ideology as it functions in historical materialism. As he has deprived himself of that concept from the outset, once the essential difficulty of the 'link' between ideology and the relations of production comes up, he is silent, condemned to designate the site of a problem in a 'mystified' way.

Let me make myself clear.

1. The concept of ideology as it functions in historical materialism – in Marx and his successors – is not in fact the pure inverse of science. Foucault is quite right; the question he poses about the 'regime of materiality' of ideology is a real (materialist) question of an urgent theoretical necessity for dialectical materialism. As we know, ideology has a consistency, a material – notably an 'institutional' – existence, and a real function in a social formation. Everyone knows that in the still descriptive schema of the structure of a social formation given by Marx, ideology (or: ideologies) appears in the 'superstructure'. The superstructure, determined 'in the last instance' by the economic infrastructure, is said to have a 'reciprocal effect' on the infrastructure. As such, ideology cannot disappear merely because of the appearance of science. It is clear in what sense Michel Foucault is right to want to work 'at a different level' from that of an epistemology of 'rupture'.

'Rupture is not for archæology the barrier to its analyses, the limit that it indicates from afar, without being able either to determine it or to give it specificity; *rupture* is the name given to transformations that bear on the general regime of one or several discursive formations.'[36] To determine ideology as an 'instance' in all social formations is in fact to accept the obligation to think ideology no longer only in strictly Bachelardian style as 'a tissue of tenacious errors', hatched in the secrecy of the imagination, as the 'formless magma' of the 'theoretical' monsters which precede science – and often survive it in a pathological existence – but to accept the obligation to think the constitution, functioning and function of that instance as a material, historically determinate instance in a complex social whole, itself historically determinate. To have attempted this, it seems to me, is what constitutes the quite exemplary value of *The Archæology*.

2. It remains that this attempt results in a failure: the analyses 'come to grief' on the blind distinction between discursive practices and non-discursive practices. In reality, if what I have just said is correct, there is nothing surprising in this: it can be shown that Foucault would like to resolve *three* distinct problems with this single distinction. Three problems which can only be *formulated* in the concepts of historical materialism. Three problems whose effects Foucault encounters in the form of perplexity, without having even been able to pose them.

Problem 1 concerns the relation between an 'ideological formation' and what Foucault calls 'social relations', 'economic fluctuations', etc. In short, what I have several times designated as the problem of the 'interlocking', so-called. In other words: in a social formation, what type of relations does ideology have with the economic infrastructure? A naive question, it will be said, which a Marxist can easily answer by the classical schema of the infrastructure and the superstructure. In fact this answer, although easy and, fundamentally, correct, is surely inadequate. For it is still *descriptive*: even if it has the inestimable advantage of 'showing' what is the *materialist* order of determination; even if it has a well-tried polemical value against all the idealist conceptions of history for which it is ideas that conduct the world; even if, for these decisive

36. ibid., pp. 176–7.

reasons, it has to be resolutely defended as a theoretical acquisition of Marxism, insofar as it enables us to draw a line of demarcation between the two 'camps' in philosophy, between our enemies and ourselves – it must still be recognized that it does not give us the means to think the mechanism that links ideology, as *a system of hierarchized relations producing an effect of subjection* on the 'subjects', to the mode of production (in the strict sense), i.e., to the constituted system of the relations of production and productive forces.[37] It is precisely such a mechanism that Foucault makes it imperative on us to think theoretically; by the notion of 'interlocking' he designates the site of an urgent theoretical problem: to move, from the descriptive theory of the relations between ideology and the infrastructure, to that theory *as such*. We know that only historical materialism can resolve this problem. Without being able to provide the solution here, I can at least add a specification of the terms of the problem: if it is true, as the classical schema suggests, that it is the infrastructure which is determinant, we must ask what it is in the mechanism governing the relations of those two systems – the productive forces and the relations of production – that makes a system of ideological subjection necessary? One day this question will indeed have to be answered: it is to Foucault's credit that he has 'rediscovered' it – though in displacement – and more fully demonstrated its urgency.

Problem 2 concerns the status of the 'false sciences' which are the particular object of Foucault's previous work. He insists: General Grammar, Natural History, etc., may well, by recurrence, in the eyes of the constituted sciences, be called 'ideological'; no doubt it can even be shown that there are close ties between these 'ideological' disciplines and the system of ideological relations existing in a given society at a given moment in its history. All *The Archæology* tends to prove it. It is nonetheless true that General Grammar or Natural History do not have the same *status* as religions, moral or political ideologies as they function in the social formation under consideration. An index of this difference: these disciplines adopt – whatever we think – the title 'sciences'. In short, Foucault wants to avoid a

37. Cf. on this question Althusser's article 'Ideology and Ideological State Apparatuses', in *Lenin and Philosophy and Other Essays*, NLB, London, 1971, pp. 121–73.

'reduction' that I should willingly call 'ideologistic', and basically mechanistic. He proposes in fact a distinction between two 'forms' of ideology; making sure not to see in it merely a 'formal' distinction (the ones are systematized, the others not), but on the contrary, considering that there is a 'difference of levels' between them. I shall take this to mean that he is thereby designating a distinction which can be formulated in the concepts of historical materialism as the distinction between 'practical ideologies' and 'theoretical ideologies'. Althusser has given the following – provisional – definition of practical ideologies:

> By '*practical ideologies*' I mean complex formations of montages of notions-representations-images on the one hand, and of montages of behaviours-conducts-attitudes-gestures on the other. The whole functions as practical norms governing the attitudes and concrete adoptions of positions of men with respect to the real objects and real problems of their social and individual existence, and of their history.

How are we to think the 'articulation' of these practical ideologies with the 'theoretical ideologies'? What is a 'theoretical ideology'? Such are the questions – formulated in materialist terms – that Foucault poses in other terms. It is here that the canonic notion of the *archive* acquires all its meaning and import. To show this it would be necessary to examine the chapter entitled 'The Historical *a priori* and the Archive'[38] line by line. In justification of his use of the first expression, Foucault writes: 'Juxtaposed, these two words produce a rather startling effect: what I mean by the term is an *a priori* that is not a condition of validity for judgements, but a condition of reality for statements.' Whence it follows that the *archive* – understood in a radically novel sense – is 'first the law of what can be said, the system that governs the appearance of statements as unique events'. And more generally: 'It is the general system of the formation and transformation of statements.'

But this general system, as we have seen, is not autonomous; the law of its functioning is itself constrained by a different type of 'regularity', that of the non-discursive practices. I shall say that the

38. *The Archæology of Knowledge*, pp. 126–31.

formation of the objects of theoretical ideologies is subject to the constraints of practical ideologies. More precisely, I suggest that practical ideologies assign theoretical ideologies their *forms* and their *limits*. By proposing to work at the level of the archive, Foucault is thus inviting us to think the mechanism which regulates these effects; he is posing us this problem: by what specific process do practical ideologies intervene in the constitution and functioning of theoretical ideologies? or again, how are practical ideologies 'represented' in theoretical ideologies? Here again Foucault is posing a real – and urgent – problem. The answer *The Archæology* gives it is once again no more than a sketch to be reworked on the firm ground of historical materialism.

Problem 3 concerns what type of relationship there is between a theoretical ideology and a science. Here Foucault has much to contribute: he shows that it is impossible to resolve the problem if it is posed in terms of *objects*. To compare the objects of a theoretical ideology with those of a science is to condemn oneself to the description of a *rupture* which explains nothing. By establishing the necessity of proceeding 'via' the category of '*savoir*' – as he has elaborated it – he poses the problem correctly. This problem is not the problem of the relations between a determinate science and the theoretical ideology which seems to 'correspond' to it, but that of the relations between a science and the system of theoretical ideologies and practical ideologies constituted in the form I have been discussing. Now, if, as we have just seen, practical ideologies are 'represented' in theoretical ideologies by assigning them their *forms* and *limits*, it has to be admitted that a science can only emerge thanks to a *play* in this *limitation* process; that is why Foucault proposes to replace the term *rupture* by what I believe is the happier one of the *irruption* of a science. This irruption occurs *in savoir*, i.e, in the material space in which the system of practical and theoretical ideologies acts. According to Foucault, it is by this means that the insertion of a science into a social formation must be thought; it is by this means that it is possible to avoid both the idealism for which science falls from the sky and the economistic-mechanicism for which science is merely a reflection of production.

It is time to show in a concluding example how such a type of analysis may function. Let me take that of the relations between Marx and Ricardo. Foucault writes the following striking passage:

Concepts like those of surplus value or the tendency for the rate of profit to fall, as found in Marx, may be described on the basis of the system of positivity that is already in operation in the work of Ricardo; but these concepts (which are new, but whose rules of formation are not) appear – in Marx himself – as belonging at the same time to a quite different discursive practice: they are formed in that discursive practice in accordance with specific laws, they occupy in it a different position, they do not figure in the same sequences: this new positivity is not a transformation of Ricardo's analyses; it is not a new political economy; it is a discourse whose installation took place vis-à-vis the derivation of certain economic concepts, but which, in turn defines the conditions in which the discourse of economists takes place, and may therefore be valid as a theory and critique of political economy.[39]

The best commentary that could be given on this analysis is to confront it with a passage from the Afterword to the second German edition of *Capital*.[40] Marx writes:

Insofar as Political Economy remains within that (bourgeois) horizon, in so far, i.e., as the capitalist regime is looked upon as the absolutely final form of social production, instead of as a passing historical phase of its evolution, Political Economy can remain a science only so long as the class-struggle is latent or manifests itself only in isolated and sporadic phenomena. Let us take England. Its Political Economy belongs to the period in which the class struggle was as yet undeveloped. Its last great representative, Ricardo, in the end, consciously makes the antagonism of class-interests, of wages and profits, of profits and rent, the starting-point of his investigations, naively taking this antagonism for a social law of Nature. But by this start the science of bourgeois economy had reached the limits beyond which it could not pass.

What makes Foucault's text of such exceptional interest is revealed here: it is clear why the objects of Ricardo and Marx derive from the

39. ibid., p. 176.
40. *Capital*, Vol. I, translated by Samuel Moore and Edward Aveling, Foreign Languages Publishing House, Moscow, and Lawrence and Wishart, London, 1961, p. 14.

same 'discursive formation', why that theoretical ideology, classical political economy, is determined in its constitution by a system of *limits* produced by the constraints of practical ideologies; it is thereby clear how inadequate is the epistemological point of view of the rupture (or break). But also visible is what is *missing* from *The Archæology*: a class point of view. In fact, it is because Marx took up the point of view of the proletariat that he inaugurated a 'new discursive practice'. In other words: practical ideologies are traversed by class contradictions; the same in true of their effects in theoretical ideologies. Hence only a modification in the system of contradictions which is constituted in this way makes it possible to move from the ideology to the science. These reflections, which have been suggested to me by *The Archæology*, rudimentary as they are, go beyond Foucault's undertaking. They go beyond it of necessity and their absence accounts for the displacement of all the Foucauldian concepts. For this reason, *The Archæology* remains itself a theoretical ideology. Now, according to what I have just said: it is ultimately to a class position that we have to refer in order to understand it. We can now see the meaning of Foucault's *choice* between historical materialism and his own constructions: this theoretical choice is ultimately political. We have seen the effects of this choice in detail: it assigns to *The Archæology* 'the limit it will not be able to go beyond'. Let the 'archæologist' change terrain, on the contrary, and there is no doubt but that he will discover many further treasures. One last point: he will then have ceased to be an 'archæologist'.[41]

41. These lines were written in April 1970.

Appendix to Part Two

SHORT BIBLIOGRAPHY OF WRITINGS ON EPISTEMOLOGY
AND THE HISTORY OF THE SCIENCES
BY GEORGES CANGUILHEM AND MICHEL FOUCAULT

I. GEORGES CANGUILHEM

Books:

Essai sur quelques problèmes concernant le normal et le pathologique (An Essay on
some Problems concerning the Normal and the Pathological), Publications de
la Faculté des Letters de l'Université de Strasbourg, fascicule 100, Clermont-
Ferrand, 1943; reprinted by the Société d'édition 'Les Belles-Lettres', Paris,
1950; reprinted with 'Nouvelles réflexions' as *Le normal et le pathologique*
(The Normal and the Pathological), Presses Universitaires de France, Paris,
1966.

La formation du concept de réflexe aux XVIIᵉ et XVIIIᵉ siècles (The Formation of
the Concept of the Reflex in the Seventeenth and Eighteenth Centuries),
PUF, Paris, 1955.

La Connaissance de la vie (Knowledge of Life), Hachette, Paris, 1952; second
revised and expanded edition, Librairie Philosophique J. Vrin, Paris, 1965.

Études d'histoire et de philosophie des sciences (Studies in the History and Philosophy of the Sciences), Vrin, Paris, 1968.

Articles not included in the above volumes:

'Note sur la situation faite à la philosophie biologique en France' (A Note on the
Situation Produced in Biological Philosophy in France), *Revue de métaphysique
et de morale*, Paris, 1947.

'Sur une épistémologie concordataire' (On a Harmonizing Epistemology), in
Hommage à Gaston Bachelard, PUF, Paris, 1957.

'La diffusion scientifique' (Scientific Diffusion), *Revue de l'enseignement supérieur*,
1961, no. 3, Paris.

Canguilhem has also contributed to a number of *Thalès* on *L'histoire de l'idée de
l'évolution*, 1960; and to René Taton, ed.: *Histoire générale des sciences*, PUF,
Paris, 1957–64.

Translations into English:

'The Role of Analogies and Models in Biological Discovery', in *Scientific Change* (a Symposium on the History of Science, University of Oxford, 9–15 July 1961), ed. A. C. Crombie, Heinemann, London, 1963.

Articles on the history of animal physiology in the eighteenth and nineteenth centuries in René Taton, ed.: *A General History of the Sciences*, translated by A. J. Pomerans, Thames and Hudson, London, 1963–6, Vol. II, pp. 527–39 and Vol. III, pp. 414–21.

Studies of George Canguilhem:

Pierre Macherey: 'La philosophie de la science de Georges Canguilhem: épistémologie et histoire des sciences', *La Pensée*, no. 113, January/February 1964, pp. 54–74.

2. MICHEL FOUCAULT

Books:

Maladie mentale et psychologie (Mental Illness and Psychology), PUF, Paris, 1954.

Folie et déraison, histoire de la folie à l'âge classique (Madness and Unreason, A History of Madness in the Classical Age), Plon, Paris, 1961; reprinted as *Histoire de la folie à l'âge classique*, Gallimard, Paris, 1972.

Naissance de la clinique, une archéologie du regard medical (The Birth of Clinical Medicine, an Archæology of the Medical Gaze), PUF, Paris, 1963; second revised edition, PUF, Paris, 1972.

Les mots et les choses, une archéologie des sciences humaines (Words and Things, an Archæology of the Human Sciences), Gallimard, Paris, 1966.

L'archéologie du savoir (The Archæology of Knowledge), Gallimard, Paris, 1969.

L'ordre du discours (The Order of Discourse), Leçon inaugurale au Collège de France prononcée le 2 décembre 1970, Gallimard, Paris, 1971.

Translations into English:

Madness and Civilization: a History of Insanity in the Age of Reason (abridged translation of *Histoire de la folie*), translated by Richard Howard, Tavistock Publications, London, 1967.

The Order of Things: an Archæology of the Human Sciences (translation of *Les mots et les choses*), Tavistock Publications, London, 1970.

The Archæology of Knowledge (translation of *L'archéologie du savoir*), translated by A. M. Sheridan Smith, Tavistock Publications, London, 1972.

'Orders of Discourse' (translation of *L'ordre du discours*), translated by Rupert
Sawyer, *Social Science Information/Information sur les sciences sociales*, Vol. X,
no. 2, April 1971, pp. 7-30.

The Birth of Clinical Medicine (translation of *Naissance de la clinique*), translated
by A. M. Sheridan Smith, Tavistock Publications, London, 1973.

Studies of Michel Foucault:

Roland Barthes: 'De part et d'autre', *Critique* no. 174, November 1961, pp.915-
922; reprinted in *Essais Critiques*, Éditions du Seuil, Paris, 1964, pp. 167-74.

Jacques Derrida: 'Cogito et histoire de la folie', *Revue de métaphysique et de
morale*, 1963, no. 4, pp. 460-94; reprinted in *L'écriture et la différence*,
Éditions du Seuil, Paris, 1967, pp. 51-97.

François Dagognet: 'Archéologie ou histoire de la médicine?', *Critique* no. 216.
May 1965, pp. 436-47.

Georges Canguilhem: 'Mort de l'homme ou épuisement du cogito?', *Critique*
no. 242, July 1967, pp. 599-618.

Jean Wahl: 'La philosophie entre l'avant et l'après du structuralisme', in *Qu'il
est-ce que le structuralisme?*, Éditions du Seuil, Paris, 1968, pp. 299-441.

Gilles Deleuze: 'Un nouvel archiviste', *Critique* no. 274, March 1970, pp. 195-
209.

Index

Printed in the United States
by Baker & Taylor Publisher Services